EDWARD STOTT

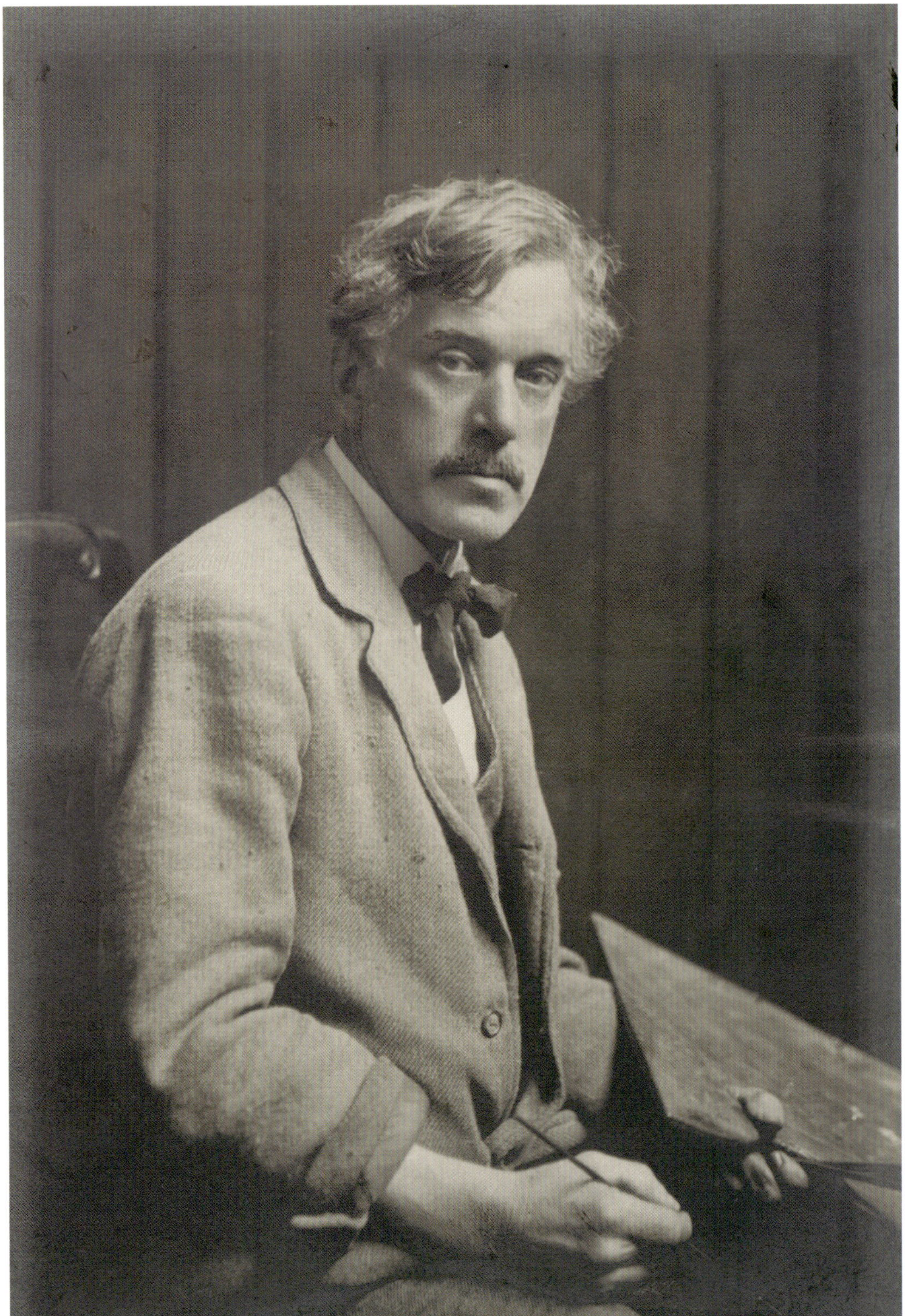

Valerie Webb

EDWARD STOTT

(1855–1918)

A Master of Colour and Atmosphere

Sansom & Company

First published in 2018 by Sansom and Company
A publishing imprint of Redcliffe Press Ltd.
81g Pembroke Road. Bristol BS8 3EA
www.sansomandcompany.co.uk
info@sansomandcompany.co.uk

ISBN 978-1-911408-22-2
British Library Cataloguing-in-Publication Data
A catalogue record for this book is available from the British Library

Design and typesetting by Design Deluxe, Bath
Printed and bound by Cambrian Print Ltd.

Front Cover: Edward Stott, *The Fold* (also known as *The Penfold*), 1895. Oil on canvas, 60 x 55.5cm. © Touchstones Rochdale

Frontispiece: Photograph of Edward Stott, by James Russell & Sons, date unknown. © National Portrait Gallery, London

Back Cover: Arthur Kynaston, *Portrait of Edward Stott, A.R.A.*, ca. 1895-1900. Oil on canvas, 40.5 x 30.3cm.
Photo © Royal Academy of Arts, London;
Photographer Andy Johnson

CONTENTS

ACKNOWLEDGEMENTS

Many people and institutions have helped to make this publication possible. The timely support and assistance I received, particularly with regards to the granting of permissions, image licensing and copyright requirements, has made this time-consuming part of the project relatively easy to manage.

The publication, however, would never have come to fruition if it had not firstly been for Professor Sam Smiles suggesting that I research Edward Stott and, secondly, for the patience and perseverance of my supervisors, Dr. Matthew Potter and Professor Ysanne Holt. My thanks also go to Professor Christiana Payne and Dr. Lesley Twomey for a stimulating viva, and encouraging me to publish and consider the idea of a commemorative exhibition.

Generally, I would like to thank the staff at the British Library (Humanities 1), Geoffrey Redman at Chichester Reference Library, Getty Research Institute Library in Los Angeles, Horsham Library, National Art Library at the V & A, Rochdale Resource and Heritage Centre, Archivist Elizabeth Stazicker at The King's School, Ely, and Jane Dore at Worthing Reference Library.

My thanks also go to those curators who allowed me to view paintings by Stott in their collections that are not in the public domain. These are Gallery Oldham, Manchester Art Gallery, Touchstones Rochdale, Towner Art Gallery in Eastbourne, and the Watts Gallery in Compton.

Now to the big task of thanking and acknowledging all those people who granted permissions, and organized the licensing and release of images. Aberdeen Art Gallery & Museums Collection (Museum Support Staff), Bonhams, Bridgeman Images (Sian Phillips), British Library (Chris Rawlings), Christie's, Robert Farrow for giving me permission to use his photograph of Stott's window, Ferens Art Gallery, Anthony McIntosh for giving me permission to use his photographs of Stott's memorial, National Portrait Gallery, Rochdale Local Studies Centre (Janet Byrne), Royal Academy (Jennifer Camilleri), Sotheby's, Touchstones Rochdale (Anna Bates), Towner Art Gallery (Sara Cooper), Tate Images, University of Hull Art Collection (John Bernasconi), and Williamson Art Gallery & Museum (Colin Simpson and Philip Eastwood).

My thanks also go to Dominic Milmo-Penny of Milmo-Penny Fine Art, and Frank Kaminski of Kaminski Auctions, who provided me with two images which unfortunately I could not include. However, I appreciate the time and trouble they took in assisting me.

Thank you to Clara Hudson and her team at Sansom & Company who have been supportive, instructive and helpful.

Finally, I would like to thank David McAllister for the constant help and support he gave during the PhD process, and for the continuing assistance whilst I brought this book to realization.

INTRODUCTION

EDWARD STOTT'S ARTISTIC CAREER spanned three historical periods: late Victorian, Edwardian and modern 'Georgian'. Art production during this time, which covers the 1880s through to 1918 when Stott died, was competitive and somewhat complex. This becomes evident when focussing on the genre of landscape painting and its close association with images depicting scenes of rural life. What emerges is a variety of competing styles which, in turn, reveals a number of influences, affinities and changing allegiances, all of which were visible in exhibiting circles that were also becoming increasingly competitive. At the beginning of the 1880s, new art venues were springing up. Whilst the Institute of Painters in Oil Colours, which formed in 1882, consciously set out to emulate the Royal Academy, the progressive New English Art Club which formed in 1886, and the New Gallery which opened its doors in 1888, aimed to provide alternative exhibiting environments to the Academy and to encourage innovation and experimentation. This re-energising of the art world was centred in London, and can be seen to stem mainly from the experiences in France received by those British artists who had trained in Paris, one of whom was Edward Stott. As an art student attending the atelier of Carolus Duran, and then the École des Beaux-Arts where he studied under Cabanel, Stott was exposed to such French influences as Jules Bastien-Lepage who painted in the style of rustic naturalism, the Impressionists, and the earlier influences of the Barbizon School. In particular, works by Jean-Baptiste Camille Corot and Jean Françoise Millet. Whilst in Paris, Stott exhibited four paintings at the Paris Salon: *The Helping Hand of a Small Friend* (1882) (also known as *In the Fields, Auvers-sur-Oise*) and *Solitude* (1883), both of which were shown at the Salon of 1883, and *The High Grasses* (1883) and *The Return to the Poultry House* (1884), which were shown at the Paris Salon of 1884.[1] Stott had some success at the Salon because his paintings attracted the patronage of a visiting buyer from America.

On his return to England, Stott initially exhibited with the Institute of Painters in Oil Colours and the Grosvenor Gallery, before shifting allegiance to the New English Art Club and the New Gallery. He exhibited only occasionally at the Royal Academy in the early years and it was not until he became an Associate of the Royal Academy in 1906 that he began to exhibit exclusively at the shows. As Stott's exhibiting career developed, he attracted regular patronage and his work began to be consistently and favourably reviewed by the art critics. He also acquired something of an international reputation, and it would be true to say that he was highly regarded as an artist in his day. Today, his reputation as an artist, together with his body of work, is largely forgotten. Apart from publications by Kenneth McConkey and Ysanne Holt, who make reference to Stott, his contribution to landscape painting generally, and scenes of rural life specifically, has been largely unexplored.[2] The last exhibition of his work was held in 1976, organised by the Fine Art Society, and was a joint exhibition with works by William Stott of Oldham. An exhibition dedicated to Stott's career is long overdue, as is a sustained study of his life and work.

This publication is the first in-depth monographic study of the life and work of Edward Stott whose career spanned over thirty years. Taking a chronological and thematic approach, it brings the life and work of Edward Stott to the fore, and by situating his work historically and contextually, has allowed for an extensive re-evaluation of his commitment and contribution to the history of English landscape painting and rural life. Supported by a cast of artists, many of whom have also been largely forgotten, not only has Stott been resurrected but they too are being remembered.

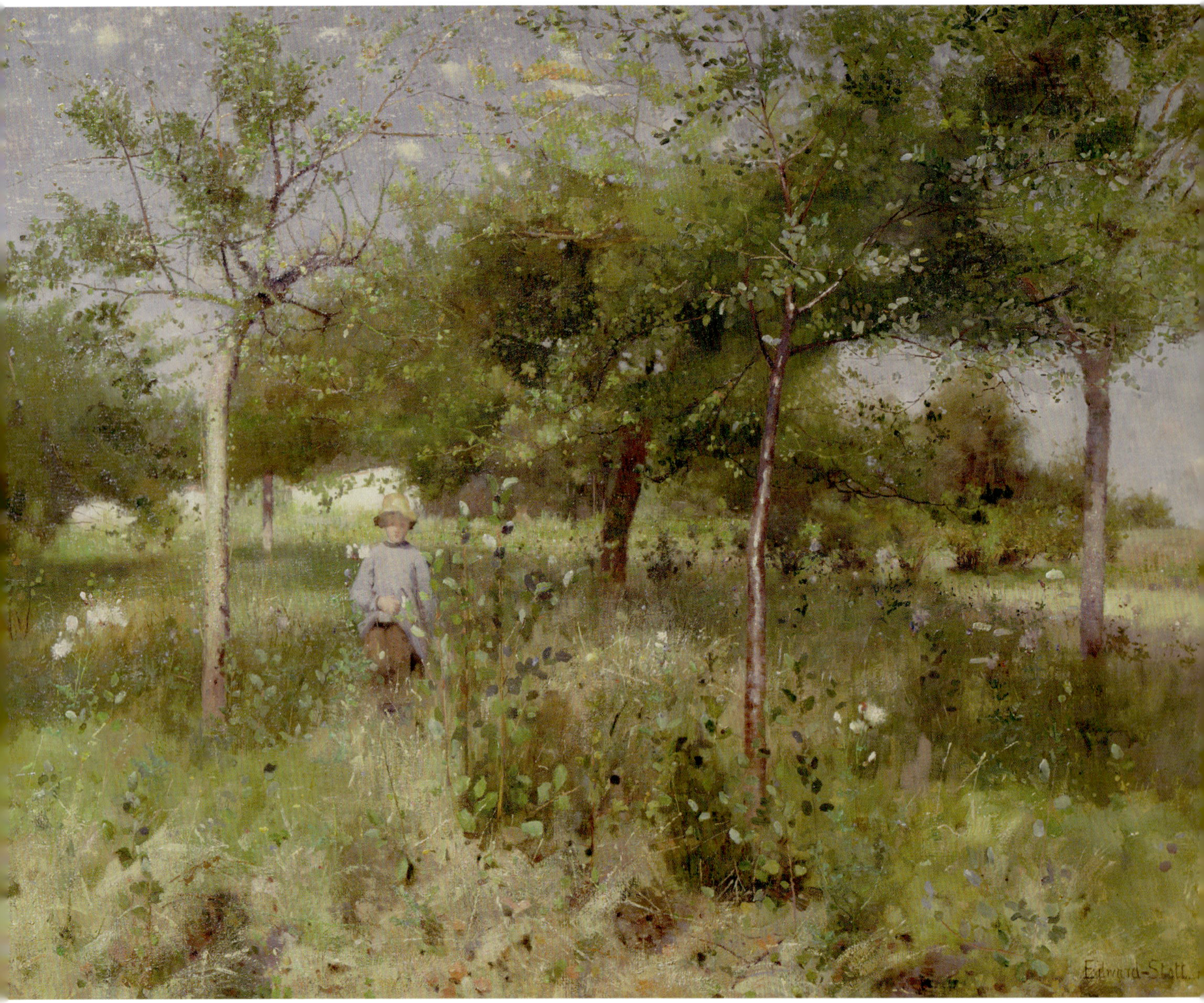

1. Edward Stott,
The High Grasses,
1883. Oil on canvas,
45.1 x 59.6cm. Private
Collection/Photo
© The Fine Art Society,
London, UK/Bridgeman
Images

1

THE EARLY YEARS

Rochdale and Paris

WILLIAM EDWARD STOTT WAS BORN on the 25th April 1855 to Samuel and Jane Stott (née Pilling), of Quarry Hill, Wardleworth, Rochdale, in the County of Lancashire.[3] His father was a partner in the firm of Messrs. Stott and Pilling at Howards Mill (also known as 'Shappers'), Cheetham Street, Rochdale and also held prominent positions in Rochdale's political and municipal circles. In the first Borough Council elections, Samuel Stott received 1149 votes and was elected to the Town Council as a Councillor representing the Wardleworth Ward.[4] In 1865, when Edward Stott would have been aged 10, his father was raised to the status of Alderman. As well as serving as a Justice of the Peace, he was also twice elected Mayor,[5] from 1863 to 1864, and then from 1865 to 1866. Samuel Stott's years as Mayor occurred during a difficult time in the history of Lancashire's cotton trade. Although there had been a boom trade in the years of 1859 and 1860, the years 1861 to 1865 experienced a cotton famine. Known as the Lancashire Cotton Famine, this depression in the textile industry had catastrophic consequences for the Lancashire cotton mill owners and workforce.[6] Two further events would have placed additional financial burden on Samuel Stott's business and family life. On the 12th November 1868, when Edward was aged 13 and attending Rochdale Grammar School, a fire broke out at Stott and Pilling's mill causing £7000 worth of damage. Just 18 months later, on the 17th May 1870, a second fire broke out with damage estimated at £30,000.[7] It is not known how these events affected Edward Stott personally. However, rather than follow in his father's footsteps and enter the family business, he was determined to pursue his ambitions to be an artist which were met with disapproval and resistance from his parents.

2. Samuel Stott, Senior. Date unknown. Local Studies Centre, Touchstones Rochdale

3. Edward Stott, *Self-Portrait*, date unknown. Oil on canvas, 30.4 x 20.9cm. Touchstones Rochdale

In 1870, Edward Stott was sent as a boarder to The King's School, Ely, where he won the Mathematics Prize (Division II) that year, followed by the Drawing Prize in 1871.[8] According to the obituary published in the *Sussex Daily News* of 21st March 1918, Stott started painting when he was four-years-old, his artistic nature seemingly coming from his mother's side.[9] His talent is evident from a self-portrait he painted as a young man. (Fig. 3). In the painting he appears diffident, serious and slightly melancholic and one can imagine, therefore, that such a quiet and reserved persona would have been quite at odds with the dominant personality of a successful Victorian patriarch such as Stott senior. This, in fact, proved to be the case. Edward Stott wanted to pursue an artistic career, but spent five years working for his father in the Manchester office. His spare time and holidays, however, were spent sketching.[10] Stott's friend, J. Stanley Little, has written of how Stott would rise early on a Sunday and spend the whole day in the fields making sketches.[11] During this time, Stott came to the attention of W. Knight Keeling who was the first and third President of the Manchester Academy of Fine Arts.[12] Keeling occasionally visited Rochdale, where Stott showed him some of his sketches and, as a consequence, Stott went on to study at the Manchester School of Art where he attended the evening classes.[13]

Despite opposition from his father, Edward Stott was determined to pursue a career as an artist. His parents gave him no financial or moral support, and Laurence Housman records that Stott's wish was 'looked upon coldly by his own family, and... [he] was left to follow his bent with nothing warmer than passive disapproval as a send-off.'[14] However, limited financial support came from an unknown benefactor and this enabled him to study in Paris. Stott had also been given a letter of introduction to a friend of Charles August Carolus-Duran by someone from the firm of Thomas Agnew and Sons, thus assuring Stott's entry into Carolus-Duran's studio in Paris.[15] It is not known why Stott chose to go to Paris to study rather than to, say, the Royal Academy Schools or the Slade School of Art in London. However, as Jeanne Sheehy found in her research into art training in London and on the Continent, many students, like Stott, who came from the provincial schools of art by-passed London. The Royal Academy had a restrictive selection process, and the Slade was fee-paying, and students might, therefore, have found it easier to get accepted into the Paris ateliers. There was also the added fact that it was perceived to be prestigious to have attended a foreign school, particularly one based in Paris.[16] Paris was the most popular destination due to its variety of independent ateliers, its perceived supremacy in the arts, and the chance of progressing onto the École des Beaux-Arts. Stott may have chosen Paris because certain Schools of Art in England, in the provinces and in London, were 'feeders' into the more important establishments in terms of an artist's future career. In the provinces, Sheehy found that students who studied at the Lincoln School of Art under the tutoring of the Headmaster, E.R. Taylor, went on to study at Verlat's studio in Antwerp. When Taylor later became the Headmaster of the Birmingham School of Art, his students also went on to Antwerp.[17] A similar link

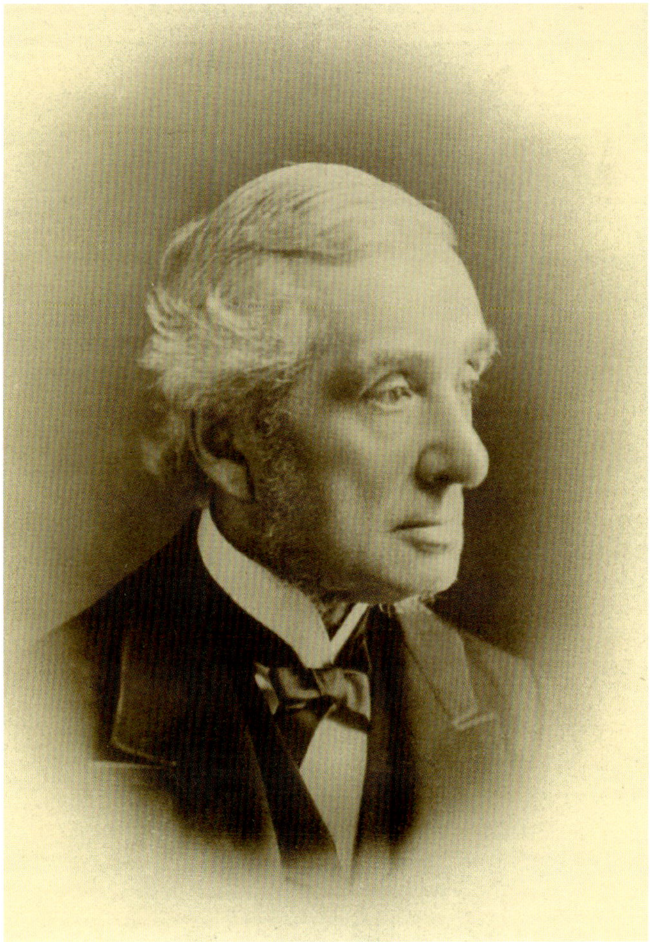

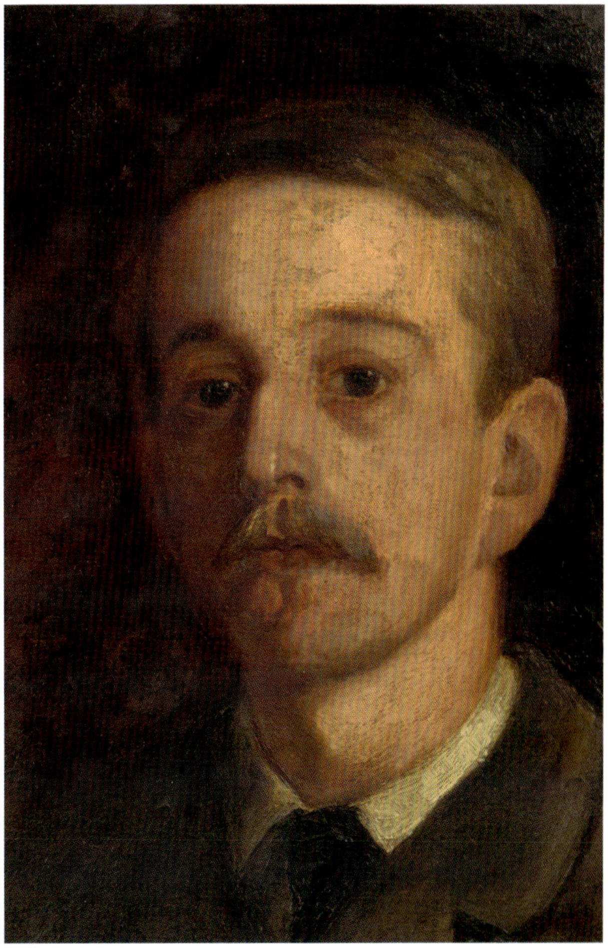

can be made between Manchester and Paris: Edward Stott, William Stott of Oldham and Fred Jackson, all went to Manchester and then to Paris. Edward Stott went to the atelier of Carolus-Duran and then the École des Beaux-Arts to study under Alexandre Cabanel, whilst William Stott of Oldham went straight to the École to study under Jean-Léon Gérôme and Léon Bonnat. As regards Fred Jackson, he went first to the Oldham School of Art and subsequently to Manchester, before attending the École where he studied under Jules Lefebvre and Gustave Boulanger.[18] As to London, the National Art Training School based in South Kensington (formerly the Government School of Design until its move to South Kensington in 1854), was considered to provide a natural progression onto the Royal Academy Schools.[19] Tutoring at the Royal Academy Schools and the Slade School of Art was based on the Parisian system[20] and as it was considered to be an important part of an artist's training to complete a period of study abroad, many students from the Royal Academy Schools and the Slade went to Paris at some point.[21]

PARIS AND THE ATELIERS

IN 1883 EDWARD STOTT WAS recorded as living at 87, Rue de Seine. The Rue de Seine was in the VIe Arondissement which ran parallel to the Rue Bonaparte where the École des Beaux-Arts was situated, with the Louvre and the Tuileries just across the river. From the Rue de Seine, Stott moved into the XVe Arondissement staying at 10, Impasse Fremin, Rue des Fourneaux (now Rue Falguière), where his lodgings were located between the ateliers and the abbatoir. There is very little archival information specific to Stott's life as an art student in Paris, but general information on student life at that time can be gleaned from recollections of fellow students such as George Halkett, Shirley Fox, and Philip Wilson Steer.[22] Added to this are the reminiscences of Albert Ludovici who studied in Paris in the late 1860s and 1870s, and a handful of articles that appeared in the *Magazine of Art* written by 'Barclay Day'.[23] With specific reference to the studio of Carolus-Duran, Arthur Kennedy's article in *The Contemporary Review* proves insightful, as does Albert Boime's study of the École des Beaux-Arts.[24]

Stott's initial training took place at the atelier of Carolus-Duran. As was the case with most ateliers, acceptance was granted by a letter of introduction and samples of work. Arthur Kennedy writes that Carolus-Duran's atelier attracted an international mix of students, 'half full of Americans, English, and other aliens.'[25] This idea of an international community of art students is confirmed by Barclay Day who studied at the atelier of Léon Bonnat. He recalled that about forty students were registered, with a mixed age range from 18 to 38-years-old, and comprised many nationalities from different backgrounds. According to Day, within the studio the students were all equal with the common ground of art between them. Furthermore, as they all wore the uniform of the 'brown-holland blouse', this removed all traces of class difference – at least as regards outward appearance.[26] Yet, considering the mix of students in Bonnat's studio who came from a varied socio-economic background, the idea of a 'classless society' is debatable. Day's contemporaries consisted of the son of a count, a baron, 'several *bourgeois*...who worked when they liked', a wine-grower who attended intermittently and, among other nationalities, three Englishmen and four Americans.[27] Furthermore, the idea that the students were all equal and that a community spirit prevailed, is somewhat contested by Albert Boime. He found that hierarchies existed within the private ateliers, and that they could be 'a hotbed of seething conflicts and resentments.'[28] This was certainly the case with students who had received municipal grants from their home towns and who often found themselves on the receiving end of jealous students who had not received any financial assistance.

Across ateliers, the structure and regime was much the same. On admittance into Carolus-Duran's studio, Stott would have paid his subscription and entrance fees to the *massier* who was the chief student elected by his fellow artists. This was a contribution towards studio funds and to cover the cost of the easel and stool.[29] His name would have been entered in the register, whereupon he would have become a recognised member of the atelier. It is not known what fees were charged by Carolus-Duran, but it was likely to have been in the region of 30 francs per month.[30] The hours of work in the studios were usually four hours a day, with the starting time determined by the time of year. In the summer months, work began at 7 a.m. In the winter months, an hour later. Many students supplemented their day training by attending evening classes at other studios, or visiting the Louvre during the day for copying exercises. Stott attended the studio of M. Colarossi after his classes with Cabanel at the École des Beaux-Arts had finished, whereas Steer would visit the Louvre in the afternoons where he would copy the work of Old Masters such as Van Dyck.[31]

Space inside the ateliers appeared to be utilised and accessorised in much the same way. The rooms were usually lofty and lit by a large north-facing window. Studio furniture and accessories were basic. Racks were arranged against the walls to hold the canvases, drawing boards and portfolios. On shelves above the racks lay the plaster casts. The rest of the furniture consisted of a clock, a cast-iron stove on which there was a basin of hot water to keep the atmosphere from becoming too dry, a metal fountain or bowl filled with water, and soft black soap for washing the brushes. There was a table, an address book for models' and pupils' details, and the 'Réglement' which contained ten simple rules regarding studio etiquette, which was pinned to the wall over the table. There would be a table or platform on which the model posed, and in semi-circles arranged around the model there would be rows of easels and straw-covered stools. The front stools and easels were low, thus making it difficult for those students at the front to draw the whole figure, which meant that their focus was on the head or upper part of the body. Behind the front row, there was a gradation in seating height. Those students furthest away from the model would usually stand and work at larger easels, which resulted in their being able to draw the figure in its entirety.[32] It is apparent that there was a hierarchy at play in the seating arrangements, with the more advanced students located at the back which gave them the opportunity to paint or draw the whole figure, but only after initially being 'front row' students. As Shirley Fox remembered, the ateliers were very busy at the start of the day with students trying to secure the best place, with several of the more important students already selecting their places and becoming annoyed with those who attempted to crowd them.[33] Steer, in a letter home to his mother, wrote that 'Last week I got rather a bad place so my work was not very satisfactory but I hope to do better this week as I have a good place. One has to get to the studio very sharp on eight on Monday if you want to get a good place as it is a question of first come first serve.'[34] It was often the case that the choice of seating would be determined by the *massier*. In theory, places were supposed to be allotted in the order of those artists who obtained awards in the previous Saturday's competition.

Whilst this occasionally happened, the *massier* would have first choice of where to sit and then he would read out the list of names of those who would get seating after him.[35]

A requisite part for any new student would be the 'initiation' ceremony in order to become fully accepted into atelier life. The ceremony generally comprised paying the *massier* a sum of money, known as the student's 'footing', whereupon he would then be called to 'show his figure', tell a story and sing a song. As Ludovici recalled, even if the performance was good, the student would be 'hooted off the platform', and anyone who tried to avoid the initiation would be severely ridiculed and humiliated.[36] Steer recounted in a letter home his experience of the initiation ceremony on his first day at the École des Beaux-Arts:

> On Tuesday I made my first appearance at the new atelier which was rather a serious undertaking according to all accounts but the reality was not so bad. All I had to do was to get on the platform...and sing a song which was not heard because as soon as I commenced they all began screaming and yelling. If they see you are good tempered over it they don't carry it very far.[37]

Shirley Fox remembers that he was subjected to lots of ribbing and insults. On one occasion, when a particularly unpleasant proposition was put to him, William Stott of Oldham, who was seated in front of him at the time, turned around to reassure the young student and, giving him a 'broad grin and sly wink', said that nothing bad would happen to him.[38]

Visitation and instruction from the 'master' differed from atelier to atelier. Stott's tutor, Carolus-Duran, would visit twice a week, arriving at 9 a.m. He would correct his students' work and proceed to lecture on what was uppermost in his mind concerning art at the time.[39] He would also provide demonstrations, putting his ideas into practice. Arthur Kennedy remembers Carolus-Duran preparing to paint the model's head. First, he drew it on the canvas in charcoal and had it 'fixed' before beginning to paint. Kennedy writes that the drawing of the head was as interesting to watch as the actual painting process, because the soft charcoal on a half-primed canvas was a very effective medium with 'Darks of velvety depth...obtained in the first moment, and modelled up with a finger-touch into the most delicate half-tones appreciable in the second.'[40] According to Kennedy, the drawing element for Carolus-Duran was the 'sternest preparation for the painted end-product; a preparation which involved the placing of masses and lines, rubbing out, making alterations and, once finished, showed extraordinary precision.'[41] The fluid nature of this process, which clearly accommodated creativity, was far removed from the rigidity of the stippling method taught at the Royal Academy and the Royal College of Art, of which the aim was to produce a smooth surface.[42] The thoroughness of Carolus-Duran's teaching, and the specific training Stott received, sufficiently prepared him for entry into the École des Beaux-Arts, and influenced his artistic process throughout his career. The instruction of Carolus-Duran was thorough. Not only did he correct his students' work, he also incorporated a lecture on matters pertaining to art, and provided helpful demonstrations to put his ideas into practice. Thus, under Carolus-Duran's tutelage, his students would have been well versed in theory and practice.

Not all atelier masters were so thorough. At Bouguereau's atelier, the 'esquisse' (sketch or outline) that Steer had been attempting of Clytemnestra showing the bodies of Agamemnon and Cassandra to the crowd, drew forth the comment from Bouguereau that it was "trés gentile" but not horrible enough.'[43] It is not known, however, if Bouguereau enlightened Steer as to how he should make his scene more 'horrible'. At the Académie Colarossi, which Stott attended in his spare time, there was no test of competency. As George Halkett recalled of visits to the studio by Messrs. Collin and Courtois, they 'were unfailingly good-natured, and one might easily have completed a course of study, as bare of knowledge as when one began.'[44]

Having instruction in drawing was an essential part of atelier life, and it was vital that a high degree of accomplishment was attained before being accepted into the ateliers of the École des Beaux-Arts. Halkett revealed that Stott took this aspect of his training very seriously and, by all accounts, was an assiduous student at the École in Cabanel's studio. Not content with studying during the day, Stott spent his spare time at Colarossi's. Clearly with only minimal instruction this particular studio was not first-rate for teaching. However, it may have proved useful for Stott to attend there where he would have been left to freely explore and experiment with his drawing technique. Halkett remembered Stott 'In this happy-go-lucky company of mediocre accomplishment...oblivious of the clouds of tobacco-smoke and of clanging tongues, a solitary figure charcoal in hand, striving...in pursuit of that illusive and unnameable essence...'[45] He also recalled that Stott's studies consisted of a maze of delicate lines, 'through which a shadowy figure seemed to be struggling for birth... with an elemental sense of life and movement.'[46] As some of Stott's pencil and charcoal studies produced after he had left Paris reveal, he was able to capture the essence of a scene or figure with the barest of detail and minimal sketching, which shows how his early training impacted on his later drawings. One example, among many, would be *Study for 'The Cider Press'* (date unknown) (Fig. 4).

Although much of an art student's training was carried out within the confines of the atelier, and then supplemented with copying exercises at, say, the Louvre, in some instances students were encouraged to venture outside and draw from life. Long before the Impressionists practised *plein-air* painting, students were encouraged to leave the studio.[47] Albert Ludovici, who attended M. Charles' evening classes, would visit the quarries or quays and make rapid sketches of the working men in different poses. He recorded that he found this to be an invaluable exercise because it was more interesting than the academic drawing from the studio model.[48] Corot, who was a member of the Barbizon group, was also encouraged to visit the environs of the Forest of Fontainebleau by his tutor Michallon.[49] Painting and sketching

4. Edward Stott, *Study for 'The Cider Press'*, date unknown. Black & white chalk on brown paper, 33 x 17.8cm. Cecil French Bequest, Hammersmith and Fulham Council, London/ Bridgeman Images

outside would allow the students to put theory into practice; to see the human form in action, or to let students see at first hand the changing colour values on a given setting or surface due to climatic and atmospheric conditions. This was certainly the case in Carolus-Duran's studio, where the veracity of colour and tonal values was just as important as the ability to draw. Commenting on a landscape that had been submitted to him, he remarked 'if all those houses had caught the remains of the sunlight, there would certainly have been one that was brighter than the rest. You have made them all of the same value', and of the trees in the same painting, Carolus-Duran again reinforced the importance of correct colour values when he exclaimed, 'You have trees at varying distances of the same value; they would all be different in Nature.'[50] Only by sketching in the open air could a student fully understand the values which Carolus-Duran was aiming to capture. Consequently, under Carolus-Duran's tutelage, Stott would have had impressed upon him the importance of working from the 'motif', and the equal importance of the changes in colour and tone dependent upon the various situations the scene presented. This was something Stott took careful notice of. As Halkett revealed, even on social occasions, Stott thought constantly about art. Speaking of the dinners that were taken at Thirion's restaurant in the Boulevard St. Germain, Halkett recalled that Stott's conversation was always about art and he 'was the eager disputant on tones and values and motives, and always so absorbed that I am very sure that most meals at Thirion's left him in delightful uncertainty as to what he had eaten and drunk.'[51]

Edward Stott's commitment to his studies paid off. After spending two years at the atelier of Carolus-Duran, he entered the École des Beaux-Arts to study under Cabanel where his contemporaries were Philip Wilson Steer, Arthur Rendall, Herbert Dalziel, Shirley Fox and Solomon J. Solomon.[52] Cabanel's studio was considered to be the strongest in terms of work, and Boime confirms this when he writes that he was one of the most successful masters of his time, revealing himself to be 'modern' in his sketches and therefore on a parallel with the more progressive artists of the period. Furthermore, 'his procedural combination of informal contours and loose slashing strips of pigment affected his most promising pupil, Bastien-Lepage.'[53] Contemporary sources such as Fox and J. Stanley Little, reveal that Cabanel was a much-liked and respected teacher who encouraged independent thinking in his students. Fox remembered that Cabanel was as different as possible in temperament and disposition to his previous master, Gérôme, who tended to dominate and treat all his students alike in his instruction, so that their work was apt to be of the same character. In contrast, Cabanel was 'Gentle and sympathetic', and allowed his students to 'follow their own bent modifying and adapting his advice to their individual requirements.'[54] J. Stanley Little recounts that Stott regarded Cabanel highly, describing him as a '"charming old man, sympathetic and patient. He always tried to guide the student, instead of endeavouring to mould him. He discovered where the strength and aptitude of the particular pupil lay, and administered a stimulant. I consider him

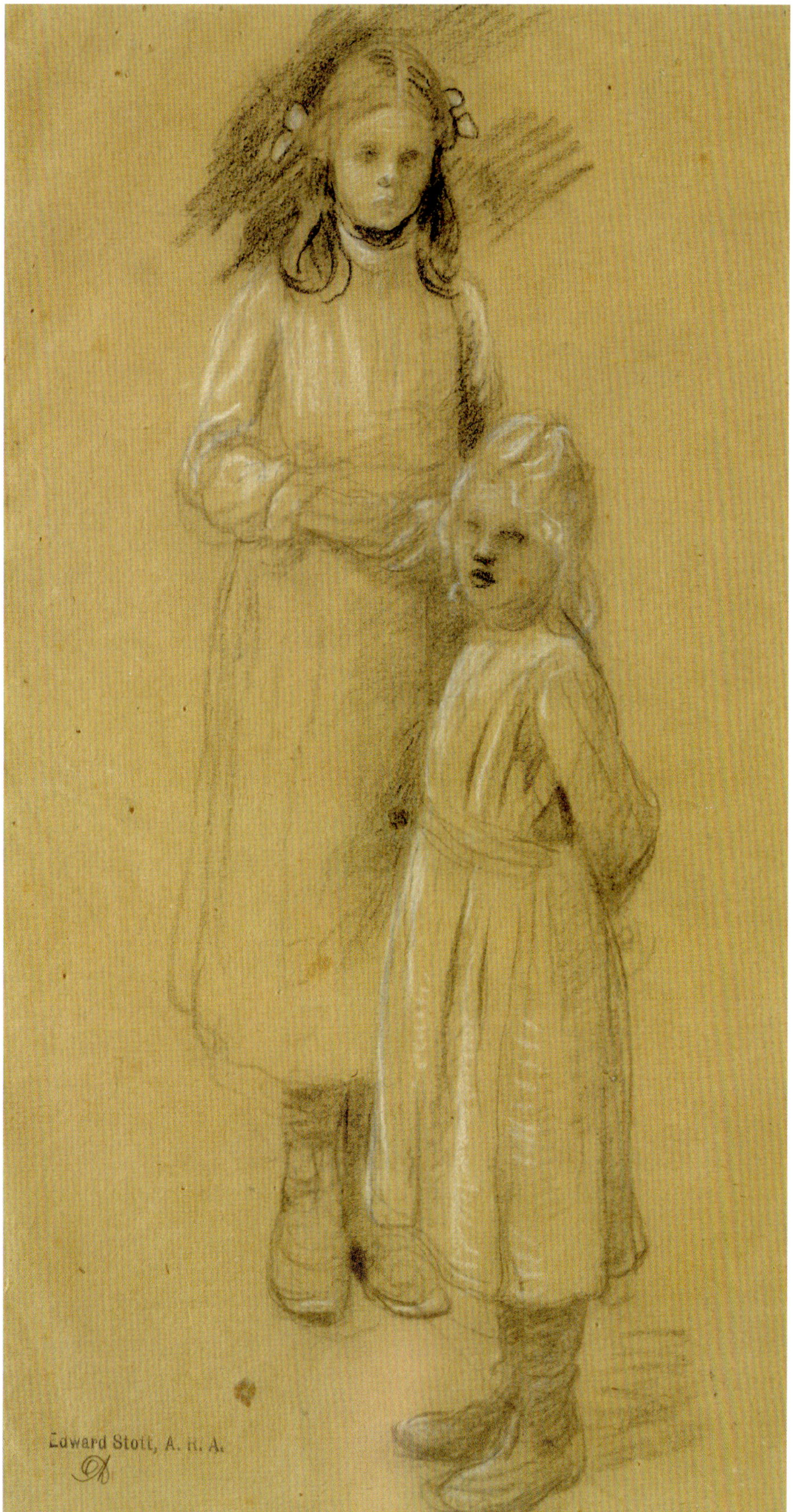
Edward Stott, A. R. A.

an ideal master; he was academic, of course, but he had a fine sensitive taste and a more liberal-minded man could not be".'[55] It can be speculated therefore that the seeds of Stott's striving for independence and autonomy in his search for a 'signature' style and defining subject matter, were planted whilst at Cabanel's studio.

Life at the École was a continuation of the initial training at the Atelier d'Eleves, but with competitions taking on a more crucial role. One new ruling, introduced in 1884, which was to have repercussions for foreign students, was the introduction of a French language examination.[56] Steer, who had never managed to become fluent in French, was unable to pass the examination and left the École. Edward Stott, who clearly achieved some fluency, was able to continue with his studies. Training at the École was formal, structured and competition-led. Based on the curriculum of 1816, students would have taken daily exercises in drawing from a live model and plaster casts, taken courses in anatomy and perspective, and entered into a series of competitions. As Boime states, the first task of the master was to prepare students for the successful participation in the *concours des place* at the matriculation register. This was necessary in order to enter the minor semestrial competitions, and which were a requisite for those French students wishing to enter for the prestigious Prix de Rome.[57] As mentioned previously, by the time students became registered, they would already have undertaken a wealth of drawing experience prior to graduation and the École des Beaux-Arts therefore did not actually teach the principles of drawing, but offered advanced pupils – 'those who could represent the live model in a professional manner' – a place to practise under the watchful eye of the masters who, in turn, judged the competitions.[58] The custom was for every student, regardless of attainment, to make their début in the Antique, and work in this way until the students were considered proficient enough to work from the live model. In effect, this constituted a student's 'rites of passage'.

Edward Stott flourished under Cabanel's teaching. Whereas at Colarossi's it appeared he took advantage of the relaxed atmosphere to experiment with his technique and rarely finished his drawings, under Cabanel's tutelage he was expected to complete his work. As Halkett remembered, 'he was not the man to shirk any mechanical aid to study' and many of his completed works at this time, which were 'the fruit of his work with Cababel, were sweet and dainty and wistful, stamped already with the individuality of his later pictures.'[59] Fox gives a brief but interesting insight into Stott's time in the studio. One of Stott's contemporaries was Solomon J. Solomon, whom Fox considered to be the better artist. Of Stott, Fox wrote that he was 'a far less brilliant student…although his work was always earnest and sincere, it was never such as to stand out prominently among that of his fellow-students as did Solomon's.'[60] He also revealed that Stott was unacademic, and searched for the subtle and less obvious rather than aim for proficiency and dexterity of execution. Nevertheless, whilst at the École des Beaux-Arts, Stott achieved a certain amount of success with his work. Not only did he win the second *recompense* during his second year, his work attracted the attention of an American art buyer when he sold two studies to the New York Art League. A few months after this, he received – and declined – an offer to go to St. Louis to found an art school based on the Parisian system.[61] A.C.R. Carter revealed that all of Stott's Salon paintings were purchased by an American art dealer who was attending the Paris Salon.[62] For Stott, whose continuance in Paris was dependent upon having the necessary funds, the sale of these works would no doubt have given him some much needed financial assistance. An anonymous typed note in the Stott Archive reveals that when Stott was in Paris he lived on 6p a day. He would boil his eggs in his coffee to save gas, as well as collecting bits of bread left at the easels of fellow students which were used for rubbing out. The money he saved in this way went on his studio fees and materials.[63]

THE PARIS SALON

THE HISTORY OF THE PARIS SALON is complex. From its original formation in 1725 to, at least, 1890, its ever-shifting structure and artistic preferences for the academic versus the progressive went through many changes which were closely linked with French politics.[64] During Stott's period in Paris, the politics of the Third Republic (1870-1940) dominated. The French government had withdrawn its official support of the Salon in 1881, which led to a group of artists who called themselves the Société des Artistes Français taking over responsibility for the shows. Within the Société, and directly representative of the politics at the time, a sub-group of artists emerged who combined both academic and progressive features in their paintings. Boime calls this sub-group the *juste milieu* of the Third Republic.[65] These artists 'gratified...the public taste for modernism combined with traditionalism by modifying the disquieting features of impressionism and rejecting the polished technique of the academic painter. The public could appreciate the impressionists' doctrine of light and colour when it was made palatable by more solid draughtsmanship.'[66] Probably the most well-known artist in this group was Jules Bastien-Lepage.[67] John Forbes-Robertson, reviewing the Paris Salon of 1881, commented on Bastien-Lepage's work which, with its 'open-air and naturalistic effect...makes everything around it look conventional and artificial.'[68] He also commented on the internationalism of the Salon which was 'catholic and all-embracing', with the paintings on display showing the work of artists as far apart and dissimilar as Madrid, London and New York.[69] Thus, the Paris Salon was an integral part of the art students' time at the École des Beaux-Arts, as it enabled them to showcase their work to their peers and, perhaps more importantly, attract patronage and reach an international clientele. Two years later, at the Salon of 1883, Edward Stott would have two of his 'student' works included in this geographically eclectic international arena where, as mentioned previously, he did indeed sell his work to an American buyer.

5. Edward Stott, *The Helping Hand of a Small Friend* (also known as *In the Fields, Auvers sur Oise*), 1882. Oil on canvas, 164.5 x 104.1cm. Private Collection/Photo © Christie's Images/ Bridgeman Images

Getting work accepted into the Salon was not straightforward and was also highly competitive. Those pictures not exempt from Jury selection would be voted for by the selectors and, according to the number of votes received, were allotted a reception number. Those that were voted in unanimously would be given a 'No. 1' vote which ensured a prominent centre-line position. Those obtaining second ranking would also get to show 'on the line', but in a less prominent position. Those receiving a third selection would get 'skyed' [sic].[70] Furthermore, although it seems that pictures were accepted on merit, Fox revealed that it was sometimes beneficial to have a 'friend' or master on the Jury, particularly if a picture was in the rejected pile and subject to a second chance.[71] It is not known if Stott had a contact on the Jury, or if his work was selected on merit. However, as he was successful enough to have four paintings chosen, this suggests they were selected on merit. Two works were exhibited at the Salon of 1883 – *The Helping Hand of a Small Friend* (1882) (Fig. 5) and *Solitude* (1883).[72] At the Salon of 1884, Stott exhibited *The High Grasses* (1883) (Fig. 1) and *The Return to the Poultry House* (1884).[73] As the images show, Stott was clearly interested in rural themes from the outset. As the critic for *Time* magazine remarked on the Salon of 1883, the landscape section consisted of 'Quaint mills, pools in which boys are bathing or ducks swimming, cottages…hill sides…twilight-shadows of the rising sun abound, whilst the monotony is broken by finely painted cattle or carefully drawn rustics…and by sombre or silver-lined clouds, illumined by dashes of light.'[74] Based on this list, it is evident that these formative years of art training for Stott influenced his choice of subject matter for many years to come.

THE PARIS PAINTINGS

THIS EARLY GROUP OF PAINTINGS, which reflects Stott's output as an art student, reveals the combined influences of Carolus-Duran, Corot and Bastien-Lepage, with hints of Impressionism. In terms of subject matter, it is evident that his early interest lay in the depiction of country children and scenes of rural life. Halkett wrote that Stott was 'chiefly attracted by Bastien Le Page [sic] and Édouard Frere, two men of widely different ideas, but both successful painters of children.'[75] Whilst there appears to be little affinity between the work of Stott and the overly 'sweet' paintings of Frere, apart from the superficial preference for painting children, it is apparent that Bastien-Lepage had been an influence, as had Corot. What *The Helping Hand of a Small Friend* and *The High Grasses* show is that Edward Stott had taken the teachings of Carolus-Duran on board.

The dominant palette used in *The Helping Hand of a Small Friend* is grey-green with a tonal range of dark through to light, with touches of blue-grey to add variety. Here, Stott is following Carolus-Duran's strictures on colour. As explained by Kennedy: '*Demi-teint* is the watchword of the Carolus-Duran *atelier*', with 'his emphatic

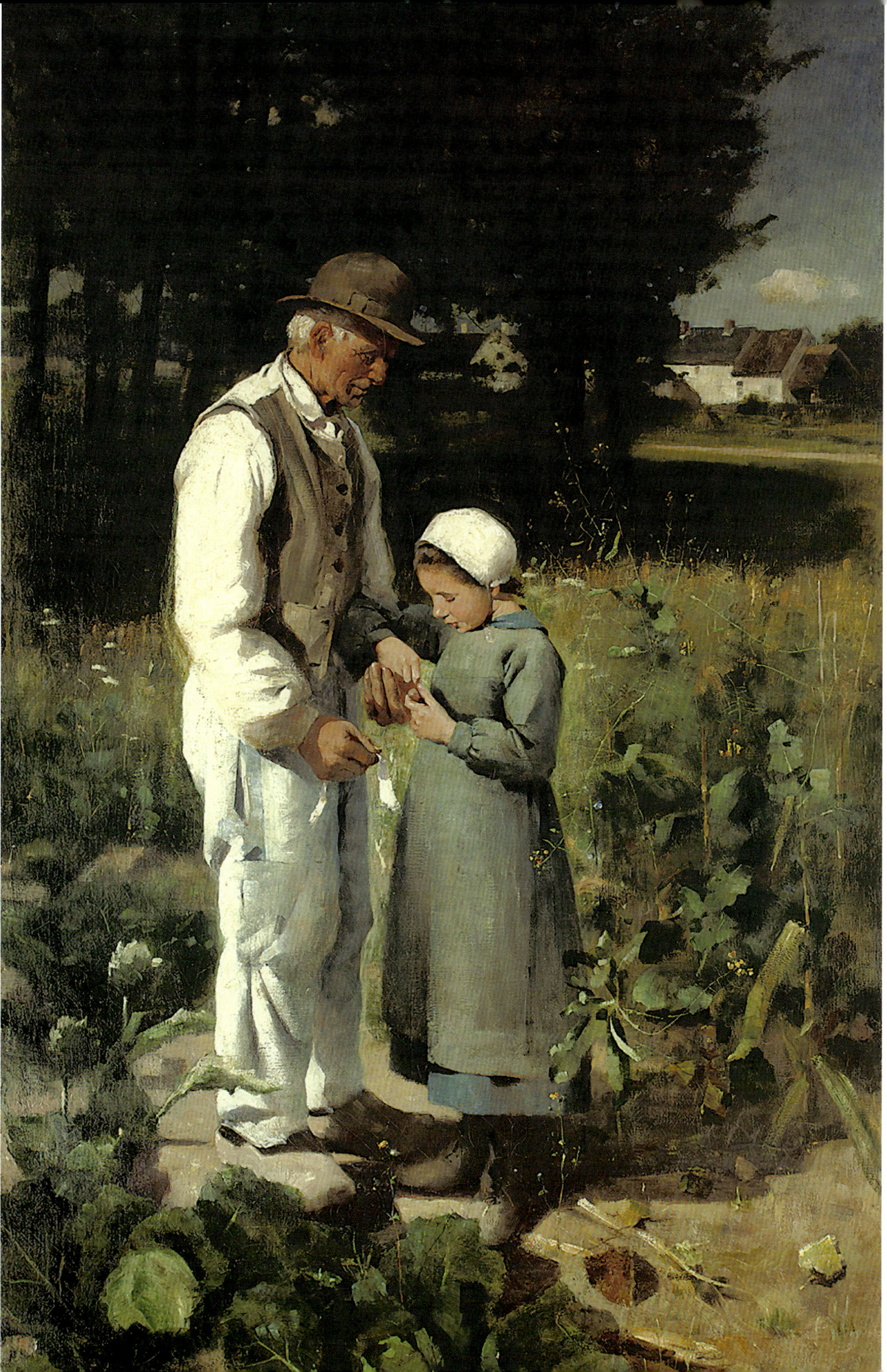

assertion that "high-lights" are not a separate thing from the *grand demi-teint* of the figure; but only a brighter tone, different from it much less than one would suppose.'[76] Stott's following of this advice can be glimpsed in the 'highlighted' circular green cabbage which stands out from the clump of dark green cabbages in the left-hand corner of the foreground. Furthermore, the whiteness of the girl's cap and elderly man's shirt is repeated in the walls of the houses in the background, but is less white to accurately denote distance. At this stage, Stott's choice of colours is restrained and aims for tonal harmony.

Spatially, and compositionally, the scene follows a logical sequence from the foreground to the background which is achieved by the segmenting of the canvas into horizontal bands of alternating light and dark, known as *chiaroscuro.* In the spatial structuring of the scene, Stott would appear to be echoing the practice of Corot. As Richard Shiff has identified, the structure of Corot's landscapes revealed that he took care over the relationship between the 'chiaroscuro values' evident in a scene and his naturalistic views.[77] Shiff also points out that the structures of Corot's landscapes became 'formularizations of the laws for the use of values' which can be traced back to Claude's 'hierarchical ordering of composite elements.'[78] The spatial ordering of 'chiaroscuro values' within a naturalistic setting can be identified in *The Helping Hand of a Small Friend* in the way that Stott has divided up the landscape into sections. Commencing with the cabbage patch depicted in shade, this is followed by the patch of earth containing the two figures and behind which is the grassy area, both portrayed in sunlight. This is followed by the dark shaded area of the trees and, finally, in the distance a row of houses in sunlight. In this formulaic ordering of the landscape, Stott has also maintained a careful regard for colour values and how they change accordingly when depicted in sunlight and shade, and in spatial terms. As a result, the visual appeal of this painting lies in its spatial and compositional unity, and tonal harmony, which combines to produce a scene where a sense of calm and stillness prevails. In the placing of the figures in the foreground, he was also echoing the compositional formula of Bastien-Lepage. In all other respects, he appears to be making a reference to the teachings of Carolus-Duran and paintings by Corot.

Stott has repeated this formulaic structuring in *The High Grasses* to create a scene that is viewed from left to right, rather than from foreground to background. What his use of chiaroscuro in this work achieves, is to 'advertise' his accomplishment in accurately conveying how the colour of the grass changes in sunlight and shadow and how its appearance varies within the depicted space from the foreground and beyond. This is evident in the visible blades of grass at the front which have been achieved by Stott's 'sketchy' brushstrokes, and where flecks of paint have been dabbed on to give the impression of plants and leaves. As the scene recedes, the tangible quality of the brushwork is less apparent and the effect is one of smoothness, as if all the minutiae of detail has been removed. In reality this is how a landscape would look.[79] Further evidence of Corot's influence can be seen in Stott's placing of the young country boy in the middle-ground and situated off-centre. This compositional device used by Corot can be seen in the positioning of the young girl in *Le Rageur, Forest of Fontainebleau* (c.1830). Furthermore, the colouring of the young country girl's clothing, which is painted in tones similar to the rock upon which she sits and the surrounding countryside, almost merges her figure into the scene. This merging of the human form with nature is mirrored by Stott in his depiction of the young country boy, whose brown trousers echo the brown tree trunk just behind him to the right, whilst his blue-grey clothing links him to the sky. Overall, his figure is fairly indistinct within the setting, and his delicate form is paralleled by the tall thin silvery tree trunks which are placed around him. This air of delicacy is also a feature found in some of Corot's works – such as *The Leaning Tree Trunk* (c.1860-65) – where his insubstantial figures are often dwarfed by the landscape settings they occupy. The tonal harmony of Stott's painting, however, refers back to Carolus-Duran.

One of the significant differences between *The High Grasses* and *The Helping Hand of a Small Friend*, is the style in which it is executed. Gone is the opacity of the smoothly applied paint which has been created using broad brushstrokes in the latter painting. Instead, in *The High Grasses*, there is a lightness of touch which comes about through the flecks of light and dark paint with which to pick out the leaves on the trees and foliage on the ground, and rapid brushstrokes used for the grass. Hence, in the delicacy of the brushwork, the insubstantiality of the forms, and the painting's tonal harmony, *The High Grasses* departs from the more prosaic rustic landscape scene of the former painting, and introduces a poetic note, similar to Corot's. As Shiff writes, the poetry of Corot's works emerges because he did not merely imitate nature, but maintained control over his technique for the sake of poetic expression.[80] Shiff quotes the French journalist and art critic, Théophile Thoré, who spoke of Corot's work as the '"opposite of imitation. It is invention, it is originality, it is the manifested sign of a particular impression. Poetry is not nature, but the feeling [*sentiment*] that nature inspires in the artist".'[81] These statements by Shiff and Thoré respectively, can equally be applied to Stott's approach to painting where he often aimed for a poetic impression rather than verisimilitude. In this respect, it was the poetic nature of his work that drew the critics' attention where Stott was often described as a 'visual poet'.

Whilst in Paris, although exhibited at the Royal Academy, Stott produced *A French Kitchen Garden* (1883) (Fig. 6), which seems to be a departure from the teachings of Carolus-Duran and perhaps striking a note of individuality. In this painting, Stott's use of colour is richer than the muted tones of the paintings discussed above, and the contrast between shade and sunlight is more pronounced: the white walls of the building provide a bright contrast to the partially shaded area, whilst the parched piece of earth in the foreground offers a contrast against the varying green hues of the vegetation. According to Kennedy, Carolus-Duran 'detested any exaggeration of the changes of local colouring', such as that used by

6. Edward Stott, *A French Kitchen Garden*, 1883. Oil on canvas, 45.1 x 59.7cm. Sheffield Galleries and Museums Trust, UK/Photo © Museums Sheffield/ Bridgeman Images

the Impressionists, whose paintings he felt were 'full of pieces of blue and orange jumping out to strike you in the eye.'[82] In terms of facture, Stott's broad flat brush-strokes create an effect of stability and earthiness. His handling of space is also more experimental. Commencing on a diagonal line at the right-hand corner of the picture which contains the patch of earth, its border directs us towards the solitary young girl positioned off-centre in the middle-ground. Compositionally, such a placing can be likened to the young boy in *The High Grasses*. The girl's upright form is mirrored by the slightly taller wooden post to the right of the painting, with a smaller post situated behind her. Here, through simple but effective means, Stott has created the illusion of space and depth. He has also achieved a sense of unity and balance in his use of horizontal and vertical forms, which are repeated in the rustic dwelling in the background. However, the painting is not without its technical deficiencies which can be seen in Stott's attempt to accurately reproduce the sky. The two blue patches to the right of the scene have the appearance of standing out in front of the trees, rather than vice versa. The painting of skies was notoriously difficult to portray correctly, and Carolus-Duran urged his students to remember how many 'thicknesses of atmosphere' there were between themselves and the distance.[83] If the students took his advice, then the blue of the sky might not appear so bright. If the advice was ignored, as Kennedy recounted, 'The result is that it does not keep its place in the picture, but comes as forward as many things meant to be close at hand.'[84] Depicting the sky as it appeared in reality involved technical dexterity, and Stott had not yet mastered this. In fact, as later examples reveal, this was a technical aspect of painting that he sometimes grappled with.

Both *The Helping Hand of a Small Friend* and *A French Kitchen Garden* portray countryside scenes of French smallholdings where the importance of family tradition and generational support was essential for their continued livelihood. In the latter work, it is interesting to note the colouring of the young girl's clothing and the way in which Stott has positioned her within the scene. If it was not for her white cap, she would merge into the surrounding vegetation. In a general sense, this reinforces her identity as a country girl and, in particular, links her specifically to the vegetable garden and the dwelling behind. This theme of tradition and generational support is something Stott would return to in his Amberley series of paintings.

In terms of subject matter and the naturalistic handling, both paintings reflect the influence of Bastien-Lepage, but *A French Kitchen Garden* also reveals an affinity with a theme popular in Scottish art known as 'kailyard' painting where the subject matter depicted is that of 'cottars and cabbages.'[85] As Laura Newton states, the trend for paintings with this kind of subject matter can be traced back to circa 1878 when the Scottish artist Arthur Melville produced *A Cabbage Garden*, which achieved some success at the Royal Academy in 1878. Melville had also visited the exhibition of French paintings at Durand-Ruel's gallery in 1878, where he would have seen works by Millet, Corot, Puvis de Chavannes and Bastien-Lepage. Possibly as a direct

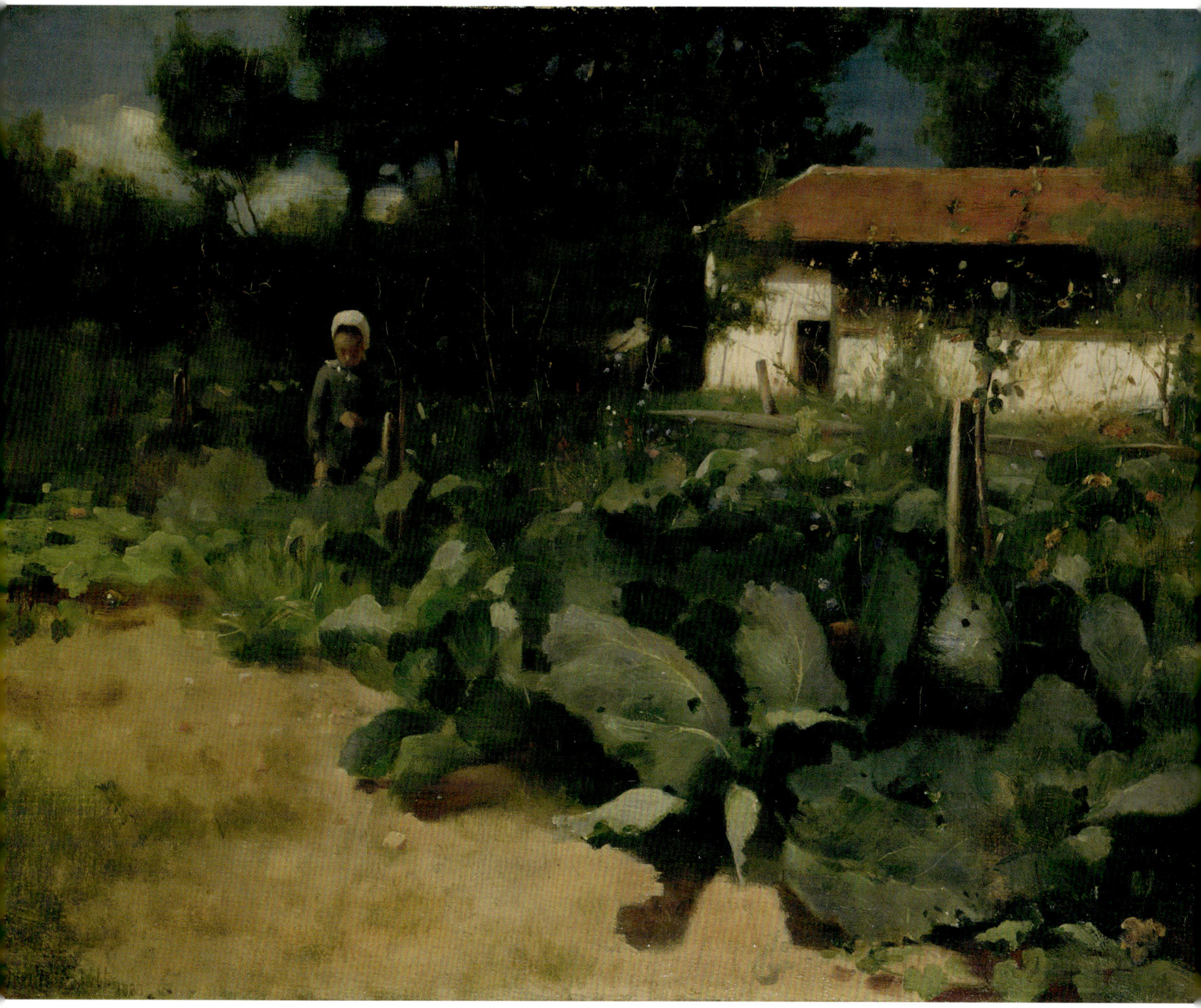

result, Melville went to France during the years 1878 to 1881, initially to study at the Académie Julian in Paris, and then to Grez which was a popular artists' colony. Melville had also exhibited a number of French-inspired paintings in Scotland during this period which 'reveal[ed] a knowledge of the Bastien-Lepage-inspired Naturalist style prevalent amongst the international community of artists at Grez at this period', which reinforces the idea that a cross-channel dialogue was taking place.[86] It is feasible, therefore, that Edward Stott was either indirectly or directly influenced in this way and *A French Kitchen Garden* was a result of this Scottish-French dialogue. As a theme, it proved to be popular amongst Scottish artists, some of whom painted collectively as the Glasgow Boys, who also went to Grez.[87] However, Roger Billcliffe has credited William Stott of Oldham with making the Glasgow Boys aware of Grez and Bastien-Lepage, asserting that:

> For the group of English and Scottish painters studying in Paris at the beginning of [the] decade there was a much more tangible link with naturalism provided by one of their countrymen – William Stott [who] had an immediate response to the work of Bastien-Lepage when he first encountered it in Paris. He met Lavery, Roche, Kennedy and Millie Dow in Paris and it was perhaps he who introduced them to Grez-sur-Loing.[88]

The privileging of William Stott of Oldham in art-historical accounts may have arisen due to the early success he had with his painting exhibited at the Paris Salon of 1882, *The Ferry*, for which he won a third-class medal, and which caught the attention of the critics back home. Furthermore, his allegiance to Whistler where he was a central figure in Whistler's circle at the Royal Society of British Artists until they had a disagreement, might also explain his preferential treatment by today's art historians.[89] Thus, any contribution that Edward Stott's painting may have made to the 'kailyard' theme, or any influence that he might have had on other artists, has been overlooked. As McConkey has pointed out of *A French Kitchen Garden*, it may have exerted some influence on the work of the Scottish artist James Guthrie who did not go to Paris as an art student.[90] There are indications, too, that Edward Stott may also have had some influence on the work of George Henry (as discussed in chapter two).

With the same Christian names and surnames, and both coming from Lancashire mill-owning families and being contemporaries in Paris, this may have resulted in some confusion and, no doubt, competition between the two artists. As Anne Dinnage recorded in her 'Reminiscences', (William) Edward Stott evidently caused some perturbation for William Stott of Oldham who approached Edward on the grounds that a 'change of name would be both graceful and convenient.'[91] Stott evidently replied, although this is possibly anecdotal, 'that he would have been charmed to make it, but for the fact that his mother had already marked his pocket-handkerchiefs.'[92] These facts may explain why they chose different locations for their 'colony' experience. Whilst William Stott of Oldham went to Grez-sur-Loing in the vicinity of Fontainebleau with some of the Scottish artists, Edward Stott headed in the opposite direction to Auvers-sur-Oise, near Pontoise, approximately 70 miles away from Grez. This may have been a tactical move on the part of Edward Stott in order to put an 'artistic' and geographical distance between them.

THE 'COLONY' EXPERIENCE

An essential part of an art student's training was to take part in the 'colony' experience; to find an inspirational place to paint, share ideas and form alliances that would, in all probability, continue once they had finished their training. Arguably, the most famous of these artists' colonies was Barbizon in the Forest of Fontainebleau which gave enduring inspiration to such artists as Corot, Millet and Daubigny in the early 1800s, where they became known as the Barbizon School. By 1875 this area had become a major tourist attraction and, as a result, over-populated.[93] The group of British, Irish and American artists from the atelier of Carolus-Duran, chose the less populated area of Grez-sur-Loing.[94] The colony of Grez-sur-Loing had its heyday between 1880 and 1885, attracting such artists as Frank O'Meara, William Stott of Oldham, John Lavery and some of the Glasgow Boys.[95] The coastal areas of Normandy and Brittany were also popular, with colonies springing up in Quimperlé, Concarneau and Pont-Aven. As McConkey found, there was often groups within groups who were linked to particular hotels and stylistic sub-sets. For example, in Brittany there was a series of colonies that attracted artists who moved around from one set to another, or from one location to another.[96] Quimperlé was a favourite location for Stanhope Alexander Forbes, Henry Herbert La Thangue and Walter Osborne. However, on occasion, these artists could also be seen working in Pont-Aven and Concarneau.

Edward Stott chose Auvers-sur-Oise which was a commune in the suburbs of Paris, approximately 17 miles from the centre. It appears to have attracted a diverse group of French painters; the Barbizon artists Daubigny and Corot painted at Auvers, as did the Impressionist Camille Pissarro, who also painted at nearby Pontoise. Two leaders of French Post-Impressionism – Paul Cézanne and Vincent van Gogh – were also inspired by the area. From this early stage in Stott's career, it is evident that the countryside appealed to him rather than coastal areas; when Philip Wilson Steer returned to England he chose the seaside resort of Walberswick in Suffolk, and Stanhope Forbes and his followers eventually formed their own art colony in Newlyn, Cornwall.[97] In contrast, Edward Stott began his search for an ideal 'sketching ground' – his 'corner of the world' – and this would always be in a rural area.[98]

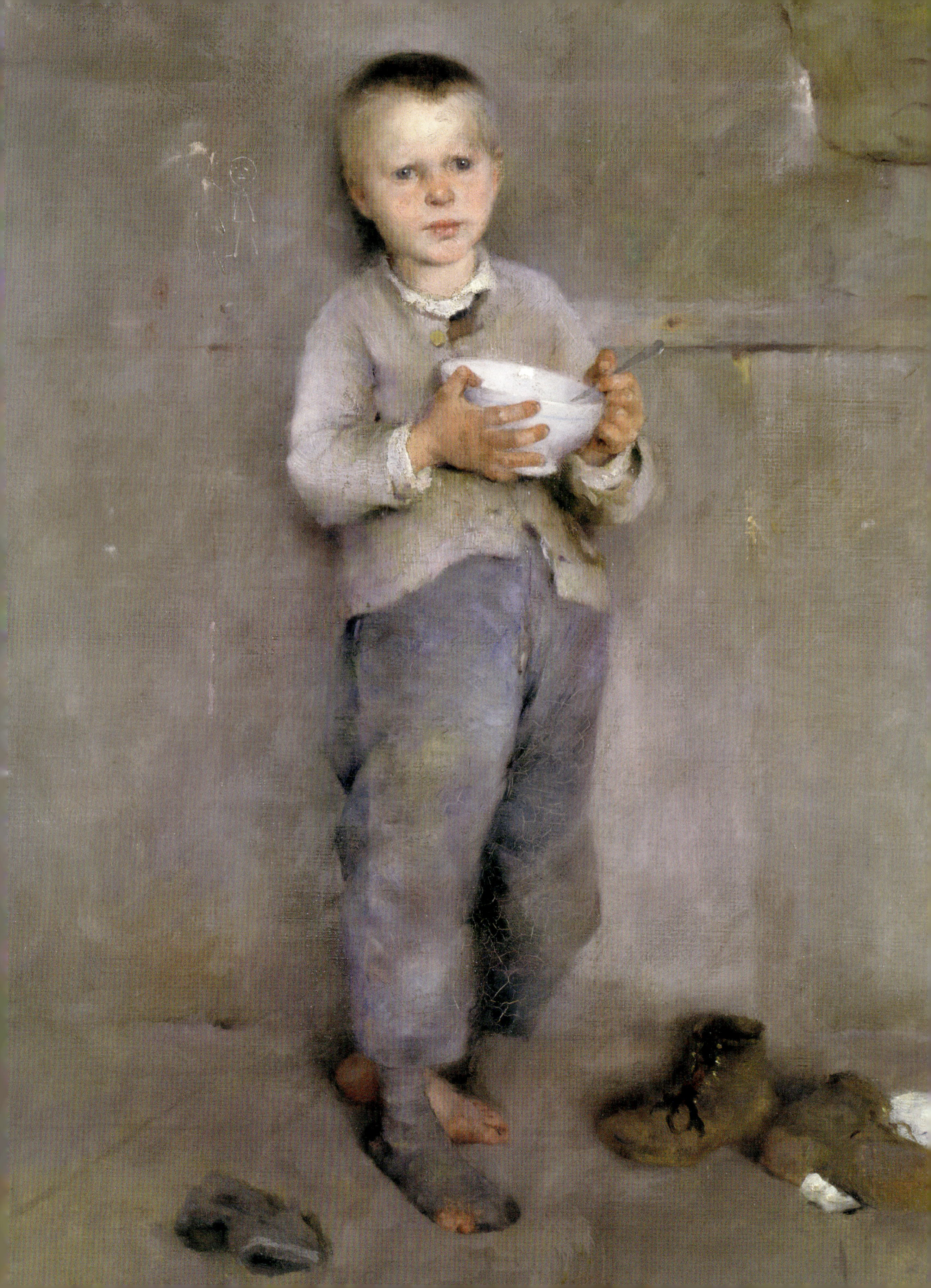

2

THE SEARCH FOR AN IDEAL 'SKETCHING GROUND' AND EXHIBITING VENUE

Upon Edward Stott's return to England from Paris he began his search for an ideal 'sketching ground'. Initially, this saw him making a brief visit to Suffolk before residing temporarily in the counties of Worcestershire and Hampshire, before finally settling in Amberley, West Sussex. As to exhibiting venues, on his immediate return he began to submit work to London-based venues such as the Institute of Painters in Oil Colours and the Grosvenor Gallery, and occasionally to Manchester. Whilst in Paris he had continued to send in work to the Royal Academy, and had at least one success with *A French Kitchen Garden.* However, as his friend J. Stanley Little revealed, his work was often rejected by the Academy. Of those

7. Edward Stott, *As Happy as a King,* 1884. Oil on canvas, 71.1 x 50.8cm. Private Collection/Susannah Pollen Ltd/Bridgeman Images

paintings that were accepted, they were often hung far from the central line and 'hopelessly cornered.' With regards to Stott's choice of themes at this point, he continued his interest in the depiction of children within the countryside but also experimented with portraiture. In terms of style, his paintings reveal the broad brushstrokes associated with rustic naturalism and, in his use of certain motifs, a continuing reference to Bastien-Lepage can be identified but in a modified form. Furthermore, Stott's take on Bastien-Lepage was quite distinct from that of his contemporary, George Clausen, who was considered the British equivalent of Bastien-Lepage. On close examination, it is evident that Stott's brand of rustic naturalism had very little in common with that of Clausen or La Thangue, with both of whom he has often been generally linked. In fact, it would appear that Stott had a momentary shared artistic vision with the Newlyn artists Stanhope Forbes and Elizabeth Forbes (née Armstrong). With their adapted brand of rustic naturalism, the paintings they produced were visually uplifting rather than socially thought provoking, and Stott's paintings fitted in with their artistic ethos. It is clear there existed more than one kind of rustic naturalism; Gabriel Weisberg, in his study of rustic naturalism in European art from 1860-1905, shows the phenomenon to be widespread in Europe and extending to America.[99] Of course, all were ultimately informed by Bastien-Lepage but the subject matter was nuanced by a range of artists and groups in order to create their own individual expressions.

EARLY ALLIANCES

IN 1884 STOTT'S SEARCH FOR a sketching ground led him to Walberswick, at the same time Philip Wilson Steer was painting there.[100] The two men would have become acquainted at Cabanel's atelier and, once back in England, it is clear they rekindled their association and both began to exhibit with the Institute of Painters in Oil Colours. Over the ensuing years they exhibited with the same organisations even if they moved in different artistic circles, and they were still in contact in the 1890s as is evident from the sketches they drew of each other.[101] However, they did have artistic differences: whilst Steer's early preference was for coastal locations such as Walberswick in Suffolk, where he concentrated on getting inspiration for what became a series of seaside scenes painted in an overt Impressionist manner, such as *Knucklebones, Walberswick, Suffolk* (1888) and *Girls Running, Walberswick Pier* (c.1888-94), Stott preferred the countryside. This is evident from an early pastel sketch of around 1884, *Sheep in a Suffolk Landscape*. It is in this early example where a connection can be made with the Irish artist, Walter Osborne, who also initially visited Walberswick and was a contemporary of Stott and Steer at the Institute of Painters in Oil Colours. Rather than go to Paris, Osborne had studied in Antwerp at Verlat's Academy. Previous to this, he had studied at the Royal Hibernian Academy in Dublin where his teacher was Augustus Burke.[102] Burke had visited Walberswick in 1883, which possibly inspired some of his former students to visit the area.[103] Stott found a kindred spirit in Osborne and a shared interest in rural subject matter. Clearly striking up a good enough friendship for Osborne to lend Stott money, from 1884 to 1885 they lodged together at the home of Mrs Gould in North Littleton, Evesham, Worcestershire, and then moved to Wherwell, near Andover, Hampshire, from 1885 to 1886.[104] Their shared interest in countryside settings, and related themes, is visible in Stott's pastel, *Sheep in a Suffolk Landscape* (c.1884), and Osborne's painting of 1885, *The Return of the Flock*, which should not be confused with a similarly titled painting exhibited by Osborne at the Institute in 1885-6. However these two examples do highlight their differing individual approaches in terms of composition. Whereas Osborne's painting presents a panoramic view depicting an archetypal 'shepherd and sheepdog' theme, Stott's focus is narrower with focal points of interest to create depth and perspective. From the small flock of sheep in the foreground, the eye is taken to the bridge which crosses the stream, and then to the windmill which is strategically placed on the highest point in the background and which looks down on the scene below. Stott has layered his landscape using horizontal bands of various shades of green which further adds to the illusion of perspective, which recalls his Paris training. He has also conveyed the idea of movement in his inclusion of a stream seen meandering beneath the diagonal bridge and disappearing into the landscape. In a more straightforward compositional approach, Osborne's canvas is divided into two thirds sky and one third landscape, in which is placed a group comprising shepherd, sheepdog and sheep, all of which have a static and posed quality.[105] In contrast, Stott's pastel has the appearance of being created 'in situ'. As he was still working in *plein air* mode at this time, it is likely that the scene was executed on the spot. This 'natural' or realistic capturing of a scene was something Stott would always strive for in order to convey the idea of immediacy or spontaneity – an 'of the moment' effect.

Two further examples attest to the working partnership between Stott and Osborne. There is a similar technique with both artists using broad flat brushwork and, once again, shared subject matter as both paintings focus on children at play within rural settings. Osborne's painting, *A Garden Party* (1883), depicts a boy and girl having a tea party within an enclosed space of a yard or garden, where they are joined by their pet rabbits which have been let out of the hutches. Stott's painting, *Tin Whistle Player* (also known as *Children by a Gate*) (1884), portrays a boy and girl within a panoramic landscape (likely to be the Vale of Evesham), where the boy sitting on the gate serenades the girl with a tune on his tin whistle.[106] The way that Stott has chosen to portray his children in a sunny wide-open landscape setting suggests connections with Stanhope Forbes, particularly during his 'Brittany' period, and Elizabeth Forbes, a connection likely to have been established at the Institute of Painters in Oil Colours with whom Stott began to exhibit on his return to England.

8. Edward Stott, illustration of *Amateurs*, 1884. © The British Library Board/Exhibition Catalogue/Institute of Painters in Oil Colours/7857.d.21

THE INSTITUTE OF PAINTERS IN OIL COLOURS

FORMED IN 1882 AS A PARENT society to the Royal Institute of Painters in Water-Colours, the Institute of Painters in Oil Colours had pretentions of being akin to the Royal Academy with many of its artists either being Associates of the Academy or full Academicians. Non-members were permitted to exhibit but, as the Institute's Articles of Agreement stipulated, their work would be chosen 'subject to the selection principles of the Royal Academy.'[107] As the list of artists contributing to the Institute exhibitions reveals, Edward Stott, Walter Osborne and Philip Wilson Steer, exhibited briefly as non-members from 1884. At this time Osborne was focusing on scenes of Lincoln and Norfolk, and also exhibited a painting called *The Return of the Flock* in 1885-6, which depicted a boy and sheepdog driving the flock down a village street.[108] Steer showed a painting with the title of *Tired Out* at the 1884-5 exhibition, which was a seaside scene with the foreground dominated by a young girl lying on the beach.[109] Stott exhibited three paintings from 1884 to 1886: *Amateurs* (1884) (Fig. 8), *The Complete Angler* (1885) (Fig. 9), and *The Harvest Moon* (1886). *Amateurs* is now lost. However, as the illustration included in the exhibition catalogue shows, the finished painting depicted a boy and girl sitting on a plank of wood placed over a stream. The critic for the *Magazine of Art*, declaring Stott to be 'publicly French', described the painting as an 'instantaneous impression of a brook, with tall grasses and white sunshine, and two urchins angling', and criticised him for failing to put 'in any values, and entirely refus[ing] to recognise the existence of any interest save the interest of paint.'[110] Whilst the description of the scene is not entirely accurate, what can be gleaned from the anonymous critic's comments is that the brushwork was possibly impressionistic and therefore viewed as having a style that was modern and influenced by French painting. *Harvest Moon* (now lost), also illustrated in the exhibition catalogue, depicts a young girl following behind a line of ducks, and was remarked upon for its 'modern skill' in *The British Architect.*[111] Meagre though these comments are, it is obvious that no connection with Bastien-Lepage was identified by the critics, which possibly indicates that Stott was beginning the gradual process of moving away from such an influence.

Interestingly, contemporary critics were not that enamoured with Bastien-Lepage's images of rural poverty. When *Les Foins* was exhibited at the Grosvenor Gallery in 1880, it received negative comments from the critics and some were vitriolic and aimed exclusively at the young woman featured in the painting.[112] Bastien-Lepage clearly divided opinion. As the critic for *The Spectator* wrote, 'round [Bastien-Lepage's] pictures there gathers constantly a little knot of worshippers or scoffers admiring or condemning in the most vehement manner.'[113] For an artist such as George Clausen who was considered to be the British equivalent of Bastien-Lepage, and whose Childwick Green series of paintings were exhibited at the Institute of Painters in Oil Colours exhibitions, his association with the French

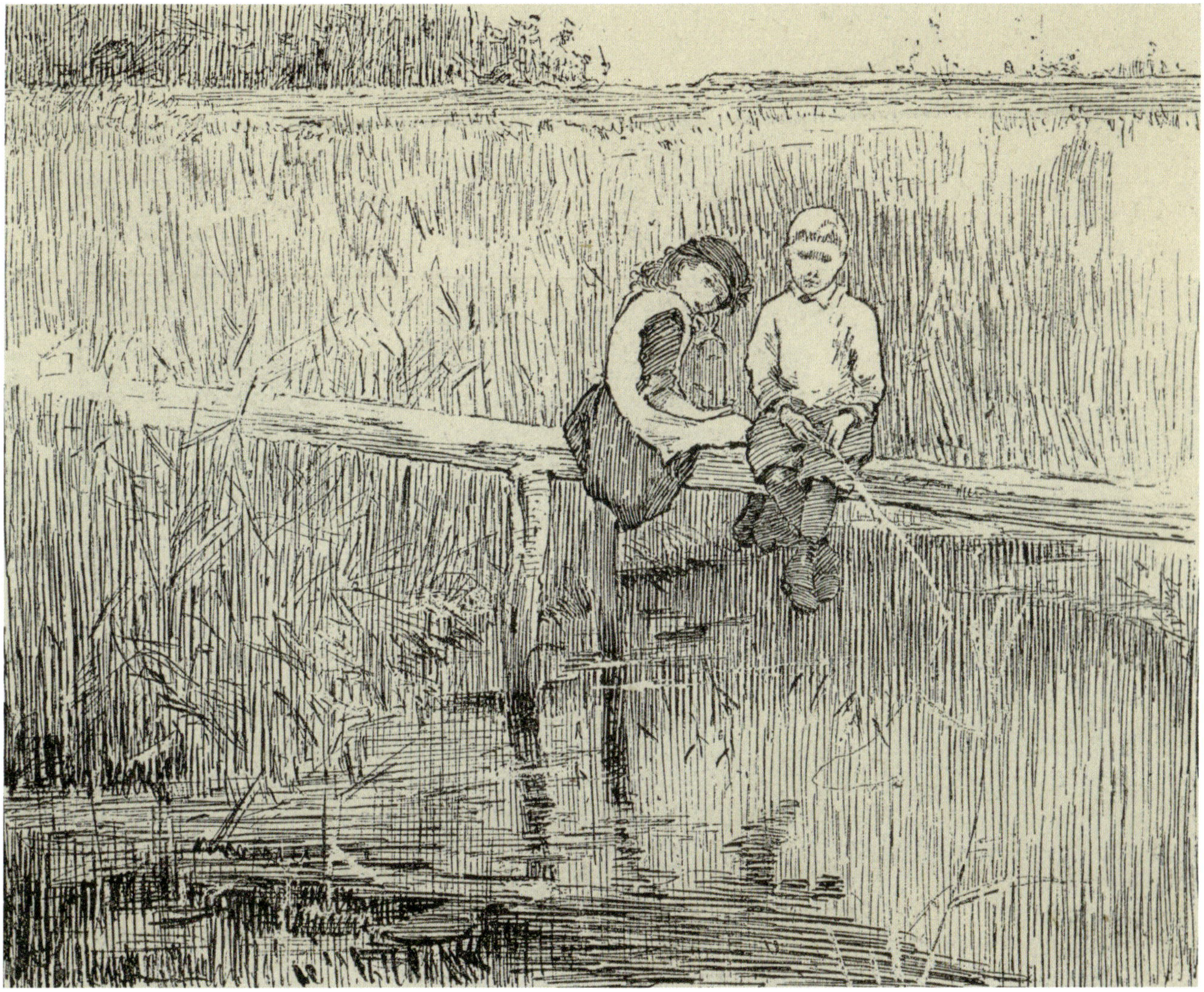

artist's work had repercussions for his own critical reputation.[114] The critic writing for *The Standard* recognized the influence of Bastien-Lepage in his painting of 1883, *Day Dreams*, which he felt was manifest in the elderly woman's lack of 'comeliness of feature' and the young woman's 'very ill-made gown.'[115] Elsewhere, critics spoke of Clausen's 'passive complacence' in his imitation of Bastien-Lepage, and his painting of 1885, *A Field Hand*, was denounced in the *Magazine of Art* for its lack of beauty and finish.[116] Whether as a result of such a negative reception, or merely to show that he could produce more visually pleasing work, Clausen changed direction with *Little Haymakers* (1885) which attracted positive comments. *The Graphic*, for example, was relieved to see that Clausen was now drawing inspiration directly from nature and that his little haymakers had a 'youthful beauty and natural grace of movement.'[117]

Favourable criticism was important for an artist's career. Julie Codell has written on the power critics held and how they provided a form of advertisement for individual artists, groups or 'schools' that helped shape reputations as a form of capital to create a market for their own knowledge.[118] Critics often wrote for more than one periodical or newspaper, and sometimes recycled and revised their contributions in terms of style, tone and politics. In this way, as Laurel Brake has shown, they could cater for a diverse audience which enabled their criticism to be broadly disseminated.[119] Hence, it is feasible to suggest that Clausen was aware of how his association with Bastien-Lepage and rustic naturalism was not enhancing his reputation. Furthermore, as Anna Gruetzner Robins has pointed out, Clausen had ambitions for financial reward and critical recognition.[120]

It seems that Edward Stott was sensitive when it came to criticism. In a letter Stott wrote to the landscape painter Herbert Harlakender Gilchrist, dated 28th October 1909, he was so affected by one of his paintings being rejected by the Royal Academy, that it caused him 'such mental anguish…that I destroyed it when I got back to Amberley…an act I admit I have ever deplored. One is not responsible for one's words and actions in such circumstances.'[121] In a letter to his friend J. Stanley Little, dated 1st November 1899, Stott wrote 'The work goes slowly but I think steadily, and I also think you will like the things I hope to get done for the spring but painting is a hard and long business… Still it is gratifying to know that the few people who have seen the things like them.'[122] Although Stott appears not to take criticism or rejection of his work too well, he was not above being critical of other artists' work. As letters held in the Getty Research Institute Library reveal, Stott could be fairly dismissive of certain of his contemporaries. Commenting on an exhibition of water-colour sketches by D.S. MacColl, he writes to Little:

> Some of them are very pretty and he has no doubt a very nice feeling for colour. Of course – to me that is – as an exhibition I cannot take it very seriously. It is the kind of thing that in a way is so easy comparitivily [sic] with more serious work. Indeed no one can relate the difficulties – technically – in oil medium for instance – to get any of the subtler qualities of colour light and atmosphere. Whereas a man… of course of average ability is able to suggest a very pretty impression of a thing with the merest wash of water colour. Still the show is distinctly worth seeing.[123]

Elsewhere, Napier Hemy's work is described as 'matter of fact and undecorative', whilst Buxton Knight is 'a good executant but has not the least bit of taste. He'll paint anything and the first thing he comes to. There's no beauty in his pictures.'[124] Stott's opinions on past artists is also interesting, in particular the work of Turner when compared to Claude. In correspondence with Gilchrist in 1909, he states that 'I have often thought that this great master, compared with Turner, is not made enough of. People forget the great part that Claude plays or has played, is all landscape work that last two and half centuries…. There is a Claude…at Petworth House. I think the finest picture, landscape, I mean, ever painted. It fairly takes ones breath away and yet you see the visiting crowds of people going past it as if it gave them more pain than pleasure.'[125] The sentiments were reiterated in 1911, again to Gilchrist, 'Yes I felt quite sorry for Turner at the Grafton show. That copy of Rembrandt's hill makes the Turner hill next door look very empty and common.... Again the Turner water colours look very poor and theatrical after looking at the Girtens [sic] and the I. Cognans. It has always seemed strange how little we hear of Claude Lorraine and yet how much is blathered about Turner. I wonder where Turner would have been if he had never seen Claude.'[126]

Stott appeared to circumnavigate such issues that faced Clausen by producing paintings that combined elements and leitmotifs of Bastien-Lepage with a style that also negotiated a refined form of Impressionism. As McConkey states in relation to artists of this period who foregrounded the principles of Bastien-Lepage, 'In most instances...artists moved from a strict adherence to the dogma of Bastien-Lepage to a more personal style which exhibited some of the features of Impressionism. Edward Stott...is interesting in this regard.'[127] Evidence of Stott's fusion of rustic naturalism and Impressionism to produce a formative 'personal style' can be identified in *The Complete Angler* (1885), which was exhibited at the Institute of Painters in Oil Colours in 1885. By including the leitmotif of a young boy carrying a stick over his shoulder, and the way in which he makes his young boy central to the scene, he is making an overt reference to Bastien-Lepage's painting of 1882, *Pas Mêche* (Fig. 10). Nevertheless, differences in the works reveal the individual artistic intentions behind the paintings. In Bastien-Lepage's painting the young boy is holding a whip and horn which indicates that he is a barge boy who ekes out a living by controlling the horses and alerting the lockmaster of their arrival. He may have an expectant look on his face but, as the translated title of the painting confirms, there is 'nothing doing' in the way of work. This painting, then, forms part of the series of works by Bastien-Lepage that focus on child poverty, whilst Stott's painting is very much about childhood pastimes, such as catching minnows or tiddlers. In terms of style, Stott has departed from the broad brushstrokes and blended colour associated with rustic naturalism. Instead, he has used impressionist brushstrokes which have been applied in a controlled and methodical manner. In his treatment of colour, he has moved away from the tonal harmonies of some of his earlier work and used contrasting colours: the use of black and white stands out against the rich green of the grass and the acid yellow of the jug, the red flower on the girl's hat, and the boy's orange hair, all strike a bright colouristic note against the green, thus drawing attention to the figures. Stott has also sacrificed realistic representation for pictorial unity – the stream which separates the background from the foreground takes the form of a black band and the colour black is repeated throughout the picture by way of the boy's and girls' clothing, thereby creating unity. This striving after pictorial unity through colour was something Stott returned to in his later paintings of religious

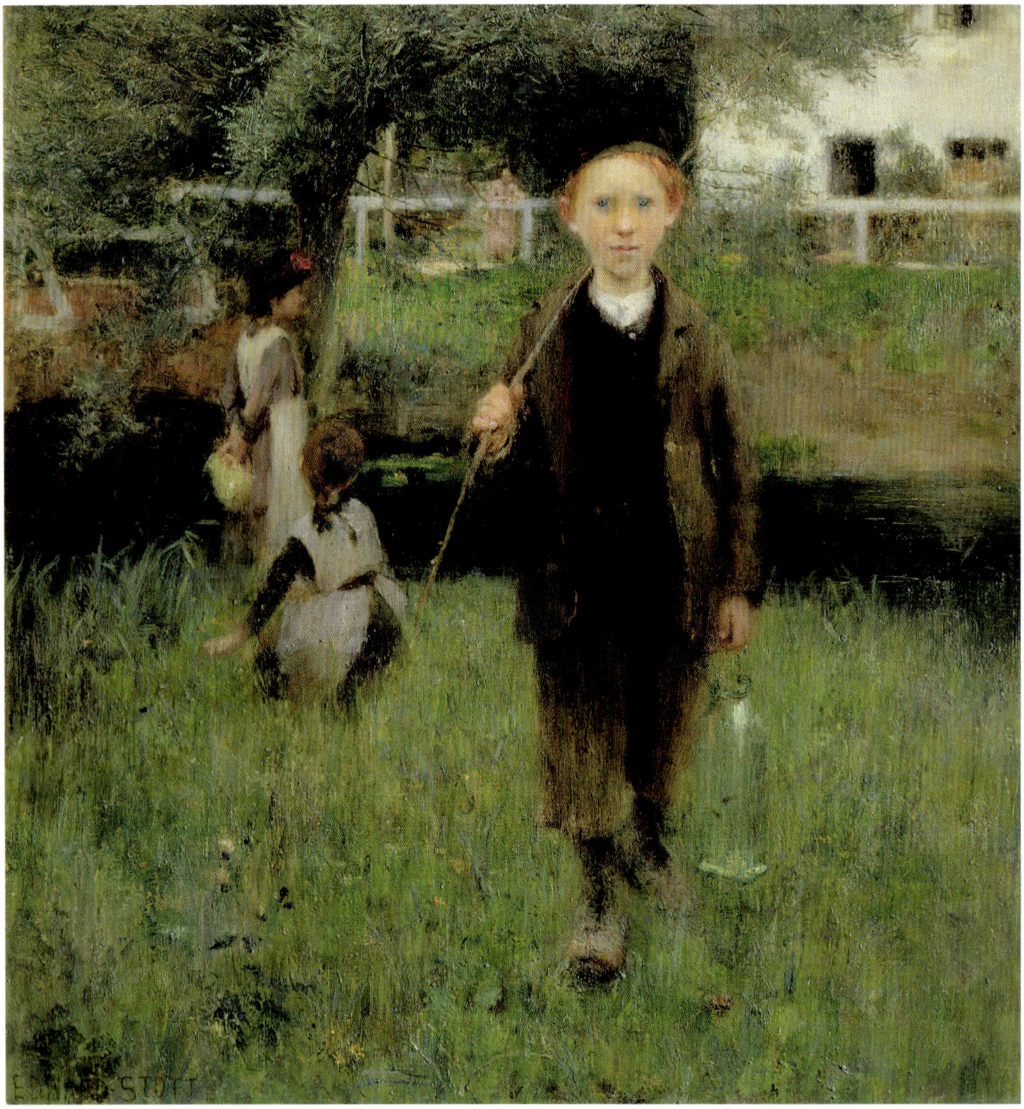

subject matter. Whilst there is undoubtedly evidence of Bastien-Lepage in this work, Stott is also leaning towards Impressionism and introducing a more adventurous use of colour. In this respect, then, *The Complete Angler* is a hybrid work.[128]

Apart from Stott, Steer and Osborne, other non-members who exhibited with the Institute included Elizabeth Armstrong (she had not yet married Stanhope Forbes), Fred Hall, and Stanhope Forbes who exhibited briefly with the Institute in 1886. All of these artists would soon cease exhibiting with the Institute. As early as 1884, there was discontent amongst members and non-members which was mainly to do with the hanging and exhibiting policies.[129] By late 1886, the Institute was in financial difficulty and many of its members – including La Thangue and Clausen – had by this time resigned.[130] Steer had also begun to exhibit at the Grosvenor Gallery in 1885, where he was joined by Stott, Elizabeth Armstrong, Stanhope Forbes and Fred Hall. There was clearly an artistic connection between Stott, Forbes and

9. Edward Stott, *The Complete Angler*, 1885. Oil on canvas, 71.1 x 68.6cm. Private Collection/Photo © The Fine Art Society, London, UK/Bridgeman Images

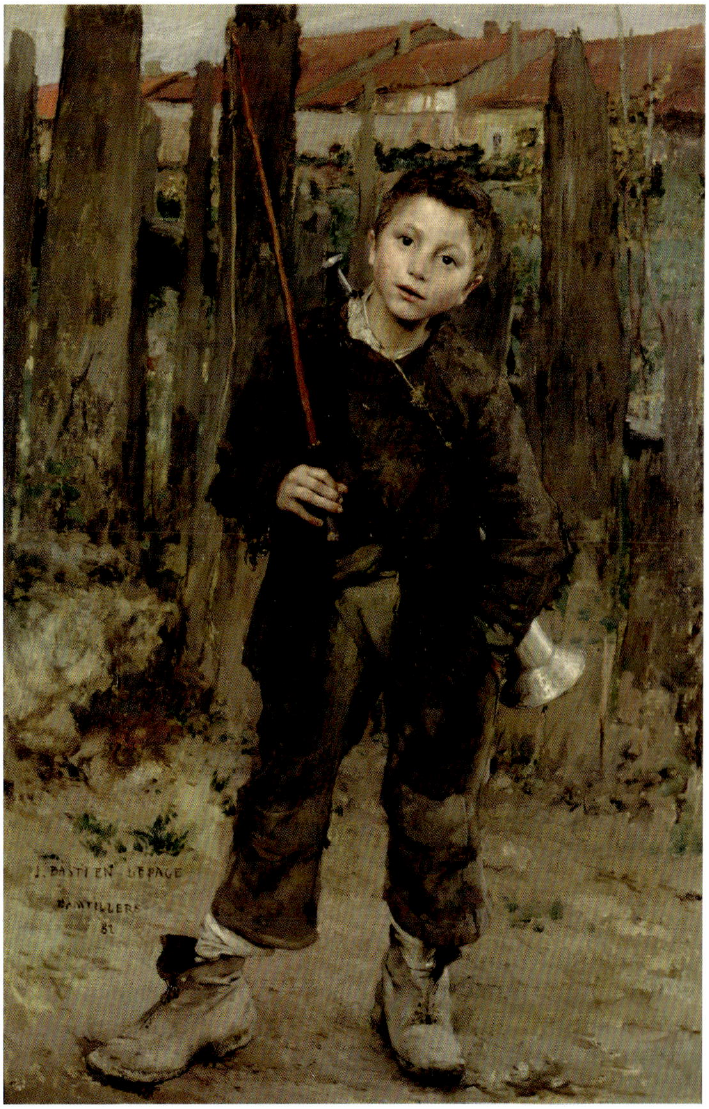

10. Jules Bastien-Lepage, *Pas Méche*, 1882. Oil on canvas, 132.1 x 89.5cm. National Galleries of Scotland, Edinburgh/ Bridgeman Images

Armstrong – albeit short-lived – as all three of them reinterpreted Bastien-Lepage's paintings of child poverty to produce works that were socially and aesthetically uplifting. Forbes, together with La Thangue, had gone to Brittany in the summer of 1882, and painted a series of scenes which focused on children playing and street scenes of women preparing for market or chatting in groups. In *The Old Convent, Quimperlé* (1882) (Fig. 11), the scene takes place on the banks of the river Odet, with the old Ursuline Convent in the background, on a bright sunny day.[131] A red-faced petulant looking boy is gazing down at a young Breton girl seated on the grass holding a paper boat, with an unconcerned look on her face. The boy stands with one hand on his hip, whilst in the other hand he holds onto a stick which is placed over his shoulder in direct imitation of the motif used by Bastien-Lepage in *Pas Mêche*, and repeated by Stott in *The Complete Angler*.[132] The light-filled setting of Forbes' painting might have provided the inspiration for Stott's painting of the tin whistle player (see p. 31).

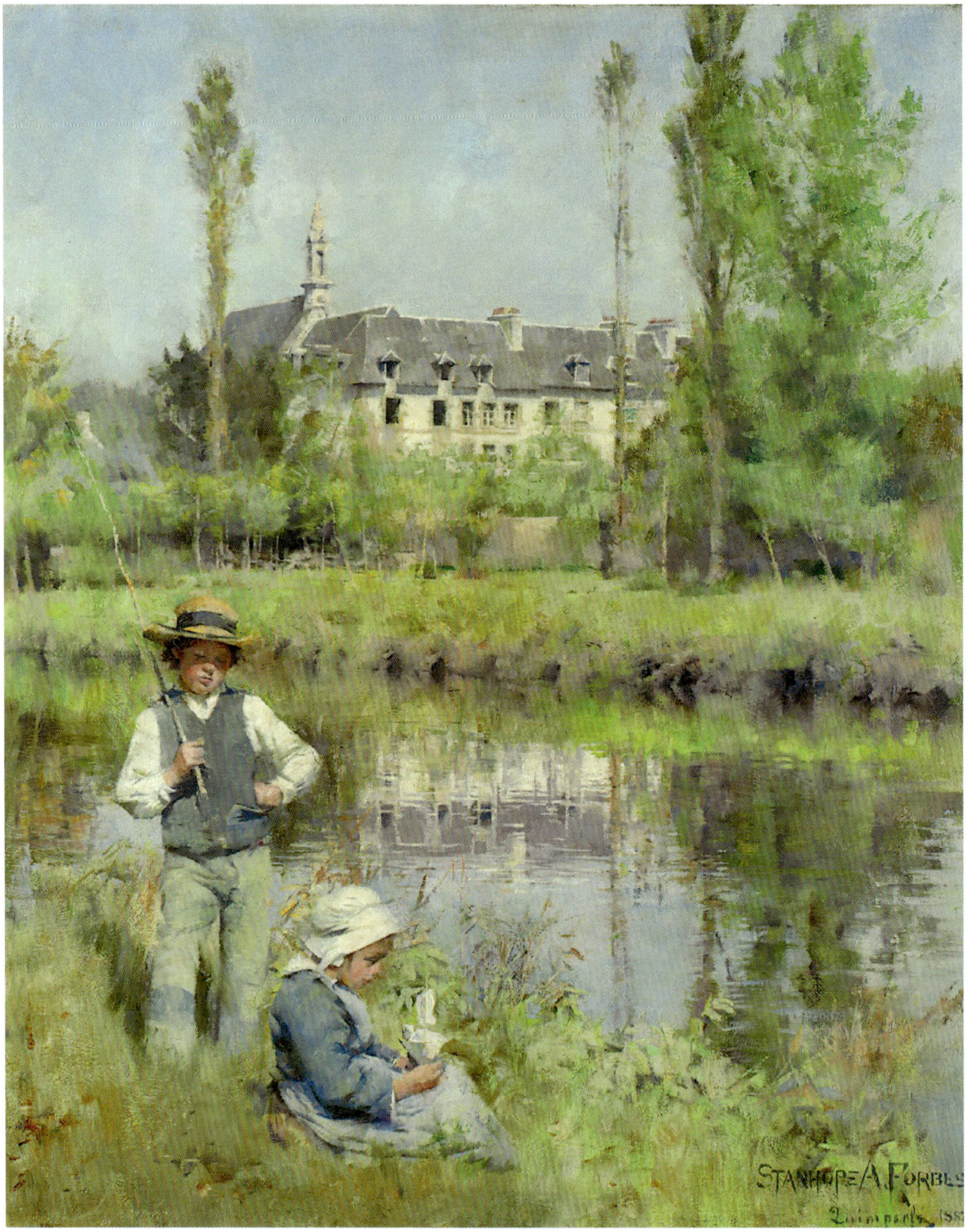

11. Stanhope Alexander Forbes, *The Old Convent, Quimperlé*, 1882. Oil on canvas, 86.5 x 76cm. Private Collection/Photo © Sotheby's London

The theme of children playing in the wide-open space of the countryside was continued by Elizabeth Forbes in a little-known pastel entitled *Hide and Seek* (c.1889 or after).[133] Whilst the pastel unquestionably acknowledges the influence of her husband, Stanhope Forbes, it also reveals an affinity with Stott's painting due to the setting, theme and the shared motif of a wooden gate. This feature also appears in a number of paintings by Forbes, and fellow Newlyn artist Harold Harvey in a later painting of 1906, *Swinging on a gate.*[134] This trio of paintings by Elizabeth Forbes, Stanhope Forbes and Stott, through their open-air settings, shared theme and motifs, reveals a complex weave of associations which is continued in Stott's painting of 1884, *As Happy as a King* (Fig. 7). In this work, the combined influences of Bastien-Lepage,

Osborne and Stanhope Forbes are apparent. The influence of Bastien-Lepage can be seen in the depiction of Stott's boy which shares a close relationship with the young boy in *Pas Mêche*. There is the shared theme of child poverty and hardship, illustrated by their ragged clothing and worn, cast-off boots. In *Pas Mêche*, the boy's boots have no laces and are far too big, whilst in Stott's painting the boots have holes and are stuffed with paper. These two examples pre-date van Gogh's series of paintings of old work boots which he produced during 1886 to 1888, of which Martin Heidegger wrote in *The Origin of the Work of Art* (1935):

> From the dark opening of the worn insides of the shoes the toilsome tread of the worker stares forth. In the stiffly rugged heaviness of the shoes there is the accumulated tenacity of [the] slow trudge through the far-spreading and ever-uniform furrows of the field swept by a raw wind. On the leather lie the dampness and richness of the soil. Under the soles slides the loneliness of the field-path as evening falls.[135]

As prosaic as a pair of old boots may seem, as an art form they have symbolic resonance which speaks volumes about the poverty, hardship and the itinerant nature of the search for work. Such symbolism, when thought of in conjunction with Bastien-Lepage's and Stott's paintings, is made poignant by the fact that the wearers of these worn-out boots are children. Similarly, the deprivation of Bastien-Lepage's boy is reflected in the drab tones of his clothing and the dreary colour of the scene as a whole. Stott has chosen equally sombre tones of blended green-grey and brown, with a smudge of muted lilac, for the interior setting of the outbuilding which is in a dilapidated state. Yet, a positive note is sounded because, as the title attests, the boy is as 'happy as a king' because he has food and shelter which is all the riches he needs at the time. Whilst there are compositional similarities between the two boys, and the shared subject of child poverty, generally Stott's paintings do not comment on socio-economic factors. More likely, he is paying homage to Bastien-Lepage who, after a long illness, died in December 1884.

With reference to Osborne, perhaps Stott and Osborne were trying to create their own identifying leitmotif. In Osborne's painting, *A Garden Party*, the boy is holding a bowl and spoon, both of which also appear in Stott's *As Happy as a King*. Stott would use this personal leitmotif in two later paintings. As to a reference to Forbes, in the blue-grey tones Stott has used for his boy's clothing, he is possibly making a connection to Stanhope Forbes' defining 'signature' colour at that time (which could be called 'Brittany blue') that informed his French paintings and continued in his Newlyn scenes. This painting by Stott then may perhaps be understood as an artistic coda to his paintings at this time which sees him working through a number of influences and assimilations, before moving onto producing work which he exhibited at the Grosvenor Gallery. At the Grosvenor Gallery, Stott continued to experiment with colour and style, revealing an affinity with paintings by the Glasgow Boys.

THE GROSVENOR GALLERY

IN 1885 STOTT BEGAN TO exhibit at the Grosvenor Gallery, where he was joined by a number of his contemporaries from the Institute of Painters in Oil Colours. Founded in 1877, by Sir Coutts and Lady Blanche Lindsay, and assisted by their two Co-Directors, Charles Hallé and Joseph Comyns Carr, the Gallery sought to promote artists who were perceived as not receiving proper recognition in the art world and were being excluded by the Academy. The ethos of the Gallery was to embrace change in the artists they chose to represent as well as recognizing the need to showcase the work of up and coming artists. As the critic for the *Glasgow Herald* wrote, the Grosvenor Gallery 'Each year brings fresh recruits, either from the rising young men or the not yet callous and fossilized followers of the Academy methods…'[136] Sir Coutts Lindsay's artistic preferences favoured the Pre-Raphaelites and Burne-Jones but, as McConkey has written, he also recognized the need for a 'broad Church' in contemporary art.[137] This 'all-inclusive' aspect of the Grosvenor's selection policy meant that paintings by established favourites such as Edward Burne-Jones, George Frederick Watts, Lawrence Alma-Tadema and Edward Poynter, were exhibited alongside paintings by younger artists, many of them who had trained in France. Thus, on the walls of the Grosvenor Gallery, the bowing out of one artistic era and the ushering in of a new one could be witnessed.[138] Undoubtedly this was a calculated move on the part of the Grosvenor Gallery to stimulate press and public interest, and the Gallery certainly appeared to court controversy. It was here that Whistler was invited in 1877 to exhibit some of his paintings, one of which was *Nocturne in Black and Gold: The Falling Rocket*. John Ruskin attended the exhibition and was not impressed by Whistler, whom he publicly denounced as being full of 'ill-educated conceit', and further described him as a 'coxcomb' who asked 'two hundred guineas for flinging a pot of paint in the public's face.'[139] Then, in 1880, Bastien-Lepage's paintings divided opinion, where his painting entitled *Les Foins* attracted negative press attention and, no doubt, would have created some shock value which possibly resulted in increased visitors to the now ailing Gallery.

The Grosvenor Gallery was very successful in its early years, but ran into difficulty in 1879 when Coutts Lindsay experienced personal and financial problems after separating from his wife.[140] With the assistance of his two co-directors, he set out to restore the Gallery's reputation and fortunes and, from the 1880s onwards, began to show work by British French-trained artists. Edward Stott was part of this sea-change, along with those other aforementioned artists. Colleen Denney has identified three main groups in this new batch: the English Rustic Naturalists such as Clausen and La Thangue, Newlyn artists such as Henry Scott Tuke, Elizabeth Forbes and Stanhope Forbes, and Irish and London Impressionists such as Frank O'Meara and Philip Wilson Steer.[141] Denney did not include Stott in any of these categories, possibly because he continued to negotiate different styles and subject

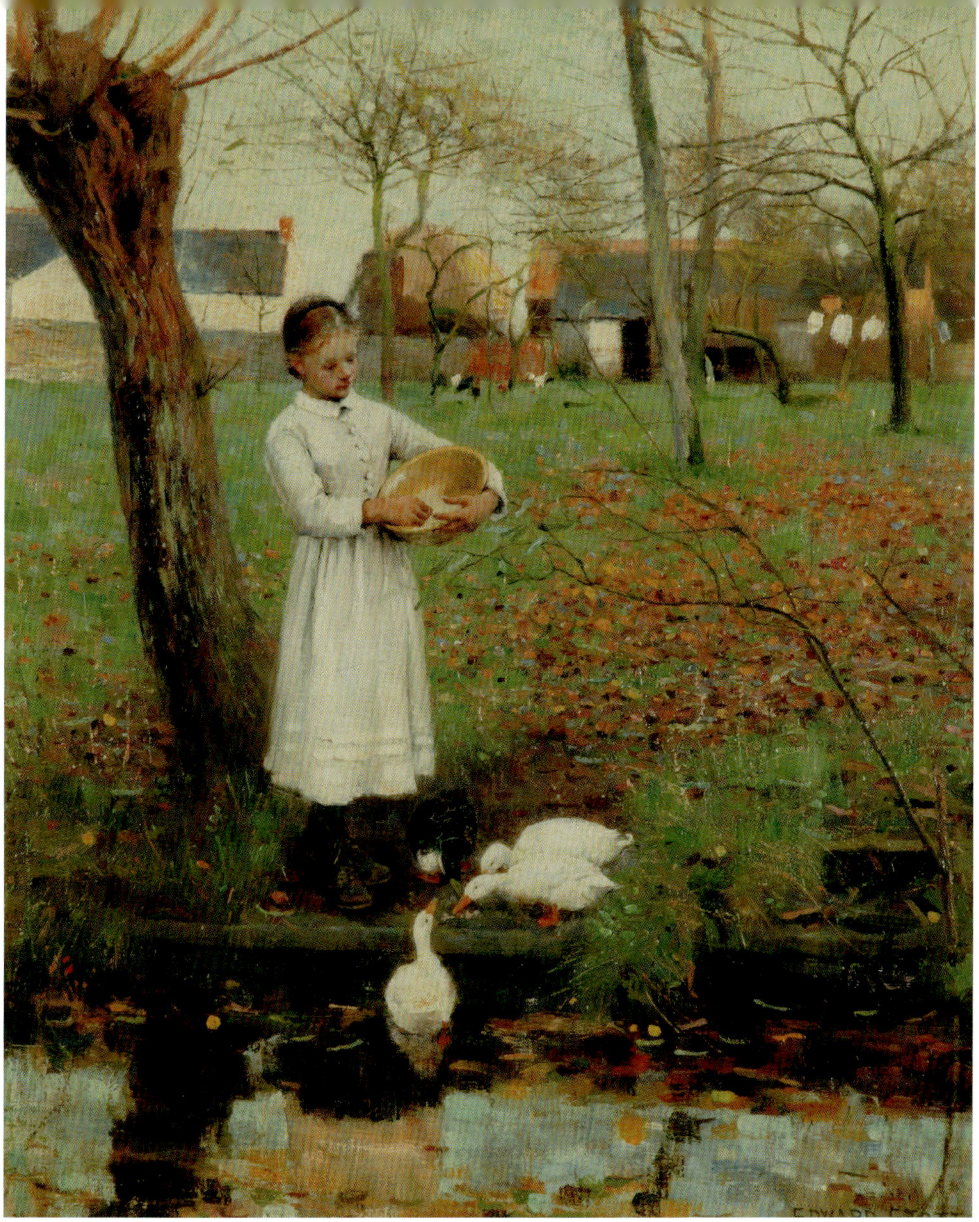

12. Edward Stott, *Feeding the Ducks*, 1885. Oil on canvas, 48 x 39.4cm. Manchester Art Gallery, UK/Bridgeman Images

matter, eluding any neat pigeon-holing. An example is served by two paintings he exhibited two years apart: *Feeding the Ducks* (1885) (Fig. 12) and *Winter's Night, Sussex Village* (1887). Although the theme of both paintings falls within the category of rural scenes, the subject matter is very different. As can be seen in the former painting, a girl is feeding ducks in a farm setting, whilst the latter work depicts a solitary house in a Sussex village street. Of the two examples, *Feeding the Ducks* is a more interesting and technically accomplished work, and shows the impossibility of adequately categorizing Stott's work at this time. Whilst some influence of Bastien-Lepage can be discerned in the foregrounding of the young girl within a rural setting, and in Stott's employment of the square-brush technique used to create the pond, he makes a departure in his use of a rich palette of green, turquoise and russet, which is offset by the bright white of the girl's dress and the ducks. Repeated dabs of white floating in the background (washing hanging on a line) create a feeling

13. Edward Stott, *Portrait of a Young Girl*, c.1885. Oil on canvas, 31.8 x 26.7cm. Private Collection/ Photo © Christie's Images/Bridgeman Images

of distance. The patterning achieved by the square-brush technique, together with the rich colours, lends a decorative note to an otherwise ordinary scene. It is the decorative quality of this painting where an affinity with paintings by some of the Glasgow Boys occurs – for example *Noon* (1885) by George Henry. McConkey has written of how Henry's work, up until 1885, was influenced by the square-brush technique and the rural subject matter of Bastien-Lepage. After meeting Edward Atkinson Hornel, his work began to display a new concern for brighter colour and a more decorative design.[142] Henry's painting, therefore, appears to be a transitional work as it combines elements of Bastien-Lepage in terms of composition and brushwork, and Hornel in the use of rich decorative colour. Consequently, Stott's painting reveals an affinity with Henry's work through their compositional, stylistic and colouristic similarities. These facts notwithstanding, there is a paradox here because George Henry lived and worked almost exclusively in Scotland, and trained there rather than on the Continent.[143] Added to this is the fact that Stott and Henry seem not to have known each other in 1885, although they may have crossed paths later in 1887 when Henry joined the New English Art Club to which Stott also belonged.[144] Neither would the two artists have met at the Grosvenor Gallery. By the time Coutts Lindsay brought the Glasgow Boys into the gallery in 1890, Stott had already ceased exhibiting there.[145] Another inexplicable coincidence also exists. Stott's illustration for *Harvest Moon* (1886), discussed earlier, bears a remarkable compositional resemblance to James Guthrie's painting of 1883, *To Pastures New*. They share a similar theme of a young country girl following a flock of farmyard birds (ducks in Stott's painting and geese in Guthrie's work), which takes the form of a processional frieze. However, as McConkey has pointed out when discussing a painting by George Henry of 1889 which shared interesting similarities with paintings by the Pont-Aven group, such coincidences can inexplicably exist.[146]

As well as continuing to paint rural themes, Stott also experimented with portraiture. Although he was never fully committed to this genre, he occasionally returned to it over the years and produced his final portrait in 1917, *The Patriarch*, (see Chapter Six). In the period 1884 to 1886, Stott produced three portraits. *'Marie' – A May Flower* (1884), was exhibited at the Royal Academy, and described by the critic for *The Art Journal* as a painting of 'A child's head, full of pearly tones and delicate modelling.'[147] Stott followed this up with *Portrait of a Young Girl* (c.1885) (Fig. 13), which appears not to have been exhibited, but at some point was purchased by Duncan Oppenheim.[148] In this portrait we can identify Stott's advancement in his use of colour for decorative purposes, and also a sense of design and pattern being introduced. Using broad bands of the colour gold for the brim of the girl's hat and the edge of her cape, Stott then combines two forms of brushwork. The square-brush technique is used to create pattern and to separate out the pastel-like colours, but smoothly blends in the colours elsewhere. The colourful and decorative image of the young girl is in marked contrast to the energetic impressionist brushwork and

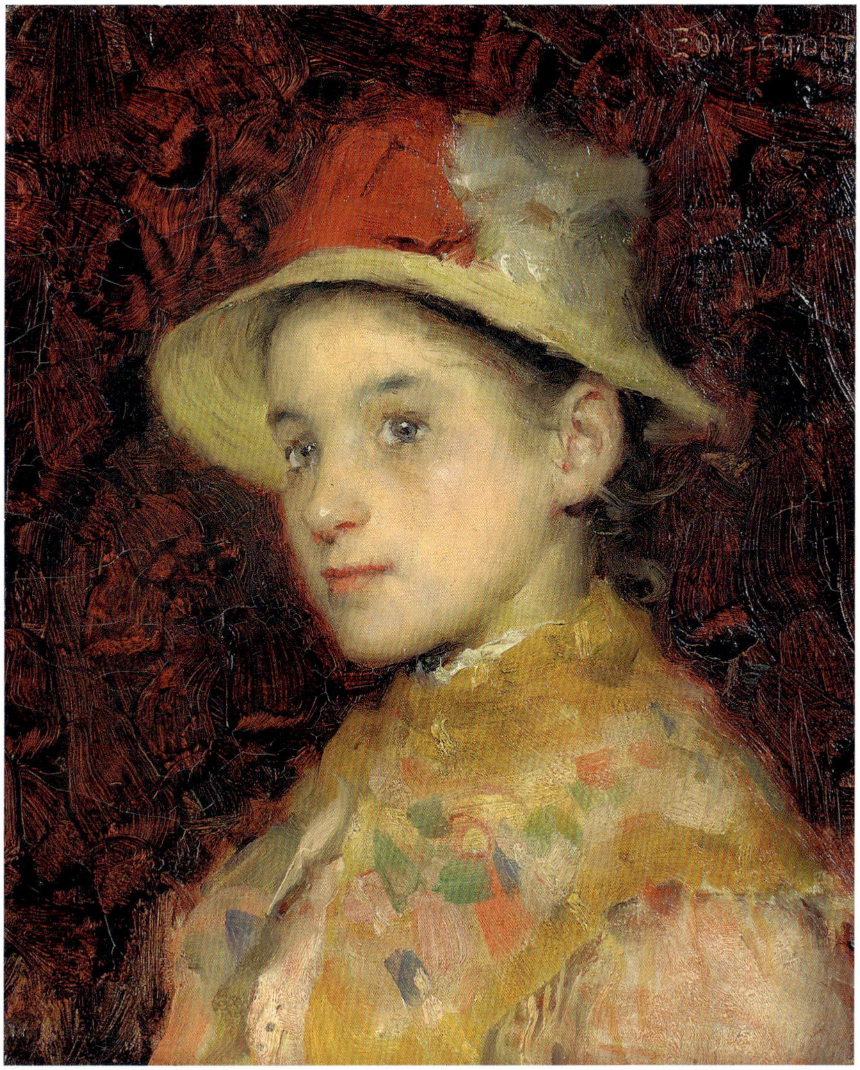

dramatic dark colours used for the background. As to the young girl's features, our gaze moves up and down taking in the red bow or flower in her hat, to the red of her lips, which draws our attention to her soft grey eyes. Stott has not only effectively captured her youthful beauty, but her colourful image is one to be visually savoured. In this painting, it is as if Stott is displaying all his knowledge and skills of facture and colour effects acquired so far. Finally, in 1886, he painted *Mollie – A Portrait* which was exhibited at the Grosvenor Gallery the same year, although nothing further is known about this work. Stott ceased exhibiting with the Grosvenor Gallery in 1886 and became a founding member of the New English Art Club where his paintings began to assimilate new ideas, and where he appeared to form new associations, whilst continuing to strive after his own personal style and defining subject matter.

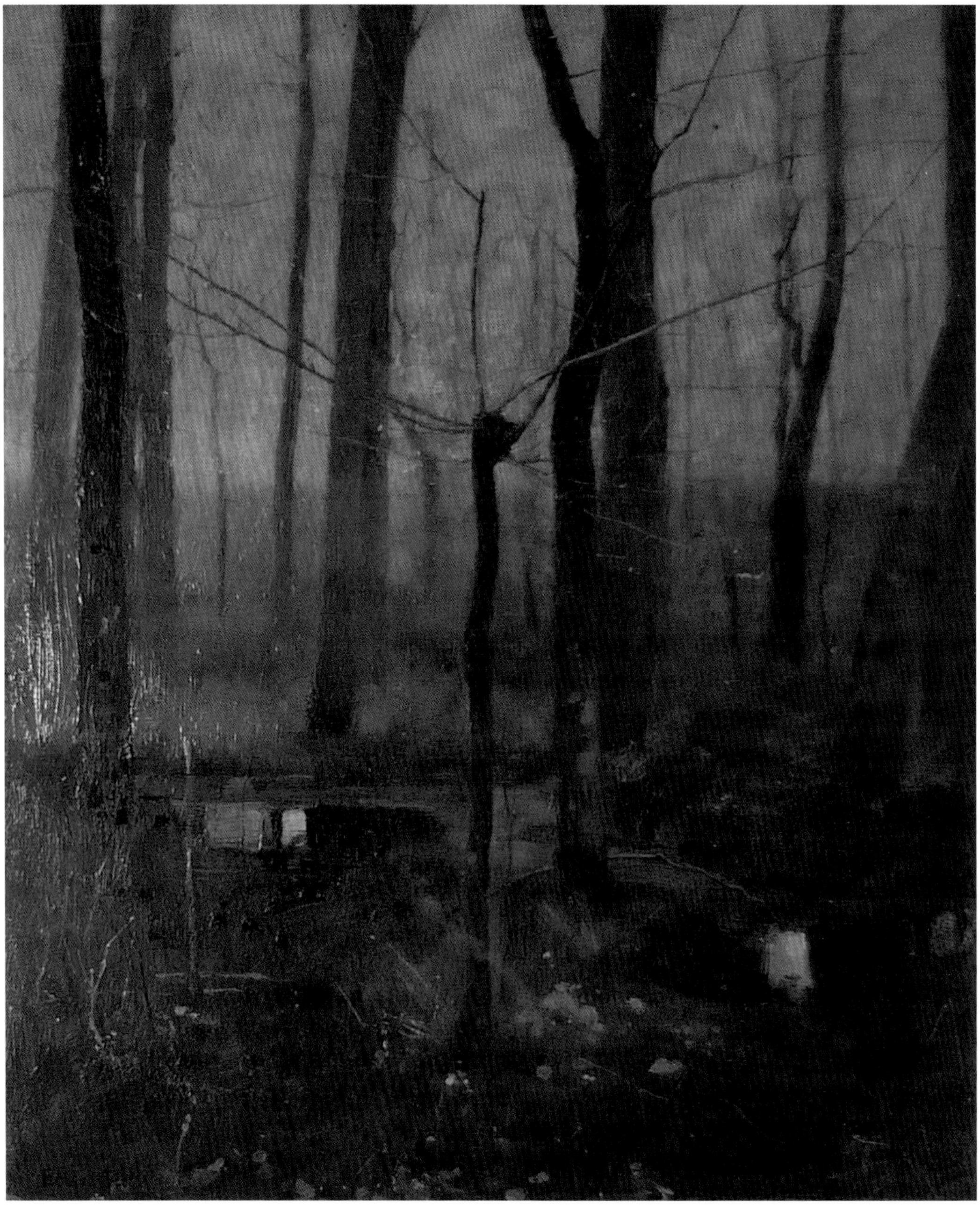

14. Edward Stott, *Alone – Early Spring Woodland*, 1886. Oil on canvas, 36 x 26cm. Brighton and Hove Museum and Art Galleries

3

NEW BEGINNINGS

The New English Art Club and the New Gallery

NEW ENGLISH ART CLUB

EDWARD STOTT'S EXHIBITING CAREER WITH the Institute of Painters in Oil Colours and the Grosvenor Gallery was short-lived as, in 1886, he became a founding member of the New English Art Club and gradually ceased showing at the other two institutions. The formation and history of the Club has been well documented, but it is worth recounting in brief the lead up to the Club's first exhibition.[149] The list of potential artists drawn up by Philip Wilson Steer and others for the fledgling new society was shown to favour the style of Salon Naturalism which was in vogue at the time.[150] Stott, who was a friend of Steer and had produced at least two paintings whilst in Paris which fitted the initial criteria, was included in the list. In January 1886, the first meeting took place at the Marlborough Gallery which was to be the exhibition space for the first show. A committee was formed with an inaugural exhibition suggested for the 5th April 1886, which was one month before the Royal Academy's exhibition. At first the Club was going to be called the Society of Anglo-French Painters, but eventually the title of the New English Art Club was decided upon. On the 12th April 1886, one week later than planned, the first exhibition of the newly-formed club took place.

15. Edward Stott, *The Ferry Boat*, 1887. Oil on canvas, 68 x 119cm. Gallery Oldham, UK/Bridgeman Images

At its inception, the New English Art Club had 50 members and, as the Preface to the first exhibition catalogue stated, these members were 'all more or less united in their art sympathies. They have associated themselves together with the view of holding an Annual Exhibition, hoping that a collective display of their works, which has hitherto been impossible, will prove not only of interest to the public but will better explain the aim and method of their art.'[151] The first exhibition contained a diverse subject matter which included, amongst others, Venetian scenes, portraits, costume pieces, social realist subject matter and landscapes. Examples of Salon Naturalism could be found in paintings by George Clausen, Fred Hall and Henry Herbert La Thangue. For instance, the overt influence of Bastien-Lepage could be discerned in Clausen's painting, *A Shepherdess* (1885), and Fred Hall's painting, *A Fisherman's Daughter* (1886). La Thangue's contribution was an unfinished study for *In the Dauphiné* (1886), which continued the influence of Bastien-Lepage in the composition of the figures and pronounced use of the square-brush technique, but also showed his continuing alliance with Stanhope Forbes in the use of grey-blue tones for the figures' clothing. Stanhope Forbes exhibited *A Fisherman's Head* and *A Cornish Street*, whilst Elizabeth Armstrong exhibited *Pale Primroses*. Edward Stott contributed a somewhat strange painting that was not typical of his output at the time called *Alone – Early Spring Woodland* (1886) (Fig. 14). The work was remarked upon by the critic writing for the *Liverpool Mercury* for its 'original treatment.'[152] As the image shows, the subject matter is a darkly wooded scene with two patches of black water in which is reflected a ghostly white shape, which could either be a reflection of the solitary person in the wood or a reflection of the dun-coloured sky. With the lack of any identifiable stylistic reference, together with the predominantly brown-toned palette and the unusual choice of subject matter (both departures for Stott), perhaps this is what the critic meant by 'original treatment'. Commenting on the first exhibition, the art critic writing for the *Pall Mall Gazette* remarked on the selection of paintings which revealed a 'quite unexpected variety of subject and treatment.'[153] The *Liverpool Mercury* attested to the Club's 'modern' status when it singled out paintings by Stott, Tuke, Clausen and Steer, stating that works by these artists could be found in the 'collections of liberal and unconservative lovers of modern art.'[154] In considering the mix of paintings exhibited by these artists, they certainly reinforce the diversity of the New English Art Club's selection policy. Clausen was still enamoured with Bastien-Lepage despite receiving negative criticism for his rustic naturalist paintings exhibited at the Institute of Painters in Oil Colours. Tuke exhibited two works, a scene of naked boys bathing (*The Bathers*) and *Basking*. Steer exhibited a painting called *Andante* (1886), about which nothing further is known except that it was skied in the exhibition.[155]

The second exhibition, this time held at the Dudley Gallery, took place in April 1887. By this time the Club's membership had increased to 80 artists, with the new members having been chosen from a list of names suggested by existing

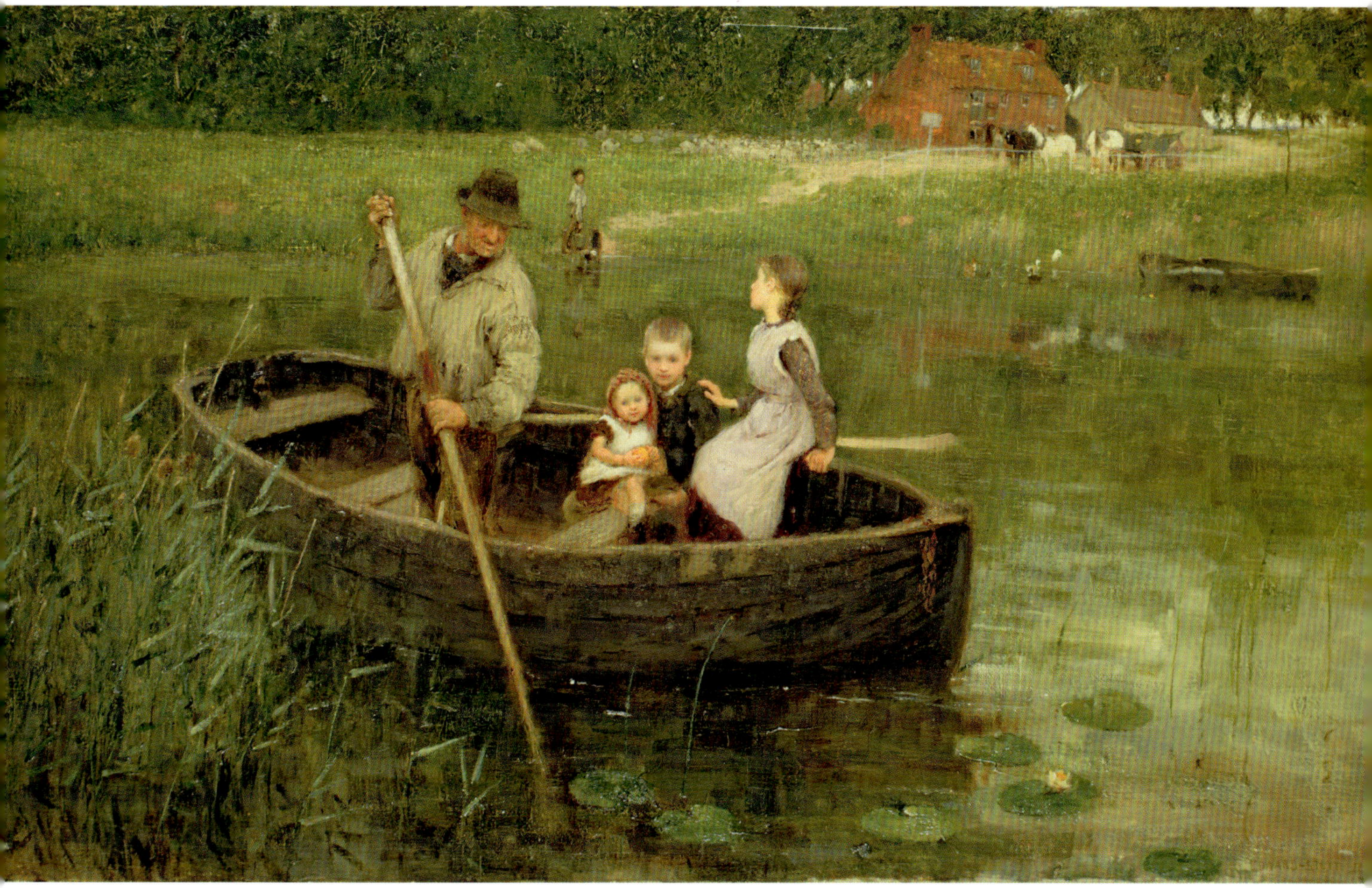

members. American artists working in Britain were now admitted, as were Scottish artists such as Edward Walton and James Paterson, and the Irish born artist John Lavery.[156] Thus, strictly speaking, the New English Art Club was no longer 'English'. Furthermore, after exhibiting only one painting, La Thangue resigned because his idea of a 'Bigger Movement' had been rejected, which left Clausen as the 'standard bearer' of rustic naturalism.[157] In an attempt at bringing some order to such a wide-ranging exhibition, the critic for the *Daily News* identified three competing styles: the rustic naturalism of George Clausen's painting, *Stone Pickers* (1887), Théodore Roussel's portrait of Mortimer Menpes which was described as 'A truly spontaneous piece of Impressionism,' and a selection of paintings by the Glasgow Boys which, from examples given in the previous chapter, were aesthetically distinctive from the other two examples.[158] Edward Stott exhibited two rural scenes. The first was a small 'oil on panel' of Winchelsea Churchyard with the scene illuminated by a low moon. In choosing to depict the scene in this way, Stott had incorporated a Milletesque leitmotif which subsequently became a trademark device for him.[159] His other contribution was *The Ferry Boat* (1887) (Fig. 15). Set also in Winchelsea, this painting represents an early consummate work by Stott. Not only

16. Edward Stott, *Ploughing, Early Spring*, 1891. Oil on canvas, 62.4 x 45.1cm. Touchstones Rochdale

does it capture an effective snapshot of one aspect of country life, it also highlights his accomplishment with tonal harmony using a predominantly green palette. With only the essentials of the scene included, and the careful placing of the figures within the allotted space, on a literal level it tells of a journey made by three children who are being ferried across the river. On a symbolic level, it shows how rural life depended on shared responsibility and generational support. This is suggested through the figure of the elderly ferryman who is safely conveying the children across the water. Similarly, just as the eldest child has responsibility over her two younger siblings, so the middle child holds safely onto the toddler. Thus, responsibility within the family is shared and they are connected to each other by the eldest child resting her hand on her brother's shoulder. The crossing is watched by the boy on horseback at the edge of the river bank who, in turn, is glanced at by the girl. In this regard, the painting succinctly conveys both a physical and gestural connection.

The idea of familial and generational support first appeared in Stott's early work of 1882, *The Helping Hand of a Small Friend* (see Chapter One), and was a theme that he would return to on more than one occasion. Whether this was because it accurately reflected the mutually supportive nature of rural communities or, on a subliminal level, was a visual 'making good' by Stott of his own lack of support from his family, is open to debate. According to J. Stanley Little, this painting was the last picture Stott painted outside, and signalled his gradual departure from the influence of Bastien-Lepage.[160] Once again, the word 'original' crops up when the critic writing for the *Liverpool Mercury* described the painting as 'an original impression...which besides being independent in execution, is full of interesting qualities.'[161] These comments could refer to all the small, but essential, details Stott has included in the scene which gives substance to the human story being told. Equally, they could refer to the manner in which the scene has been painted, which reveals a composite of styles through Stott's use of different brushstrokes. It does seem to be the case that Stott was actively experimenting with facture in order to find his own defining style. Furthermore, at this early stage of his career with the New English Art Club, there was no apparent affiliation to any one group or school.

In 1888 an influx of new artists resulted in some significant changes; these artists introduced an aesthetic which favoured an Impressionist style. As part of Whistler's circle at the Royal Society of British Artists, they comprised Walter Sickert, Francis Bate and Sydney Starr. Théodore Roussel, who was already at the New English Art Club and had exhibited an Impressionist-inspired portrait of Mortimer Menpes, and Elizabeth Armstrong were also members of this group, although Armstrong's work was not overly influenced by Impressionism. Sickert was a core member of Whistler's circle and his protégé. However, on joining the New English Art Club, he began to distance himself from his former teacher, now viewing himself as an Impressionist rather than a 'Whistlerite'. In fact, Whistler had exhibited at the New English Art Club from 1888 to 1889, but found himself out of place in an exhibiting institution run

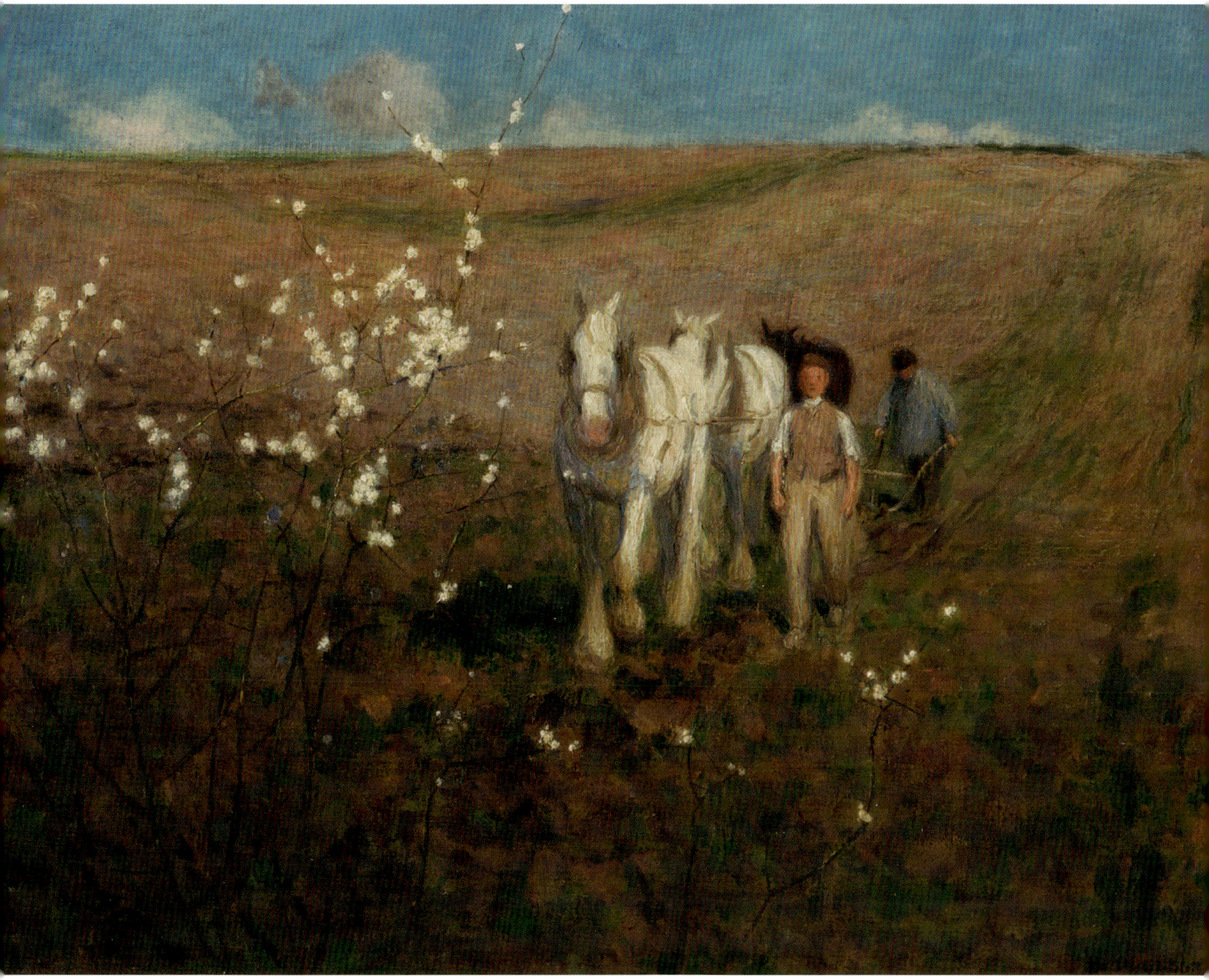

on democratic lines with no need of a President.[162] His departure released Sickert from the pupil-master relationship and Sickert became proactive in raising his own artistic and personal profile, which ultimately led to far-reaching repercussions in Sickert's drive to make the Club Impressionist-led and to create his own circle of influence. Although Sickert's machinations do not appear to have had a direct bearing on Stott, or the direction his art was taking, his aim to oust the Bastien-Lepagists – particularly the Newlyn element – resulted in some of Stott's acquaintances leaving the Club. These included Elizabeth Armstrong, Stanhope Forbes, Fred Hall and Walter Osborne, all of whom Stott had previously exhibited with at the Institute of Painters

17. Edward Stott, *On a Summer's Afternoon*, 1892. Oil on canvas, 55.9 x 71.1cm. Private Collection/Photo © The Fine Art Society, London, UK/Bridgeman Images

in Oil Colours. Sickert's dislike of Bastien-Lepage and rustic naturalism seemed to stem from what he considered to be Bastien-Lepage's lack of artistic truth, the overt commercial nature of his work, and his use of the square-brush technique.[163] The Newlyn painters were the main target of his criticism, except Tuke (who was a Newlynist at this time) who was let off lightly by Sickert possibly because they had both studied at the Slade, and shared a certain bravura when it came to their respective (sometimes controversial) subject matters.[164] Others were not so lucky. Paintings by Stanhope Forbes and Albert Chevallier Tayler were described by Sickert as 'second-hand French' 'black monochromes...[which] have neither the documentary value of instantaneous photographs, nor the higher qualities that constitute art.'[165] Although Sickert had made these statements after Stanhope Forbes had left the New English Art Club for the Royal Academy, Sickert's game plan had been to gain control of the Club's Selection and Hanging Committee, and in the process to squeeze out the Newlynist/Bastien-Lepagist element.[166] Initially the Committee had included the English Impressionists and the Newlynists, but the dislike of Stanhope Forbes by Sickert must have been reciprocal, because the Newlyn Group no longer exhibited with the Club after 1889. Despite the competitive and likely tense atmosphere that must have prevailed at the Club during these formative years, Edward Stott appears to have side-stepped the politics as he maintained a regular exhibiting presence until 1895.

As the New English Art Club exhibition catalogues show, from the Club's inception in 1886 to 1895, when Stott ceased exhibiting with the Club, he showed at least 20 works of which 13 are missing.[167] Of the remaining seven, the whereabouts of five are known, revealing an eclectic mix of styles and subject matter: *Alone – Early Spring Woodland* (1886), *The Ferry Boat* (1887), *Ploughing, Early Spring* (1891) (Fig. 16), *On a Summer's Afternoon* (1892) (Fig. 17), and *Milking Time – Early Morn* (1895) (Fig. 18).[168] There is a question mark over one further painting. Stott exhibited a painting in 1891 with the title of *Feeding Pigeons*. The whereabouts of this painting is unknown. However, another work of 1891 came up for auction at the Koedner Galleries in Florida in 2009, of which a colour reproduction was included in the auction catalogue with the title of *Feeding the Birds*. The two birds hovering in the foreground are pigeons, and this may well be the missing painting which has been incorrectly titled.

The Ferry Boat, discussed earlier, was a consummate early example of Stott's work. The next significant painting he produced for the New English Art Club was *On a Summer's Afternoon* (1892), which was exhibited in the April of the same year. In choosing to show this painting at the Club's exhibition, rather than at the New Gallery which Stott had also been exhibiting with since its formation in 1888, possibly reveals his awareness of 'trends' within the Club and a short-lived alliance with Tuke. Tuke had exhibited an earlier work of boys bathing in 1886, and in 1889 a second picture also called *The Bathers*. Edward Stott had also produced an earlier

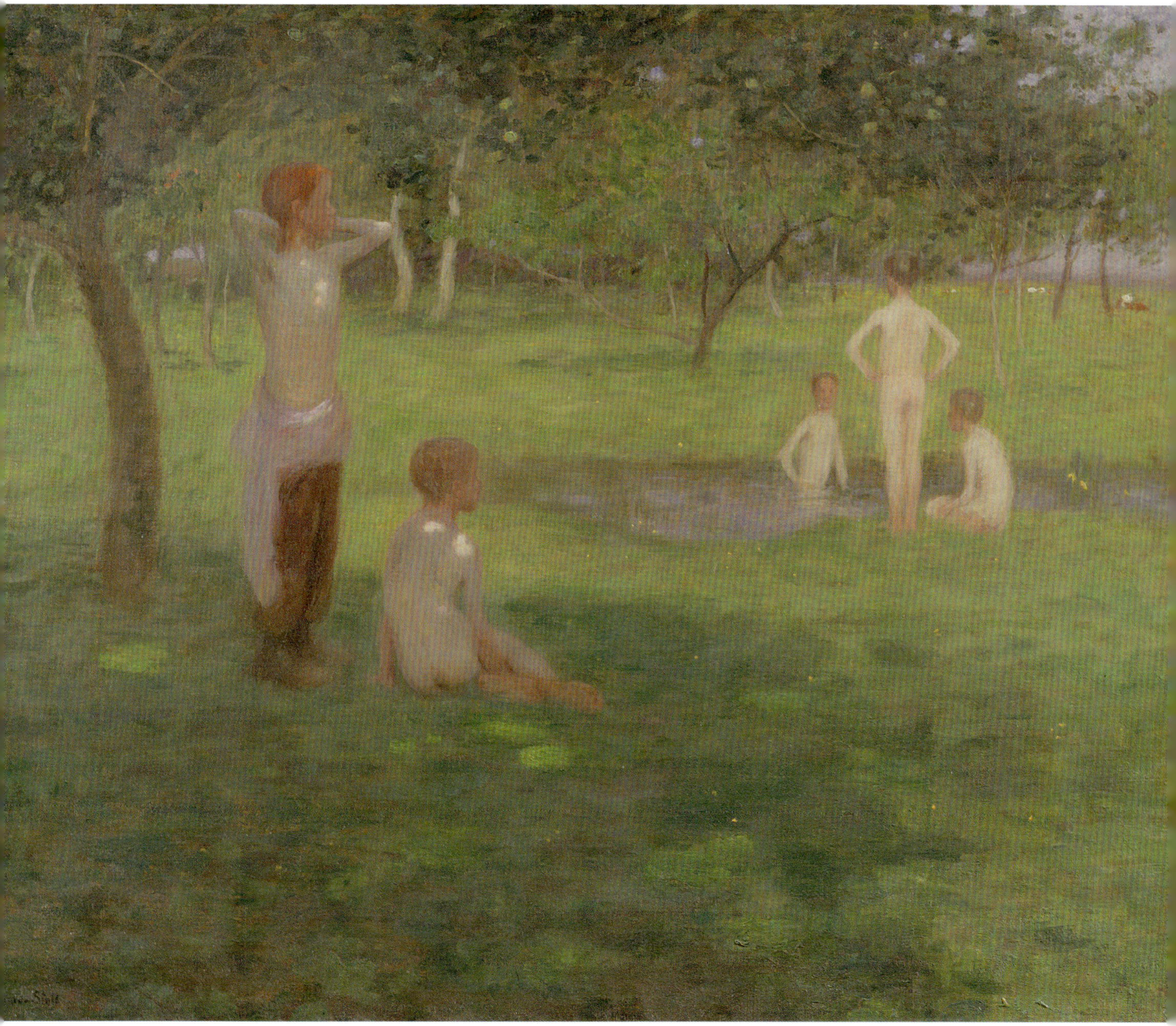

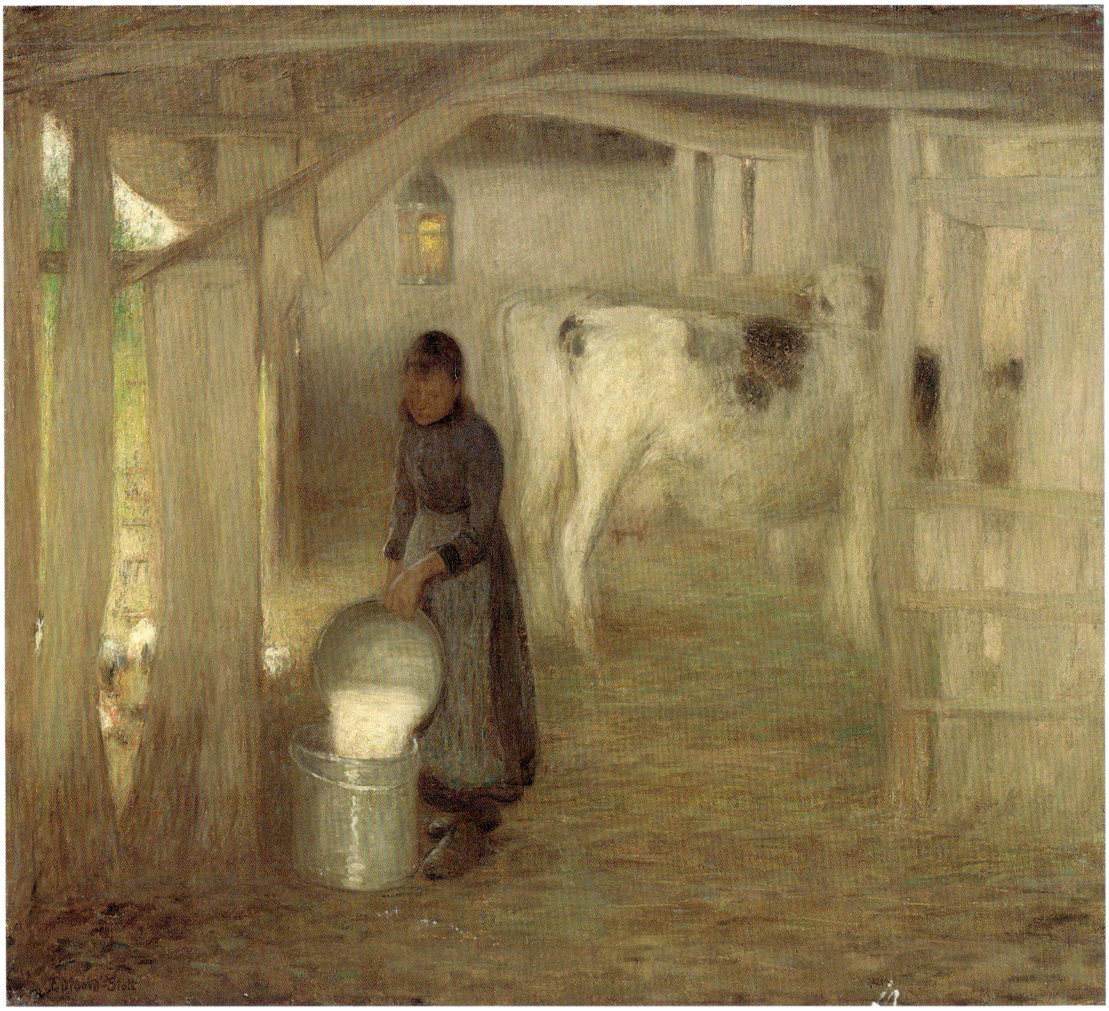

18. Edward Stott,
Milking Time – Early Morn, 1895.
Oil on canvas, 45.8 x 51cm. Private Collection/Photo © Christie's Images/ Bridgeman Images

version in 1890 called *The Bathers* which he had accepted by the Royal Academy that same year. This painting, now in a private collection, depicts a scene at sunset with five boys at the edge of a river with a hay-wain on the opposite bank, and forms part of the series of paintings Stott produced over a brief period which showed him to be grappling with the depiction of the nude in nature.[169] His painting for the New English Art Club is part of that series and, as already mentioned, reveals a connection between Stott and Tuke even though their individual treatment of the theme, and the depiction of the adolescent male form, were handled differently: Tuke's examples show that he was concerned with capturing the muscular definitions of his carefully posed boys in a way that accentuated their youthful strength and suppleness, and which possibly had homoerotic overtones in the celebration of the adolescent male body. Stott's aim was to depict the boys in a limited set of repeated poses which suggest their bodily form, rather than to portray it realistically. These models acted as vehicles for Stott in order to develop and refine his technique at suggesting the shape of the human body through a series of stock poses, making it a conceptual exercise rather than an exercise in realism.

On a Summer's Afternoon also reflects Stott's continuing preoccupation with capturing the effects of sunlight and shadow on a given scene and how colours change accordingly. This aspect of his work was recognised by the critic for the *Morning Post* who wrote that '*On a Summer's Afternoon*...is a felicitous record of sunlight and shadow in an orchard. Some boys are bathing in the narrow stream that intersects it, and others, sheltering themselves under the apple-trees from the heat, are resuming their rustic garb. The flesh-tints harmonise with the greenery around, and the general atmospheric condition is cleverly suggested.'[170] George Moore was particularly enamoured with this painting. As with the critic for the *Morning Post*, Moore appreciated the way in which Stott had conveyed the sunlight breaking through the branches and falling onto the pale bodies of the boys, noting how 'The painting of the body is that fluid, limpid execution which we admire in Dutch masters. The figure is in and not out of the atmosphere....'[171] Moore also remarked upon the originality of the painting, writing that Stott 'has achieved something which I have often seen attempted, but hardly seen achieved before....'[172] Likewise, when it was exhibited at the autumn exhibition held at the Walker Art Gallery, the critic writing for the *Liverpool Mercury* described it as 'one of the most original works' on show, and further commented that 'Mr Stott seems guided by the axiom that light draws an object as well as colours, and light puts each thing in its place. Mr Edward Stott's are among the most advanced and artistic works on the walls.'[173] The painting's originality may be due to the fact that it escapes easy definition in terms of style. Clearly Stott had begun to renounce the rustic naturalism of his earlier works and, as two of his former paintings highlight – *The High Grasses* and *The Complete Angler* – begun to tentatively explore an Impressionist aesthetic. Strictly speaking Stott was not an Impressionist and, as J. Stanley Little remarked, to think of Stott as an Impressionist was something of a misnomer.[174] In fact, in an extremely rare moment of putting pen to paper, Stott expressed exactly what he considered Impressionism to be when, in 1893, he contributed to the debate that had arisen over Sir George Reid's negative comments concerning Impressionism. The debate had taken place in *The Art Journal*, and Stott's response was as follows:

> At the term 'Impressionism' one looks for, and is willing to excuse, the derisive smiles of the ordinary outsider, but we would have expected a President of the Royal Scottish Academy to have been a little more au fait with the subject before airing his views in print. No-one doubts Sir George Reid's ability as an artist less than I, and for that reason think it the greater pity that he should write in so ignorant a way, knowing, as he must, the strong protests that it will call from those who are in the habit of being classed by art critics and the public among this school, despite the stronger dislikes they may have to the unsatisfactoriness [sic] of journalistic controversy on Art matters.
>
> Sir George evidently takes the word 'Impressionism' to mean technical incompetency, but to me it has no relation whatever with any of the technicalities of painting. To me it means a combined impression of the artist's feeling – colour and form with the charter [sic] of the subject, whether light and delicate, or strong and powerful; in short, a recording of the impression on the painter's nature.
>
> Avoiding moderns, should we have ever known Turner, Constable, Corot or Millet without their earnest and early training? And Sir George Reid may rest assured that there are those of to-day – and among the much-abused Impressionists, too – painters of their little own, who are in no way less in earnest and sincere than these four great artists were. 'Edward Stott'[175]

Impressionism for Stott, then, was a combination of feeling, colour and form, and a recording of the impression on a painter's nature. Nevertheless, Moore considered that the 'spatial envelope' in which the action occurred in *On a Summer's Afternoon* was one of the defining characteristics of Impressionism, and Sickert certainly thought of Stott as an Impressionist which, at least, meant that he escaped censure. Visiting the Royal Academy exhibition of 1890, to which Stott had sent *The Bathers*, Sickert commented on the poor hanging of the painting which was skied, and wrote that Stott was 'a poet, and an Impressionist.'[176] Yet Stott never became part of the circle of English Impressionists at the New English Art Club, where he continued to strive for originality of execution and did not settle for any one particular style or expression, thereby enabling him to maintain his independent stance within the Club. This was recognised by the critics who began to pay more attention to his work after the critical success of *On a Summer's Afternoon*. His work began to be increasingly described as 'genuine' and 'poetic', and it is evident that his 'lone star' was beginning to rise. Three paintings sent in to the New English Art Club exhibition of 1893 – *November Twilight* (1893), *Storks: Harmony in Blue and Silver* (1893), and *Blue Gold and Scarlet* (1893) – were collectively singled out for praise by the *Glasgow Herald* critic who wrote:

> Of all the pictures contributed by English members of the New English Art Club, none is more full of charm than the delightful work of Mr Edward Stott. This young painter has a genuine poetic imagination,... Year by year his work has been improving, and this year he takes a foremost place among his comrades. Perhaps he has still a tendency to a certain 'prettiness', though it might be hypercritical to hint at this...[177]

Only one of these paintings, *November Twilight*, has a surviving image by way of a black and white reproduction which reveals the scene to be one of boys fishing, and was considered by the *Daily News* as 'amongst the best' in the exhibition.[178] However, a description of *Storks: Harmony in Blue and Silver* appeared in the *Glasgow Herald*, where the scene was described as consisting of two storks at the further side of a hillside pool 'sunny, dreamy, charmingly painted, and altogether delightful', and 'painted in absolute freedom from conventionality of the academic kind, with great individuality of touch, and yet without the least eccentricity or trust upon extraneous detail.'[179] The *Daily News* also praised the painting's 'beautiful colours.'[180] The only painting not to be reviewed was *Blue Gold and Scarlet*.[181]

Edward Stott's output during the last two years of his time at the New English Art Club began to dwindle. He exhibited two works in 1894: *The Little Gleaners* (1894) and *In the Moonlight* (1894), which *The Graphic* described as a 'delicately toned and poetical little study.'[182] His final two contributions for the 1895 exhibition consisted of a pastel study of the back view of a naked child, and *Milking Time – Early Morn* (1895), for which Stott has chosen a muted palette of cream and beige tones, and the subject matter forming part of his preoccupation with scenes of country life which reflect his total immersion into the rural community of Amberley where he had settled from around 1887. The *Glasgow Herald* critic remarked of this work that 'there are a few canvases of extreme beauty like Mr Edward Stott's *Early Morning – Milking Time*', 'pervaded with delicate opalescent hues and sweet freshness.'[183] The critic for *The Saturday Review* reiterated the sentiment:

> The strength of this exhibition lies in Mr Edward Stott's beautiful study, and so delightful is this one swallow that it almost makes a summer in the Dudley Gallery by itself. It is called *Milking Time*,.... There is in the tender opalescent light all the strange silence of dawn, and in the bent figure of the girl something of that transfigured simplicity which made *The Angelus* so great a work.[184]

The linking of Stott to Millet, who was experiencing something of a renaissance, must have given Stott encouragement, as would the positive criticism. The critic concluded by saying that Stott had never produced anything 'so true in feeling so

19. Edward Stott, *Trees Old and Young, Sprouting a Shady Boon for Simple Sheep*, 1888. Version one. Oil on canvas, dimensions unknown. Private Collection/Waterhouse & Dodd, London, UK/Bridgeman Images (listed as *Springtime*)

reticent in expression,' and 'for the sake of the New English Art Club we trust that he will not also drift away from their community.'[185] In fact, this is exactly what Stott was about to do as these last two works ended his exhibiting career with the New English Art Club, although he was listed as being on the Hanging Committee for the 1896 exhibition.

Two years after joining the New English Art Club, Stott also began to exhibit at the New Gallery which opened its doors at 121 Regent Street in 1888. Stott's relationship with the New Gallery proved to be significant in a number of ways. Not only did it play a key part in the development of his career, and saw a rise in artistic status as his work began to achieve sustained critical notice, it was at the New Gallery where Stott's work began to be regularly collected by patrons of British art, such as the self-made businessman John Maddocks and Charles T. Harris.[186] It was also where Stott finally honed his 'signature' style and defining subject matter. Furthermore, his work began to show a close affinity, and/or reciprocal influence, to work by other New Gallery artists who painted rural subject matter, some of whom were also his contemporaries at the New English Art Club. These included Mark Fisher, Arthur Tomson and Alfred East. Stott also chose to display his most progressive work, which could be considered as proto-modernist in formal terms, at the New Gallery.

NEW GALLERY

THE NEW GALLERY WAS FOUNDED in 1888 by J. Comyns Carr and Charles Edward Hallé who had been Sir Coutts Lindsay's co-directors at the Grosvenor Gallery. The site of the Gallery was at 121 Regent Street and had previously been an old fruit market. Designed by the architect Edward Robert Robson, it was constructed in rapid time to ensure that it would open by the summer of 1888. The interior of the New Gallery was impressive, with supporting cast-iron columns encased with Cipolino marble to give the appearance of massive marble shafts, topped with delicately modelled Greek capitals. The architrave, frieze and cornices above the columns were covered with platinum to give the effect of 'dead' silver resulting in a matt finish. The floor of the hall was marble, with a fountain in the centre. Panels of Giallo Antico and Cipolino marble were placed around the central courtyard to form a background for the sculptures, which added to the grandeur of the Gallery.[187] The West and North Galleries, later added to by a South Gallery, were devoted to the larger oil paintings, whereas smaller works in oils, water-colours, etchings and drawings, were hung in the Balcony area around the sides of the Central Hall.[188] Many of the key artists from the Grosvenor Gallery, which eventually closed down in 1890, supported the new venture. These included Burne-Jones, Alma-Tadema and Holman Hunt, all of whom served on the New Gallery's Consulting Committee, with Watts and Frederic Leighton also transferring their allegiance to the Gallery.[189]

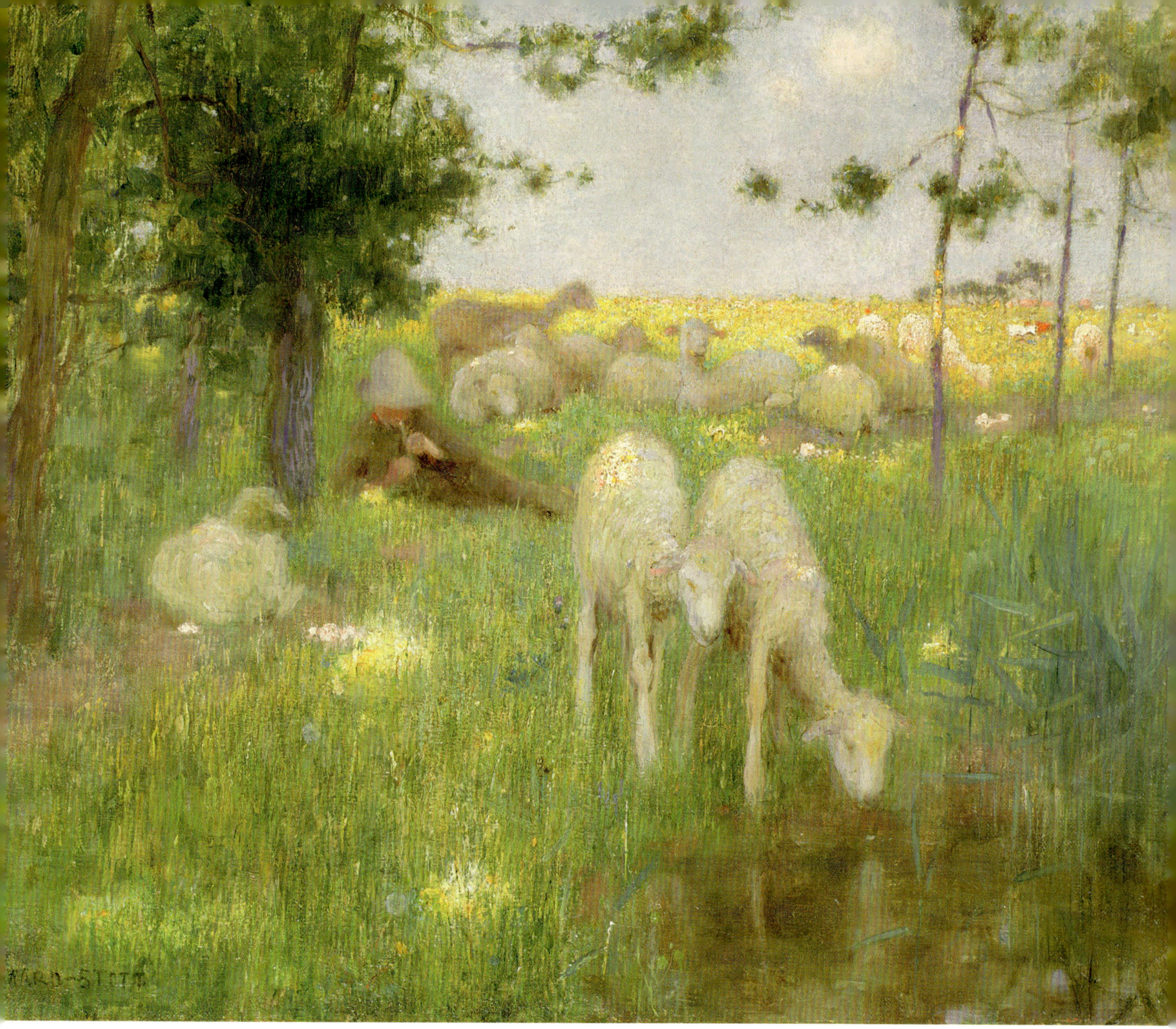

The private view of the first exhibition took place on the 8th May 1888, and opened to the public on the 9th May for three months. Not surprisingly, the New Gallery drew comparisons with the Grosvenor Gallery. The *Pall Mall Gazette* published a lengthy review with the title 'The New Gallery and the Grosvenor', with the reviewer noting that:

> It is a good, 'a very good New Gallery'. It is not a bad Grosvenor. The fact is, however, that the names of the two exhibitions in Regent-street and Bond-street severally are now really misnomers. The term 'Grosvenor Gallery' has come to be associated with a particular style – and a style which is no longer to be found in Sir Coutts Lindsay's rooms.... The so-called New Gallery...is the old Grosvenor under a different name; and the Grosvenor itself is now only an overflow meeting, as it were, from the Academy.[190]

20. Edward Stott, *In an Orchard – An Early Summer Morning*, 1892. Oil on canvas, 54.6 x 68.6cm. Private Collection/© Sotheby's London

In its formative years the New Gallery continued the early ideals of the Grosvenor Gallery in its aim to be inclusive and to be at the forefront of London exhibiting venues. This was proved when, in October and November 1888, it hosted the first showcase of industrial and applied arts by the Arts and Crafts Exhibition Society, under the direction of its founding President, Walter Crane. Not since the Grosvenor's winter exhibition of 1881, which had showed contemporary decorative art, had any attempt been made to show such work. The aim of the New Gallery was clearly to encourage artists whose work was experimental and progressive, but also to exhibit those works alongside traditional examples.

When Edward Stott joined the New Gallery, he would have reconnected with some familiar faces. La Thangue, Stanhope and Elizabeth Forbes, Fred Hall and Walter Osborne, all exhibited with the New Gallery at some point. He also found himself part of a milieu of artists such as Mark Fisher, Alfred East, Arthur Tomson and Ernest Waterlow, some of whom also exhibited with the New English Art Club, who equally showed a commitment to painting scenes of rural life and where clear reciprocal influences were at play. Broadly speaking, the subject matter comprises pastoral imagery, farming scenes, landscapes with farm animals, and snapshots of village life. In terms of specific themes, inspiration was drawn from farming related activities such as shepherding, country maids feeding domestic fowl, cow herding and other associated tasks such as fruit picking.

The theme of shepherds with their flocks played an integral part in the portraying of rural life, and proved a popular subject at the New Gallery exhibitions. Certain artists focussed on the topic of shepherds herding sheep into pens, such as Mark Fisher's painting *Winter Pastures* (1888), which he exhibited at the inaugural exhibition. Others depicted the shepherd and his flock at rest such as Stott's work which was illustrated in the catalogue and listed as *Trees Old and Young, Sprouting a Shady Boon for Simple Sheep* (1888). Now in a private collection, it has been given the title of *Springtime* (Fig. 19).[191] This particular way of depicting the shepherd and flock was continued by Edgar Chignall Wills with *The Guardians of the Flock* (1889), which bore a close compositional resemblance to Stott's painting, and Alfred East's *Labour and Rest* (1893). The title of Stott's painting was taken from Book I of Keats' poem *Endymion* (1818), of which a collection of his poems was published in 1884.[192] Referencing lines from a poem indicates that Stott was part of a trend within the New Gallery for combining art and poetry. At least two other artists who exhibited at the inaugural exhibition of 1888 used lines from poems for their titles. Alfred East's work, *The morning trembles o'er the sky, And, unperceived, unfolds the spreading day*, is from an eighteenth-century poem by James Thomson called 'The Four Seasons' and is taken from that part of the poem which deals with autumn.[193] Arthur Tomson chose for his title, *Like phantoms floating in the twilight blue, Home from their pastures troop the drowsy sheep*. These lines come from a poem by Rosamund Marriott Watson, who married Tomson in September 1887.[194] Although no image is available for

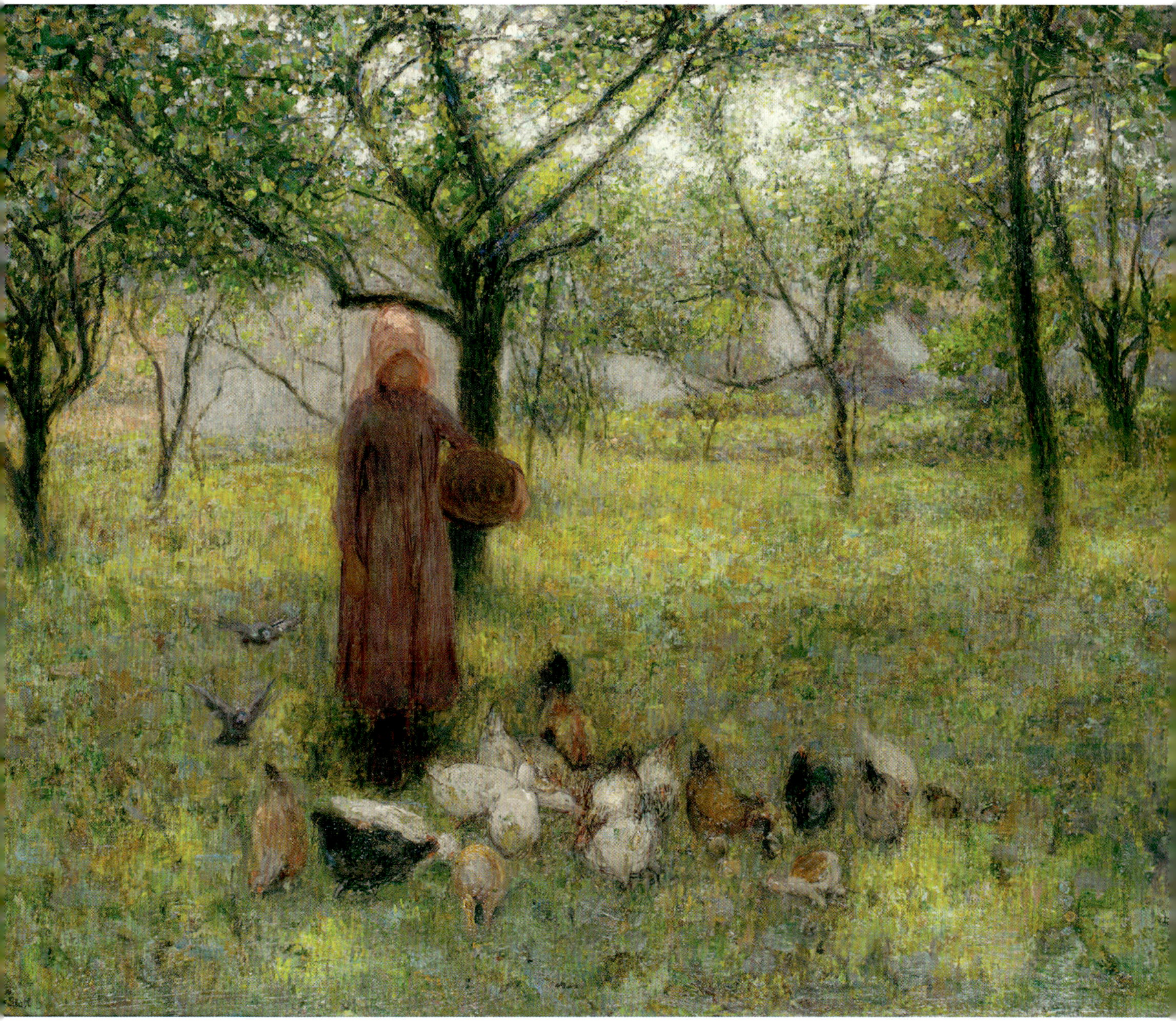

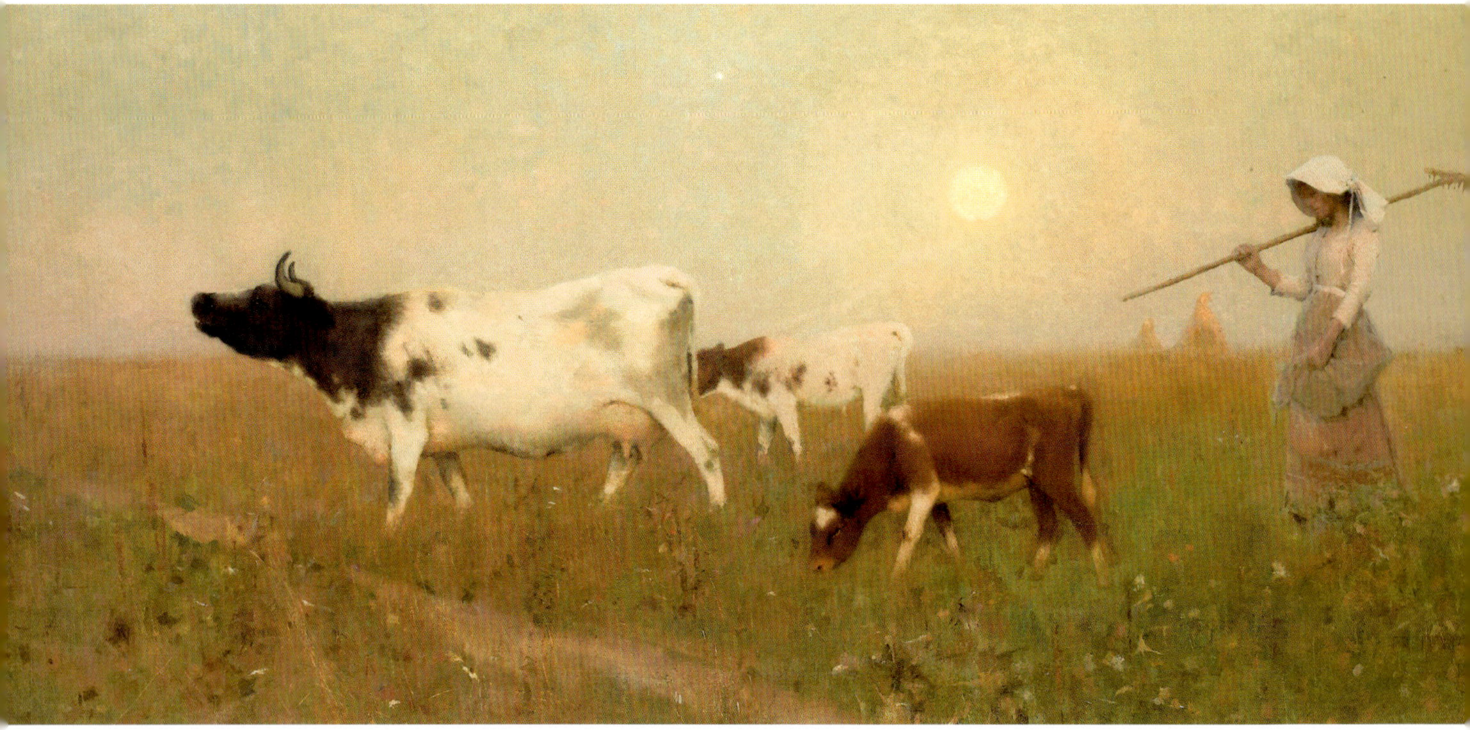

21. Fred Hall, *Twilight* (also known as *Homeward Bound*), c.1891. Oil on canvas, 91 x 97.5cm. Private Collection/© Bonhams London

this painting, the description given in the New Gallery exhibition catalogue is of a 'Shepherd with crook on the left, shows dark against the rising moon; low cliffs and seas.'[195] A further example can be found in Mark Fisher's painting, *When twilight melts beneath the moon away*, which was exhibited in 1892. This is the final line of a poem by Lord Byron called 'It is the Hour'.[196]

With regards to some of the above-mentioned artists, there was also a geographical connection to Stott. During the late 1890s, Alfred East painted scenes of Amberley such as *The River Arun* (1896), *The Vines, Amberley, Sussex* (1897) and *Amberley Bridge* (date unknown). Mark Fisher also painted in East and West Sussex, and Tomson is known to have worked in Sussex, but possibly prior to Stott. Ernest A. Waterlow, who also exhibited with the New Gallery, and was similarly inspired by scenes of rural life, also found inspiration in the Sussex countryside which included the environs of Amberley.[197] His work *Feathered Friends* (1888), exhibited at the New Gallery show of that year, provides an excellent point of comparison with a painting Stott exhibited in 1892 called *In an Orchard – An Early Summer Morning* (Fig. 20). Waterlow's catalogue entry describes 'a young Irish country maid in a brown dress, with a red and white handkerchief tied under her chin, feeding her hens. There is a dark hill shrouded in mist in the background.'[198] A connection between Waterlow and Stott can be identified in the clear compositional similarities in the way in which both country maids are depicted, including the way the flocks of birds gather at their feet. The difference arises out of the respective settings. Whereas Waterlow's illustration has more of an open-air feel to it and displays a wider vista, Stott's scene is more confined within an orchard setting in which the play of light on the ground, as the sun's rays break

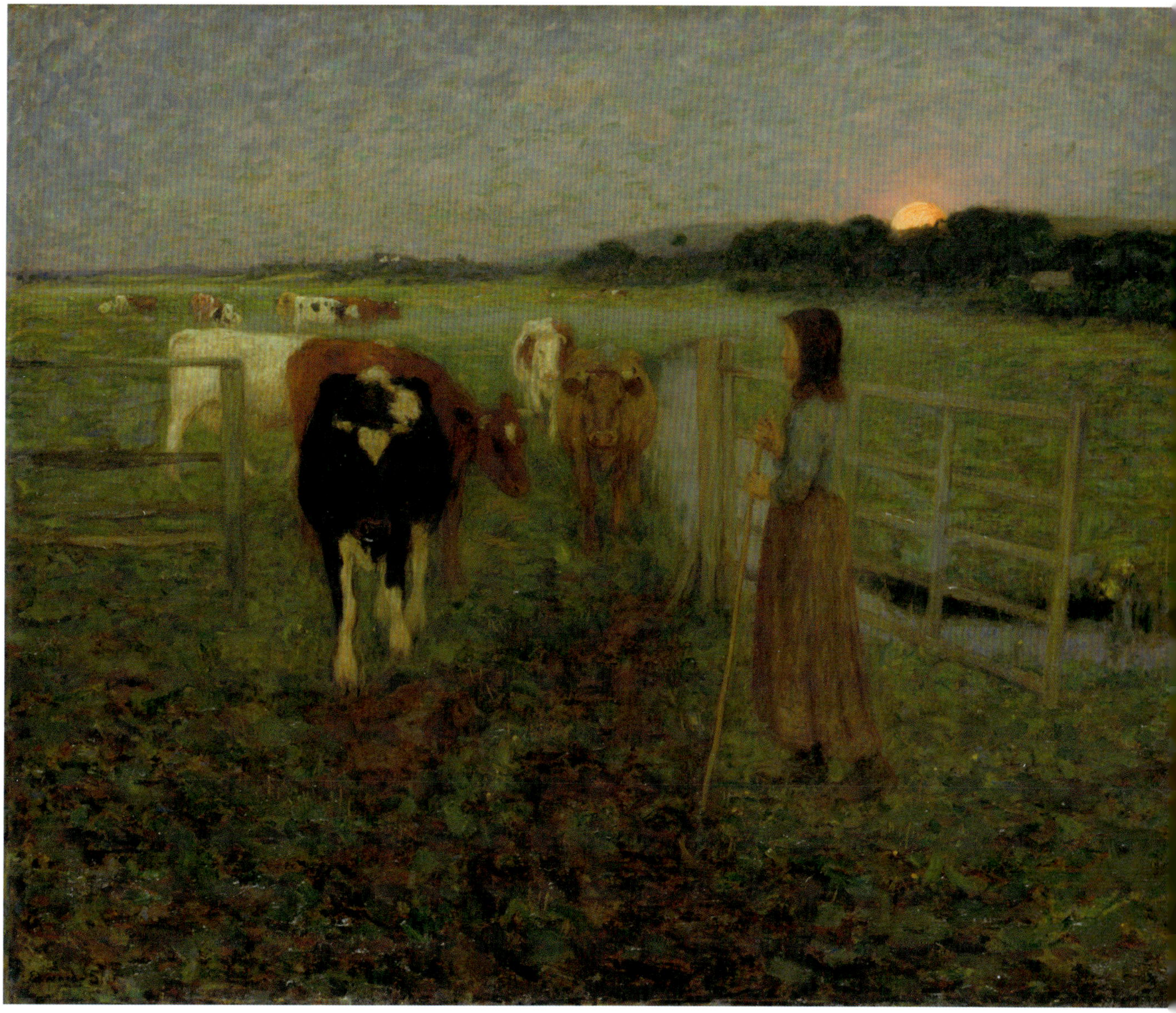

22. Edward Stott, *Changing Pastures*, 1893. Oil on canvas, 70.5 x 87.6cm. © Tate, London 2017

through the trees, simultaneously creates shadow. However, a further similarity occurs in the respective idyllic settings, and both examples give further evidence of the ideas that were circulating generally in the New Gallery exhibitions.

The third theme is those paintings which focus on cowherds. One example can be found in Stott's work of 1888, *Homewards* (whereabouts unknown). The illustration in the exhibition catalogue shows a young male herder with three calves walking across a field. George Faulkner Wetherbee contributed *A Sunny Land* (1891) which features a young female cowherd and her cows within a landscape setting, whilst Fred Hall's painting of 1892, *Twilight* (also known as *Homeward Bound*) (Fig. 21), and *Silver Mist* (1893), continues the visual alliance.[199] Edward Stott also exhibited *Changing Pastures* (1893) (Fig. 22) which focuses on a young cowherd who has led her herd from one field into another at the end of the day.

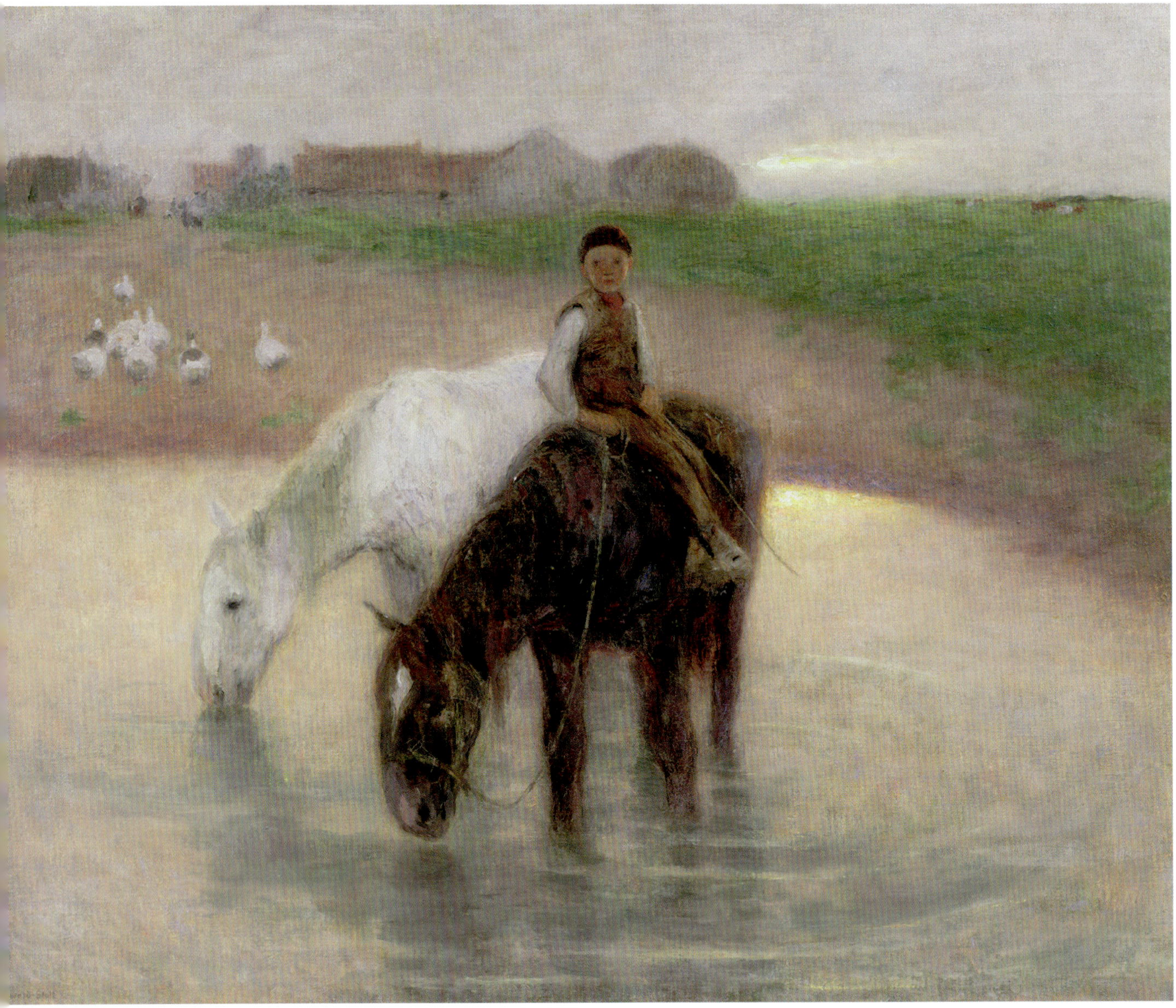

23. Edward Stott,
The Horse Pond, 1891.
Oil on canvas,
60.9 x 76.2cm.
Touchstones Rochdale,
Lancashire, UK/
Bridgeman Images

Stott was clearly part of a group of artists who, through their shared themes and subject matter, comprised a core group within the New Gallery whose work contributed to the history of English landscape painting and scenes of rural life. Edward Stott appeared to have found his niche here, where he fully developed his 'signature' style and defining subject matter which marked and informed his Amberley period. It was also at the New Gallery where Stott was at his most progressive, as it is clear that he was experimenting with style and form in certain paintings. Whereas *Trees Old and Young, Sprouting a Shady Boon for Simple Sheep* and *In an Orchard – An Early Summer Morning* have been painted in a restrained impressionist style, other works such as *The Horse Pond* (1891) (Fig. 23), *Noonday* (1895) (Fig. 24) and *The Golden Moon* (1896) show Stott to be experimenting with a form of soft-edged nascent modernism.[200] With their formal simplification, absence of non-essential detail,

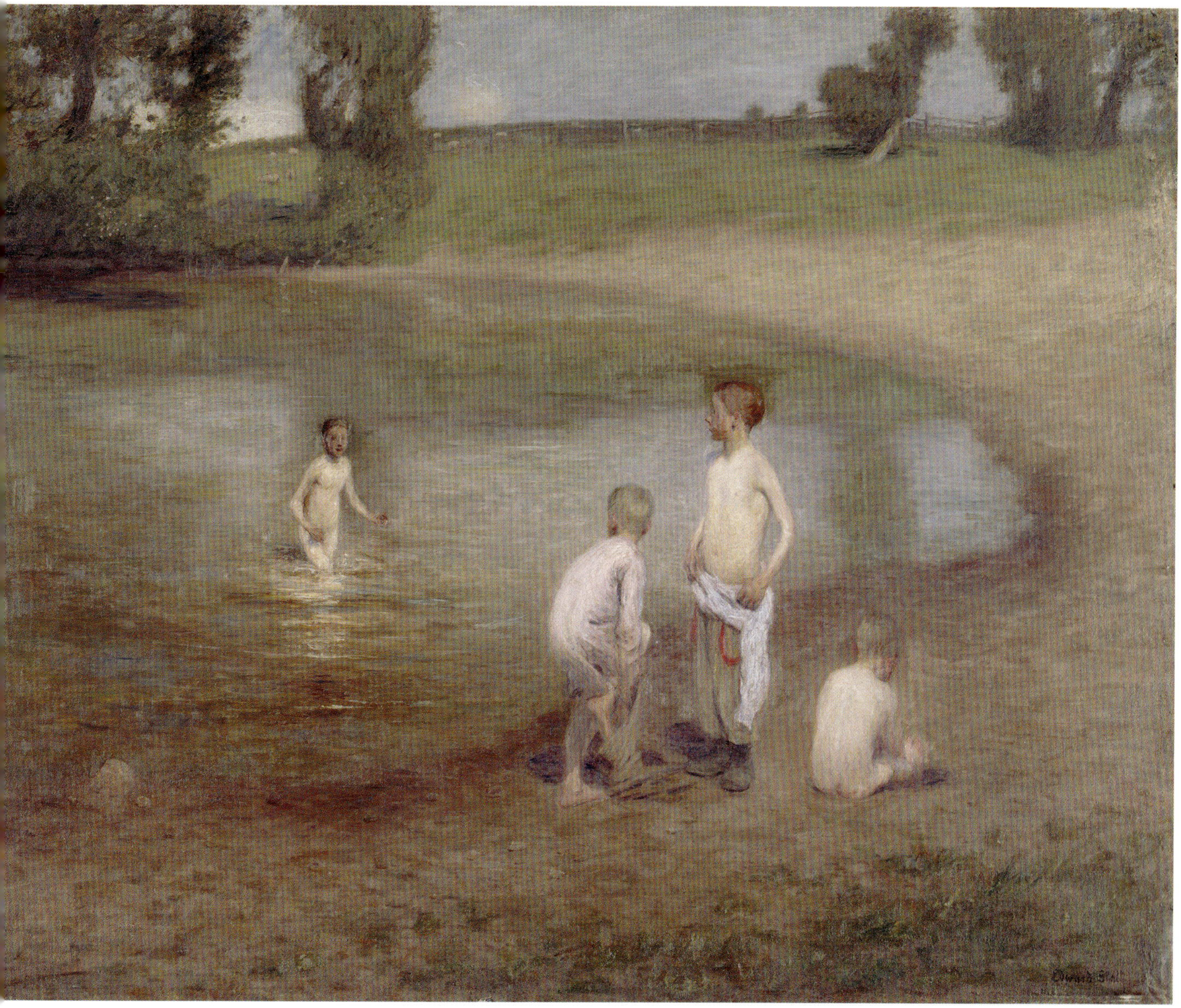

and an imaginative use of colour, Stott's work of this kind is clearly registering new artistic developments coming out of France and which he would have possibly seen when he visited exhibitions and galleries in London.[201] One of these was the International Society. Formed in 1898, with Whistler as President and Lavery as Vice President, the aim of the International Society was to show modern and progressive work, rather than academic and traditional examples, and Stott would certainly have come across paintings by modern French, Italian, German, Dutch and Scottish artists. As Ysanne Holt has identified in Stott's paintings of Amberley, which showed a distancing from modernity in that he portrayed the locality as timeless and unchanging, 'we find an essential purity and simplicity, a task that draws on timeless and ancient forms but at the same time underpins early modernism.'[202] However, striking a somewhat contradictory note, in an undated letter to J. Stanley

24. Edward Stott,
Noonday, 1895.
Oil on canvas,
71.8 x 91.5cm.
Manchester Art Gallery,
UK/Bridgeman Images

25. Edward Stott, *Echo*, 1903. Oil on canvas, 63.3 x 97.7cm. Private Collection/ Photo © Christie's Images/Bridgeman Images

Little, which was possibly written around 1900-1901, Stott comments on an exhibition he saw at the International Society. He writes 'As an exhibition I found it very dissappointing [sic]. What I find about modern work and especially about the bulk of work that one finds at the 'International', is its unintelligent [?] and self-consciousness. There seems such an indifference to try to see beauty in anything and much more to try and render the beauty and quality of paint.'[203] Stott reiterated these comments some years later in 1917, when he wrote to Bernard Osborne 'When I go to a modern show – as infrequently as possible – I feel irritated. I miss anything in the way of fine intentions, reverence, or appreciation of the innermost & beauty of things.'[204] Nevertheless, it cannot be disregarded that Stott was consciously working in a specific formal manner. Whereas the subject matter of the *The Horse Pond* depicts a sentimental image of a young farm boy with his horses, with buildings in the background, in formal terms Stott has simplified the scene by reducing it to just three areas: foreground (pool), middle-ground (field and pool edge) and background (sky). In his treatment of the scene, Stott has given a suggestion of reflection and ripples in the pond, the buildings and ducks, but overall does not aim for a realistic representation and includes only the barest of detail. In terms of colour, a touch of vibrancy is included in the bright green of the grass and an imaginative use of pink-mauve for the edge of the pond. Comparing this painting with Stanhope Forbes' work *The Drinking Place* (1900), where he has aimed for a realistic and traditional depiction of a similar scene, then Stott's example clearly looks to be formally pared down.

The next painting in the sequence is *Noonday* which was exhibited at the New Gallery in 1895. Here Stott began to incorporate his personal motif of an oval shaped pond which he used in other paintings. He has repeated the theme of *On a Summer's Afternoon* (Fig. 17), but whereas, in the previous version, Stott had aimed for tonal harmony, with *Noonday* he explored the potential of contrasting colour which caught the critics' attention. The *National Observer* remarked on the 'singular charm of colour', whilst the *Daily News* critic commented on the 'full use' of colour noting 'Here blue, mauve and green make his scheme with the flesh tones of the nude figures. How cleverly he introduces that little touch of reassuring scarlet… and how well he gives the green of the bank as seen against the blue sky above.'[205] In formal terms, Stott has defined the space through a series of elementary shapes such as the oval pond, the thin band of grass in the background which is reflected in the pond, and the 'sketchy' verticals of the trees which are mirrored in the pond resembling two columns. In turn, these 'columns' reflect the verticality of the two standing boys which bring unity to the scene. Finally, the three boys on the bank form a triangular shape. As such then, the structure of Stott's painting is predicated on a series of abstract shapes. Therefore, in comparing the earlier painting of *On a Summer's Afternoon* with *Noonday*, a shift can be identified from the realistic to the imaginative or conceptual. Furthermore, the earlier painting shows Stott's concern with the change in colour and tone caused by the play of sunlight and shadow on the

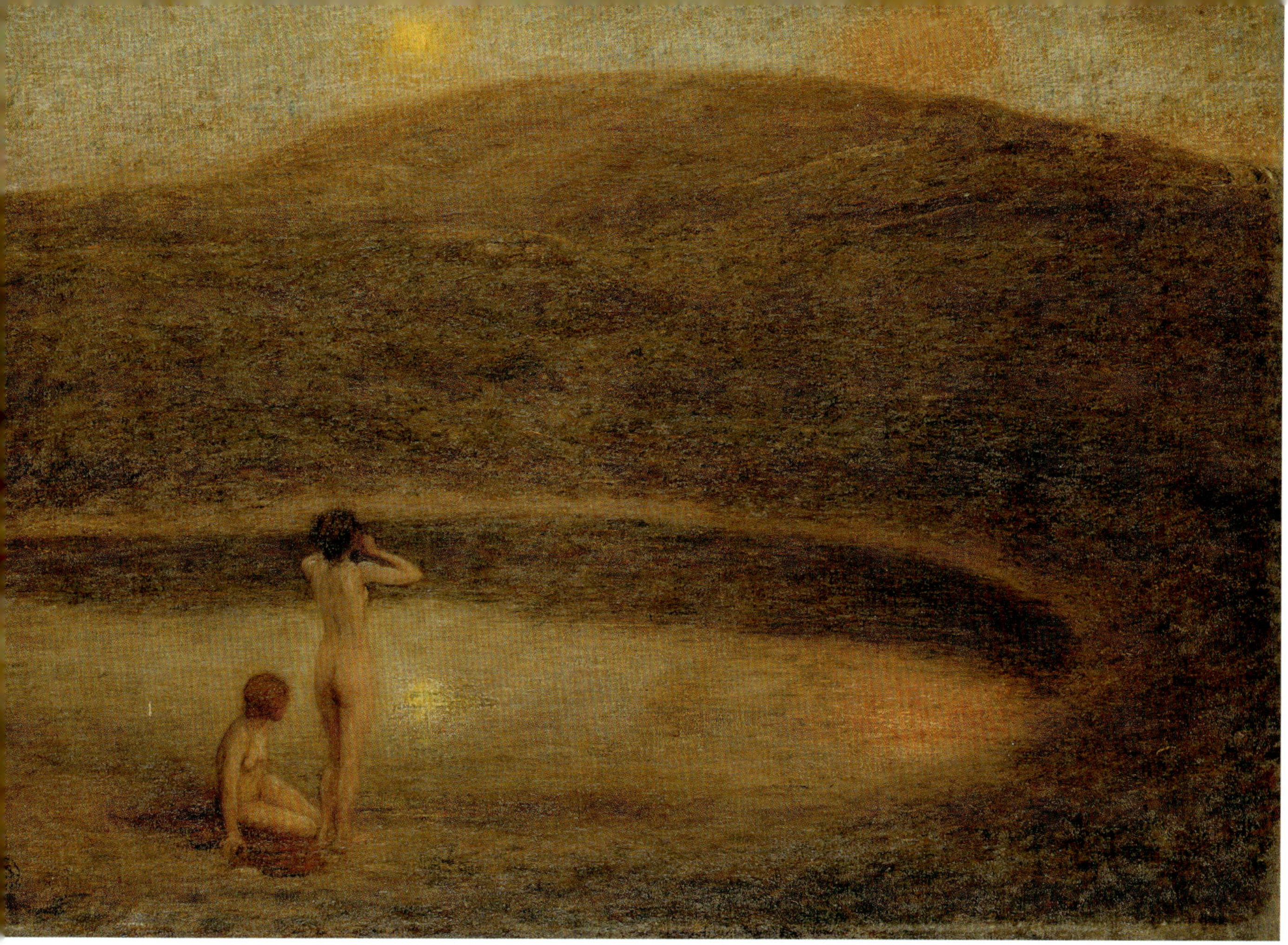

grass. In the later work, his interest now lay in the exploration of contrasting colour values, and how spatial elements and forms within a given space could be conceived of and defined through simplified means.

In 1896, Stott exhibited the first in a series of paintings in which the Amberley landscape took on a lunaresque quality, with an 'other worldly' atmosphere. *The Golden Moon* continued Stott's engagement with formalist reduction with an almost two-dimensional appearance. Three nude figures (two seated and one standing) are situated by the side of an oval pool in what is, essentially, a barren landscape. He continued this theme with a later painting of 1903 called *Echo* (Fig. 25), which was exhibited at the Royal Academy. As with *The Golden Moon*, which also had a tonally muted palette except for the bright moon, the scene in *Echo* is briefly lifted by the yellow moon and orange-red of the sun.[206] The barren nature of the landscape, together with the sombre tones and failing light, creates an atmosphere that is strange and mysterious, but is relieved by the two unclothed figures. In the final example of this series, *The Sacred Pool* (1915), which was also exhibited at the Royal Academy, reveals that Stott has reworked the scene used for *Echo* and substituted flamingos in place of people. Although not explored here, this series of paintings could also be viewed as Stott 'sampling' aspects of Symbolist art.

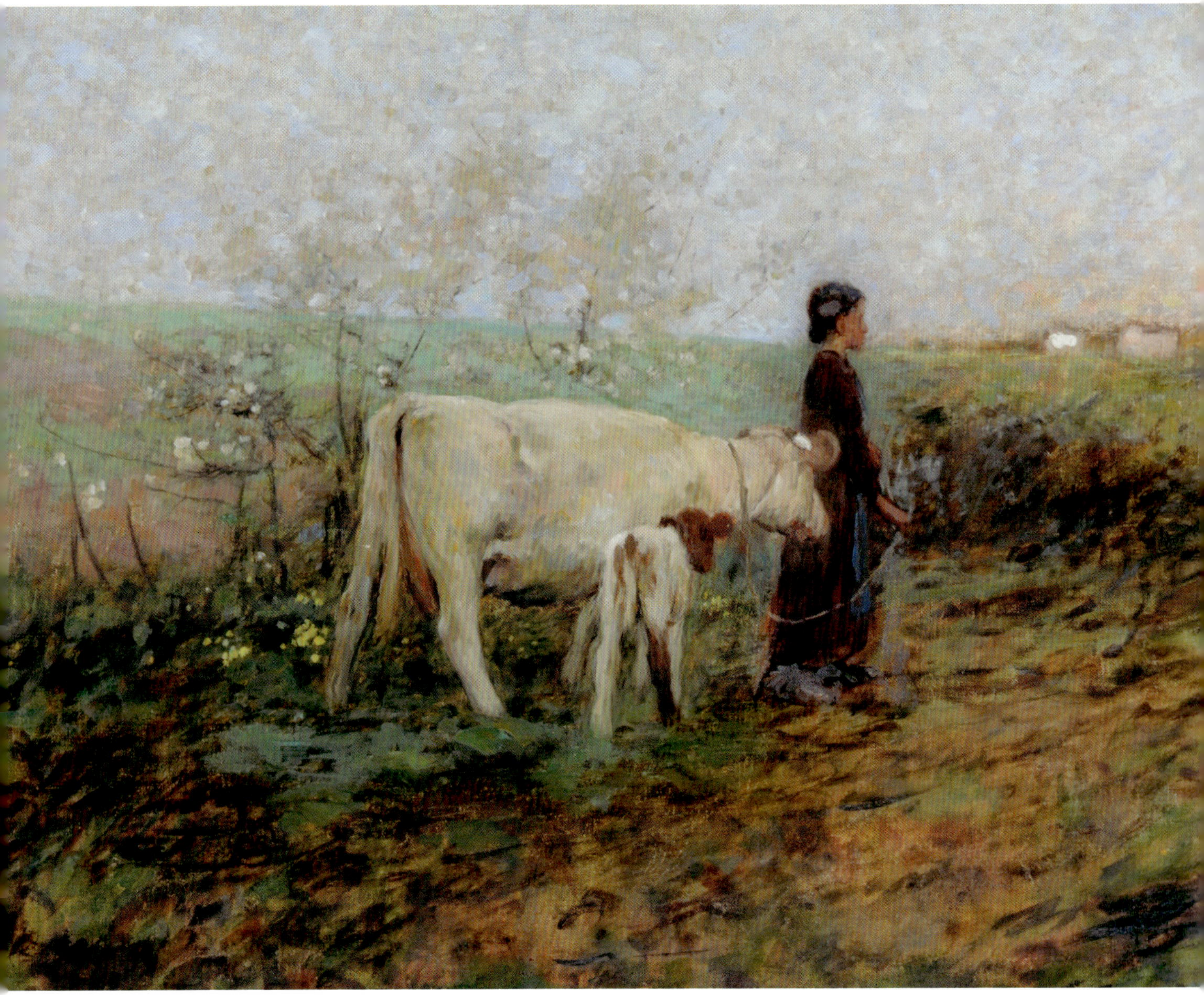

26. Edward Stott,
The Young Cowherd,
possibly 1888. Oil on
canvas. 45.7 x 61cm.
The University of Hull
Art Collection

4

AMBERLEY EXTERIORS I

'Working Life' and 'After Hours'

INTRODUCTION TO AMBERLEY

IN THE SECLUDED VILLAGE OF Amberley, Stott finally found his 'corner of the world' where he focused exclusively on the lives of the Amberley residents and, in the process, produced a lasting visual legacy and insight into the routines and structures of this small farming community.

Stott had first visited Amberley in 1885 and, as a consequence of his visit, he painted two works which were subsequently exhibited at the Royal Academy that same year: *Amberley, Sussex* (1885) and *Primrose Time* (1885) (both now lost). Anne Dinnage remembers that the Reverend G.A. Clarkson came to the Dinnage household when the family lived in nearby Houghton, and said that there was a 'great artist' living in Amberley. She recalled that she was age eleven at the time and, as she was born in 1876, this would make the year of the Reverend's visit as 1887.[207] This date is verified by A.C.R. Carter in his article on Stott which appeared in the *The Art Journal* of 1899. Carter wrote that 'It is now twelve years since the subject of this article betook himself to Amberley.'[208] This suggests that in spite of Stott's temporary addresses, he was considering Amberley as his permanent 'sketching ground' and it can be stated with some certainty that Stott was living in Amberley in 1887, and possibly as a boarder at the home of the local baker, Walter Sidney Cooter. As the Census Returns for 1891 show, Stott was recorded as residing at 67 Church Street, which was the Cooter family home.[209]

27. Edward Stott's house, Amberley, date unknown. Source: Cutting in Stott Archive, Touchstones Rochdale

Tucked away from the main road to Arundel, with its near neighbours of Houghton and Bury and on the River Arun, Amberley was a self-contained and self-subsisting village which appeared to need very little support or intervention from outside the immediate community. As Census Returns and Kelly's Directories of Sussex for the period covered reveal, the employment categories and skill-sets of the residents showed a good range of services and trades, and covered the area that comprised the three locations.[210] The area was well-served with schools, recreational facilities and at least two public houses.[211] To outsiders, and certainly from the viewpoint of contemporary social commentators, Amberley would have fitted perfectly into the ideology at the time that the countryside and village life was perceived to be unspoilt and unchanging. P.H. Ditchfield, in his study of English villages which was published in 1889, contrasted the noise and bustle of large towns and cities with the calm and peacefulness of the countryside.[212] Ditchfield also noted that, whilst the old features of the towns were disappearing to make way for modern life, the rural world was still considered to be firmly embedded in the past. It is a view such as this that has informed today's historians: the cultural historian Raymond Williams associated rural life with innocence as seen through the 'lens' of the fields, woods, agriculture, animal husbandry, and the labourers who worked at these things,[213] and Geoffrey Best has also written of how the villages and the countryside experienced little change when compared with the towns and cities, and that any changes that did occur were slow and piecemeal.[214] However, examples such as these are observations based on generalized ideas rather than studies from inside specific rural communities which were actually experiencing external changes wrought upon them, over which they had little control. Alun Howkins states that for many people outside the rural world, the twenty or so years after 1850 presented the widely-held view that the countryside was a picture of stability and harmony after earlier acts of rick burning, machine breaking and agricultural depression.[215] Yet, as he also points out, the years 1875 to 1895 were under threat with changes originating outside the rural world which could not be controlled by those in it. A good example of this can be found in Anna Gruetzner Robins' study of Childwick Green and the estate of Childwickbury in Hertfordshire. In 1883, the estate was bought by John Blundell Maple who was heir to the London furnishing firm.[216] Previously, the estate had earned its living from mixed arable and livestock farming and was a source of employment for the local people. Under Maple's ownership, this rapidly changed and much of the arable land was turned into a stud farm. Furthermore, some of the thatched cottages which had originally provided housing for the labourers were demolished.[217]

Whilst Amberley appeared not to experience the extreme disruption of traditional village life as Childwick Green had, neither was it totally immune from the slow encroachment of modern life. For example, the laying down of a railway line and subsequent building of a station resulted in Amberley being opened up to visitors.[218] The building of the station may have been welcomed by the Amberley residents,

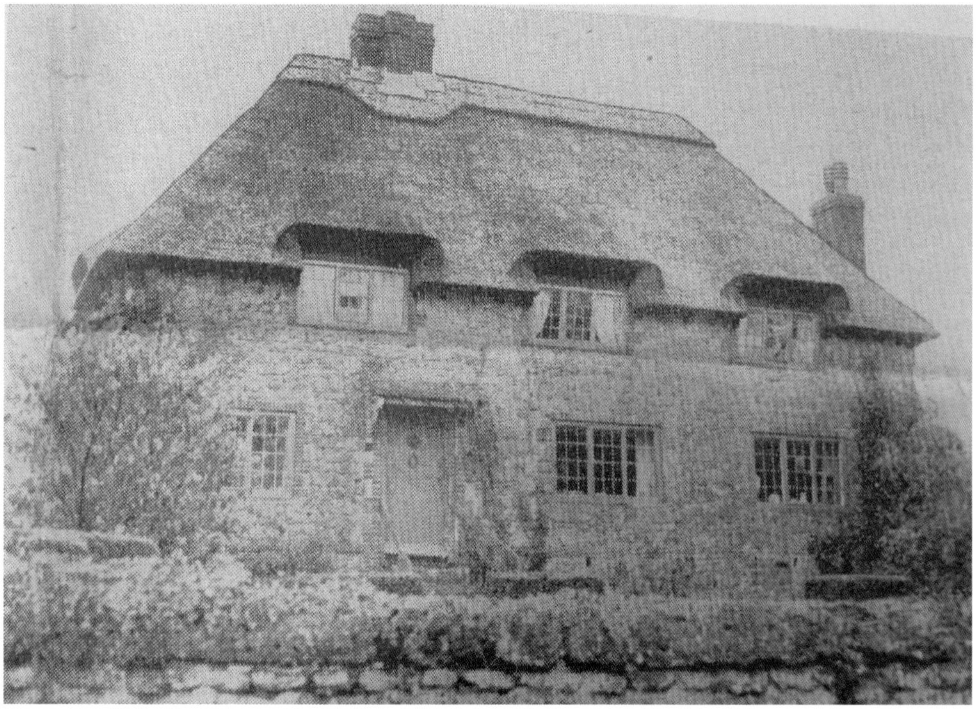

but it also resulted in hordes of visiting anglers from London who were brought by special train for fishing competitions which, no doubt, would have disturbed the peace and quiet of such a tranquil location.[219] As Ditchfield wrote, Amberley was famous for its fishing 'its trout having earned the tribute of praise from all disciples of Isaak Walton, who himself glorifies them.'[220] Stott, however, did not find inspiration in overpopulated and competitive scenes, preferring to show quiet fishing scenes such as his painting of 1893, *November Twilight*, which depicts two boys at the side of a river bank, one of whom is fishing whilst the other boy stands and watches. Amberley even experienced a pioneering hang-gliding event off Amberley Mount, by another local artist called José Weiss.[221] Edward Stott, however, did all he could to preserve the old-world charm of Amberley, buying up the thatched cottages as they came onto the market so that their character could not be changed.[222] As Anne Dinnage recalled, he stated that 'I buy them so that my eyes may have something beautiful to rest on.'[223] Stott also managed to prevent ugly signage and advertisements being hung on trees, but he could not prevent the installation of telegraph poles. He did not like to see trees or hedges cut down, and saved an old yew tree in Amberley Churchyard.[224] Of course, none of these small signs of modernisation that he could not prevent appeared in Stott's paintings of Amberley and, in this respect, it is evident that he was not averse to idealizing some of his scenes in removing all traces of modernity.

Like any rural community, Amberley also had its celebrations. Amberley Gala Day was held on the 5th June 1890, and the Queen's Diamond Jubilee celebrations took place on 22nd June 1897. Free tea for Amberley and North Stoke residents was supplied, as were barrels of ale, stout and mineral water.[225] The Angmering Band played at the Jubilee celebrations, a series of sporting events took place, and there was a firework display in the evening. Apart from one painting entitled *A Souvenir of Amberley Fair* (c.1891) (now lost), Stott appeared to show little interest in this kind of celebratory subject matter.[226]

As to the buildings at the time of Stott's residence, J. Stanley Little provides a good description:

> Of Amberley itself I may say at once that there [are] few villages so free from modern taint, and which retain so old-world an appearance. Its white and buff-faced cottage, roofed with thatch or Sussex slates covered with green-grey and yellow-brown moss and lichen, give to the entire village a mediaeval appearance, quite in keeping with its embattled castle and Early English church.[227]

Amberley today has lost none of its old-world charm, with thatched cottages maintaining the village's picturesque qualities, including Stott's cottage which was in keeping with the rest of the village (Fig. 27). The 'embattled' castle, in disrepair and tenanted by a farmer in Stott's day, is now a hotel and restaurant.[228] The Church of St. Michael's has a semi-circular stained-glass window by Robert Anning Bell in memory of Stott (Fig. 28), and the churchyard contains Stott's memorial, with sculptures by Francis Derwent Wood, who also lived in Amberley. (Fig. 29) Buildings such as churches, castles, and village halls appeared to hold little interest for Stott, although he did produce one painting called *The Village Inn* (1897), which is thought to be based on the George and Dragon Inn at Houghton, and a recently acquired sketch by the Williamson Art Gallery shows St. Michael's Church in the distance, but was never used in a painting.[229] The buildings that inspired Stott were the thatched cottages and farm buildings such as a milking shed, stable, or barn.

The village of Amberley is situated at the foot of the South Downs which is an area known for its unspoilt natural beauty, and defined by the geographical formation of chalk cliffs which often feature in Stott's paintings. Set back from the village is the wetlands known as the Amberley Wild Brooks which Stott depicted in such paintings as *Boys Bathing, Amberley Wildbrooks* (c.1892), and *Study of Amberley Wild Brooks* (date unknown).[230] In Stott's time, the Wild Brooks provided the raw material for the local basket makers.[231]

A.C.R. Carter wrote that Stott came to Amberley with the sole purpose of:

> ...forming a close communion with Nature, of understanding her beauties and defects; in short of developing the power of seeing until vision should indeed be beautific. This rare gift of visual selection is totally distinct from the microscopic capacity of connoting, like the relentless camera.... Yet he who would arrive at the true expression of Nature's worth must go through the grad-grind of these ocular gymnastics, until, by consummate practice he can conceal the labour that has built up his art.[232]

Stott's 'close communion' with nature entailed him taking daily walks through the Wild Brooks in summer, and watching the haymaking or the cattle grazing. As Anne Dinnage recalled, he would walk about eight miles a day; two after breakfast, two before lunch, two after lunch and two after supper.[233] Whilst these daily walks helped Stott to keep fit and active (he also skated, cycled, rode a horse and occasionally went on 'fad' diets to lose weight), he also used this time to get inspiration for his paintings.[234] On these walks he would make numerous sketches in pencil, charcoal and coloured chalks, and also recorded how colour changed on various surfaces depending on the time of day, or the weather conditions. As his annotated sketchbooks show, Stott's close analysis of surface conditions revealed an almost scientific approach to the process of sketching, which showed a continuation of the teachings of his masters during his time as an art student in Paris. In one sketchbook, Stott had written:

> An evening very late (June 25) 9.15 with a slight slow still from the North. Road very dry & light as the heavy part of the masonry on wall but not so light as the new mortar coping on top of wall near gate.
>
> Grass tells if anything darker than general tone of root – shaddow [sic] hues of distant long rooted grass is very narrow – narrower than many a first night value study.
>
> July 3rd – Dust in 'motion' which tells of bluish film lighter than lightest part of road & much lighter when the dust passes in front of darker objects or even grass – also note – wheel lines on road – with very slightly darker or very slightly lighter – the latter is very pretty.
>
> July 11th – (a dry night after 3 weeks dry weather) the grass is certainly darker than roofs-…left side of wall is almost as light as light patch of 'new work' right & left of doors – general appearance of walls – roofs – a mellow colour – half warm – half grey.[235]

Stott would subsequently pin up these preparatory sketches on the walls of his studio where they would act as *aides-mémoires* for when he was ready to produce a complete work. These 'on the spot' sketches would often be used in various paintings: the sketches he made of Peppers' cart horses, Lady Zouche's donkey, some of his child models, and various studies of cows and sheep, would be utilised many times over. From these sketches, some would be worked up into pastel and, on occasion, these pastel works became a complete picture and exhibited at the Pastel Society exhibitions and elsewhere. Following the pastel version, Stott would then complete a picture executed in oil. Often these canvases were then placed outside in the sun to dry, as the paint had to be perfectly dry before he began work on the picture again.

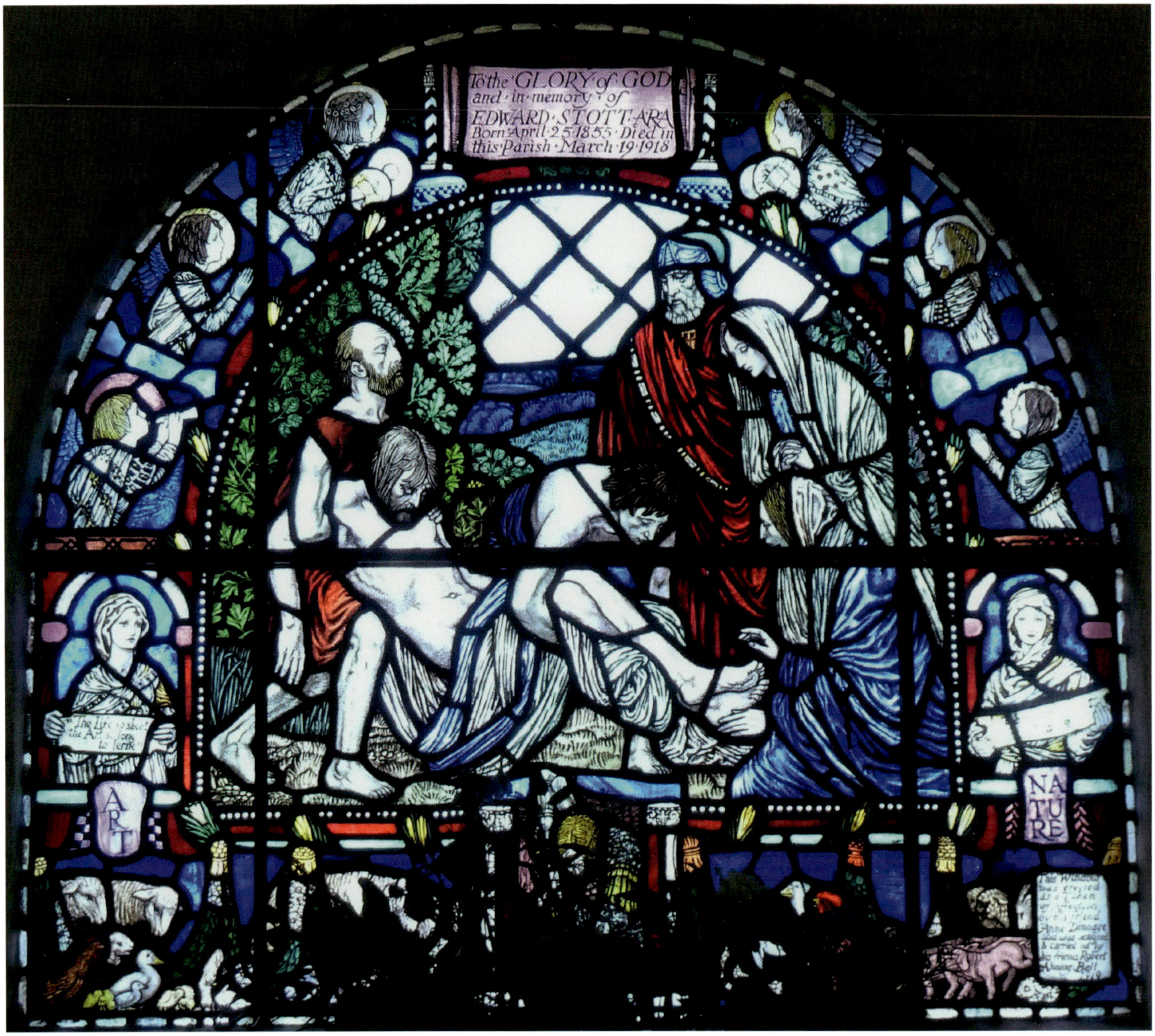

In as much as a close study of the landscape and nature was clearly important to Stott, what really gave him inspiration were the lives of the people of Amberley. As A.C.R. Carter wrote 'The idea of a picture comes to him as he watches the labourer returning from the fields, the little shepherdess tending her sheep, or the travel-stained cottagers returning home in the twilight.'[236] Stott occasionally jotted down the names of his models alongside his sketches. For example, alongside one sketch, Stott had written 'Regie [sic] Lee. His figure is quite large enough. It may be a bit smaller according to the pose.'[237] As the Census Return for 1901 recorded, Reggie Lee was the local policeman's son and was age six at the time. Alongside another sketch, he annotated 'proportions of Jonny Lisher boy in relation to size of Pepper's big cart horses.'[238] The Census Return for 1901 recorded a Lisher family

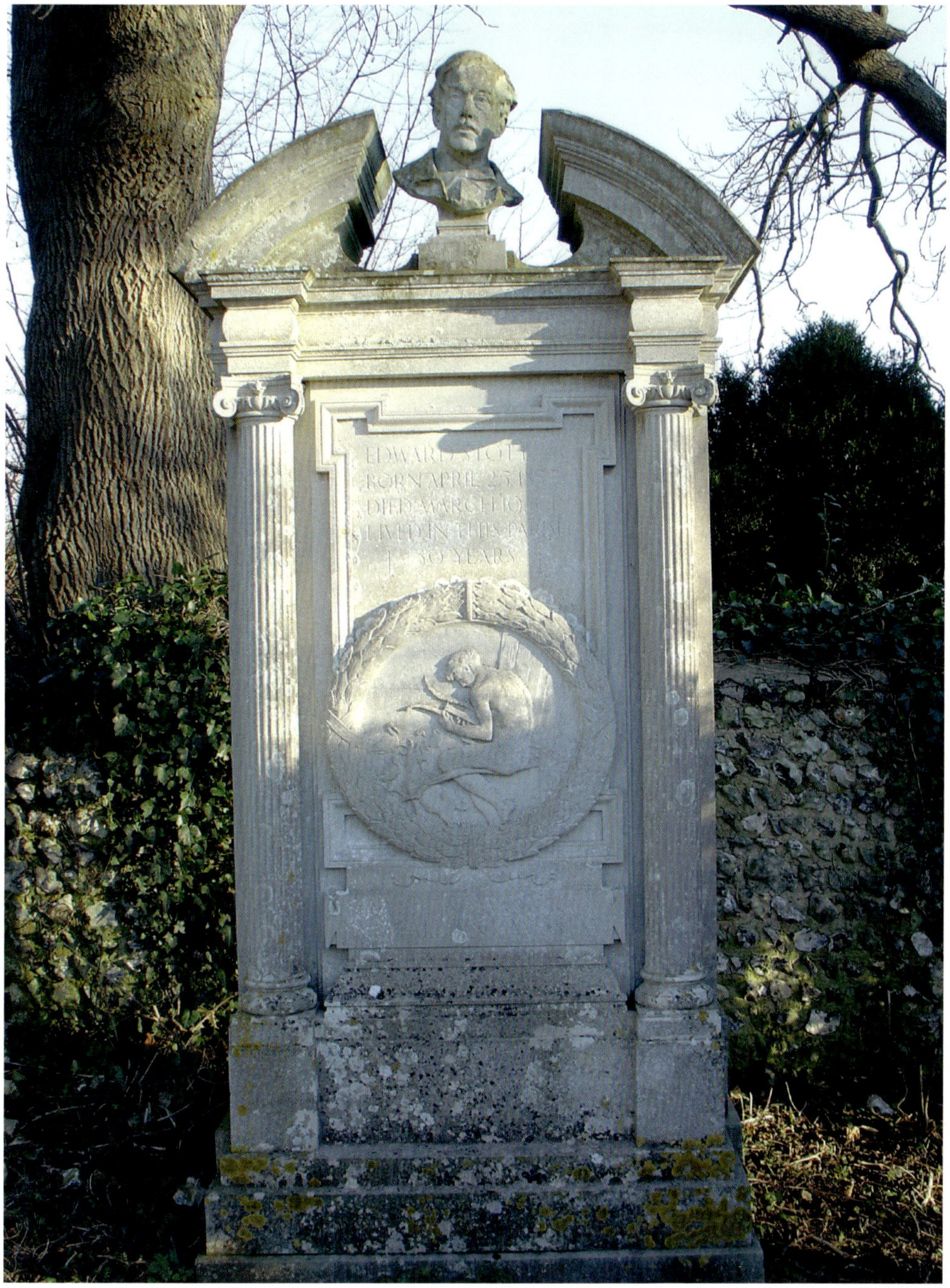

28. Robert Anning Bell, stained glass window in memory of Edward Stott, with central panel recreating Stott's painting, ***The Entombment*** (1917), 1920. St. Michael's Church, Amberley. Photo © Rob Farrow

29. Stott Memorial in St. Michael's Church churchyard, with sculpture of Stott's bust and relief of the unfinished painting, ***Orpheus*** (1918). Photo © Anthony McIntosh

living in Church Cottages belonging to St. Nicholas Church. John Lisher, aged 41, was listed as a Railway Porter and Post Worker, along with his wife Charlotte. They had three children – Leonard (age 12), John (age 5), and Mary who was aged 13. At least two of Stott's paintings – *The Horse Pond* and *The Team* – feature a horse and what looks to be the same boy model in both, who also appears in *The Harvester's Return*. The reference to 'Peppers' is Thomas Cunningham Pepper who ran the chalk quarries and associated industries such as brickmaking, lime burning and cement works, with his sons.

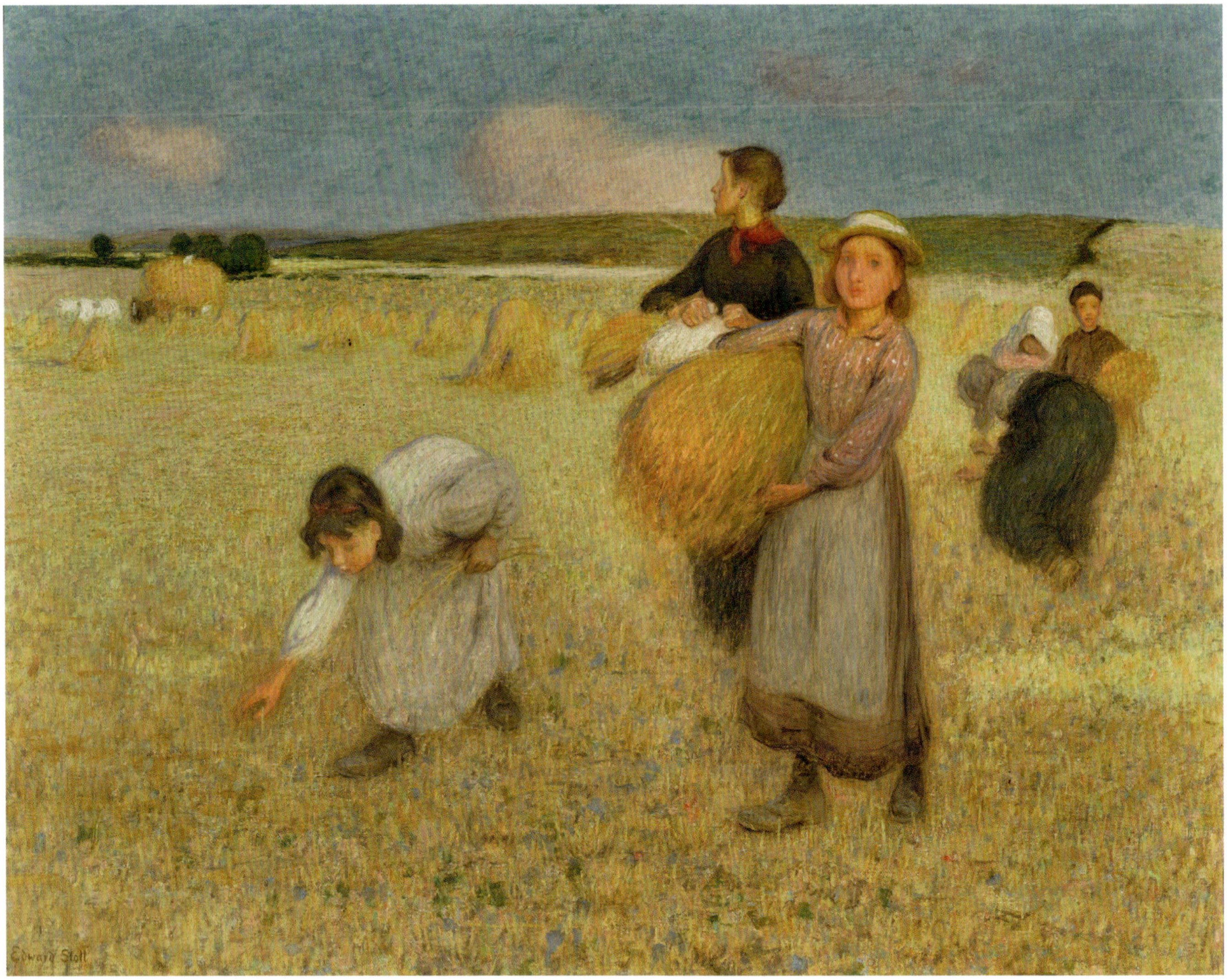

PAINTINGS OF AMBERLEY WORKING LIFE

THIS GROUP OF PAINTINGS REPRESENTS exterior scenes of rural work set within the Amberley countryside. The subject matter focusses on adults and children carrying out a number of farming-related employments which, in the main, portray solitary work. Stott's paintings of rural farm workers have generally been linked to similar subject matter painted by two of his contemporaries, George Clausen and Henry Herbert La Thangue, who have both been described as rustic naturalists. This has led to Stott also being viewed as a rustic naturalist, even though his work by the time he had settled in Amberley had not only renounced the style associated with rustic naturalism, but also the particular way in which he depicted his figures. Indeed, there is a crucial difference in terms of presentation and depiction of figures which sets Stott's paintings apart from these two artists. Nina Lübbren's study of rural artists' colonies in Europe found that in paintings which depicted rural labour, all signs of disharmony were excluded: 'Even rural labour was missing – that is, labour shown as labour.'[239] In the context of 'labour shown as labour', this would encompass intensive manual field work such as digging, harvesting, gleaning and ploughing. Stott produced only a handful of pictures which focused on these tasks, and his particular portrayal of gleaning, harvesting and ploughing, virtually erases any signs of hard labour and only hint at the effort involved. A case in point is *Ploughing, Early Spring* (1891) (Fig. 16), where the two ploughmen leading the horses down the hill appear as light and insubstantial as the white flecks of field furze which float in the foreground.[240] Only the horses give some idea of bodily substance. Another work by Stott called *Harvesters* (undated) (Fig. 30), focuses on a group of women and girls in a freshly harvested field where our attention is drawn to the colourful palette and simplified forms, rather than the arduous nature of the task which is only suggested.[241] In complete contrast, certain paintings by Clausen and La Thangue convey the labour-intensive nature of farming: the backbreaking and monotonous job of turnip picking is captured in *Winter Work* (1883-4) by Clausen, and the exhausting and perhaps fatal work of ploughing which is the subject of La Thangue's painting *The Last Furrow* (1895). In their striking realism, the arduous nature of such tasks is tangibly conveyed, and the socially thought-provoking subject matter is far removed from Stott's examples. On tasks associated with animal husbandry such as shepherding, cattle farming and poultry keeping, Lübbren defines these as 'not work', and it is the description of these kinds of tasks in this way that provides the key to understanding Stott's representation of rural work: 'One reason why shepherds, cowherds and gooseherds were preferred may have been that they *looked* to an outsider as though they weren't working at all. In fact, many of the paintings of herders come close to being paintings of peasants resting or simply standing.'[242] Stott's paintings of young cowherds, shepherds and shepherdesses, fruit pickers and poultry keepers, typify Lübbren's concept of 'not work'. It is pertinent to note here that, in his shepherd scenes, he does not paint scenes of sheep shearing or sheep dipping which involved manual strength, an example of which can be found in Mark Fisher's painting of 1892, *Sheep Shearing*.

30. Edward Stott, *Harvesters,* date unknown. Oil on canvas, 59 x 78cm. Private Collection/ Sotheby's London

PAINTINGS OF YOUNG COWHERDS

THE TASK OF LOOKING AFTER a herd of cows came with responsibility. As the *West Sussex Times* reported, in August 1891 Harriet Mills was fined 17 shillings and 6 pence for allowing two cows and a calf to stray onto the highway, and then two months later she was fined a further 10 shillings for a similar offence.[243] In Stott's ordered and organized world, his pictures of female herders saw them in complete control as they drove their herds down country paths, stood by while the cows drank from a pond, or moved the herd from one pasture to another. Thus, he was not

31. Edward Stott, *The Watering Place*, 1888. Version one. Oil on canvas, 63.5 x 84cm. Standen, East Grinstead, West Sussex, UK/National Trust Photographic Library/ Bridgeman Images

averse to idealising his scenes and, in the process, turned an essentially realistic and prosaic subject into a poetic rendition through subtle shifts in colour and atmosphere. Stott continued to experiment with his style, the changing facture of which is visible in a group of paintings he produced between 1888 and 1898. During this period, Stott produced four paintings of young female cowherds: *The Young Cowherd* (possibly 1888) (Fig. 26), two paintings with the same title of *The Watering Place* (1888) (Fig. 31) and possibly 1898 (Fig. 32), and *Changing Pastures* (1893) (Fig. 22). He would return to the theme nine years later with *Belated* (1907).

In his first painting in the series, *The Young Cowherd*, Stott has employed overt impressionist brushstrokes in the foreground, and the overall painterly effect is one of sketchiness, with only the merest suggestion of the separation of field and country path by way of a sparse hedgerow, along which a young female cowherd is leading a cow and calf.[244] In terms of colour, apart from a splash of dark turquoise in the foreground, which is repeated in a paler tone of turquoise for the field in the background, generally Stott has used traditional earth tones. Although the overall tenor of the painting has a prosaic quality, there is a delicate touch to this work and a tenderness of expression, which recalls the work of a modern Dutch artist Anton Mauve who also found inspiration in quiet pastures, scenes of cows, shepherds and farm workers.[245] A connection between Mauve and Stott was made by the critic writing for *The Art Journal*. Speaking of Stott's painting of 1901, *Winter Evening*, which shows a flock of sheep searching for food beneath the snow, the critic wrote that it was a scene that 'Anton Mauve delighted to represent.'[246] Hence, although quintessentially an English country farm scene, this painting also places Stott's work into a wider European context.

The two works with the same title of *The Watering Place* (1888 and possibly 1898), show a young female cowherd taking a break whilst her cows drink water from a watering hole. These two paintings provide a perfect example with which to show how Stott's method changed over time. In the earlier work of 1888, Stott has given us a 'close up' of a portion of the landscape in which he has placed his figure and animals, with the suggestion of landscape beyond the immediate scene. In this 'private view', the young cowherd reclines on the grassy bank with the trees offering a shady bower for herself and her cows. The gently curving trunk of the tree on the right-hand side mirrors the curve of the girl's bent arm, thus revealing that nothing is random in Stott's process. In terms of colour, apart from the deep red of the girl's dress which became something of a trademark colour for Stott, his palette is somewhat conventional. The brushwork used for the trees and background have a sketchy quality, whilst the foreground shows Stott's personal style of short layered brushstrokes with a tangible, rather than smooth, surface. By the time he painted the later version of (possibly) 1898, the traditional and conventional has given way to something more modern and formalistic; the scene has been simplified and pared down to Stott's leitmotifs of an oval pond, semi-circular patch of grass and

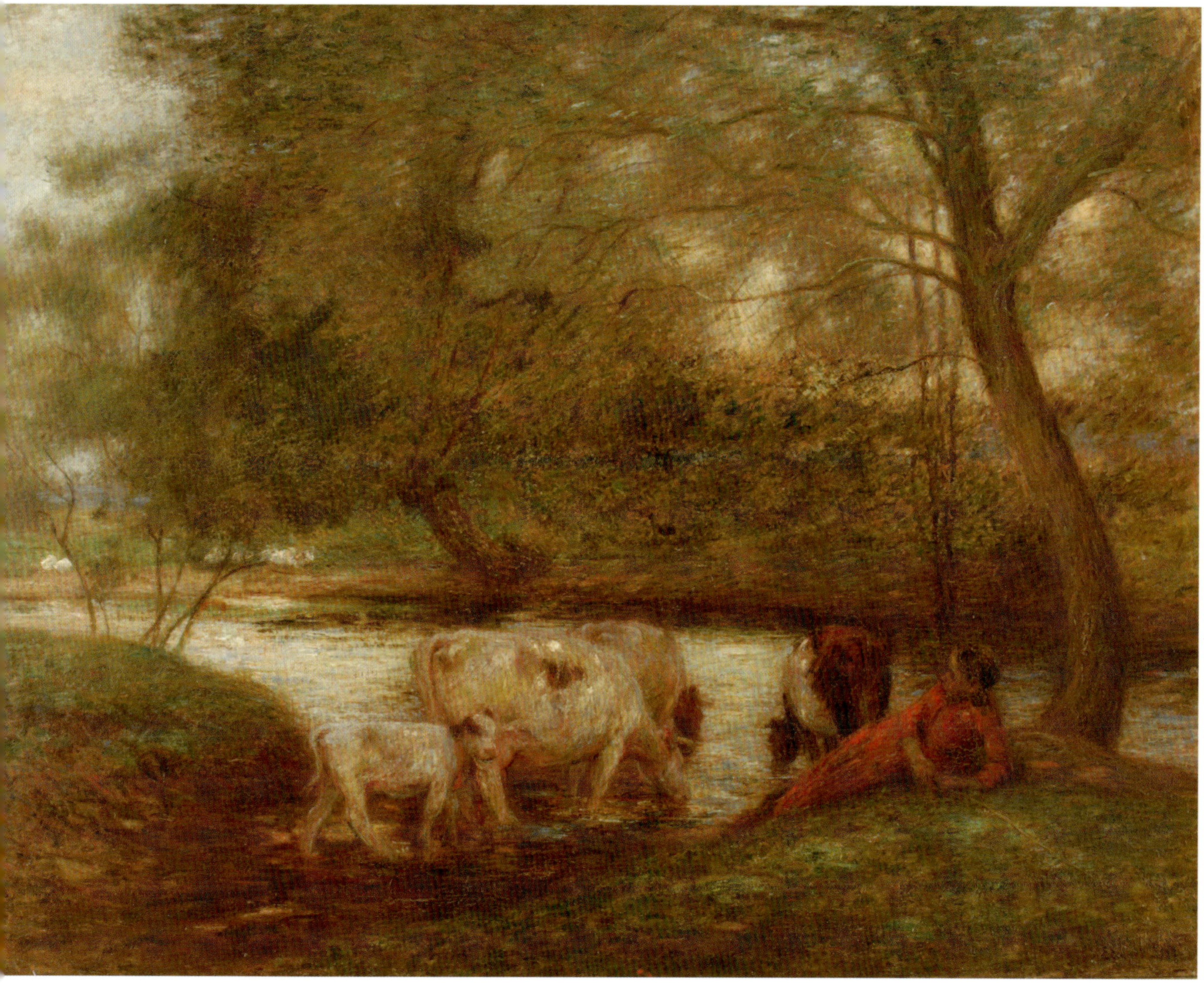

rectangular piece of ground. These elementary shapes, together with a landscape which is devoid of inessential detail, make the painting almost proto-modernist in intention.[247] The scene is also lifted out of the commonplace and into the poetic by a Corotesque 'patch' of bright colour, which appears in the form of a red bundle the young cowherd is holding. (This red accessory also appears in other paintings and is yet a further example of Stott developing his personal set of motifs.) The inclusion of this motif draws the viewer's attention to the young girl, but it also serves as a colouristic counterpoint to the creamy whiteness of the cow and the golden yellow of the pond. The painting was exhibited at the New Gallery in 1898, where the critic for *The Times* described it as 'exquisite' and 'so true in observation, so full of thought, so lovely in general effect…works of which the English School may well be proud.'[248]

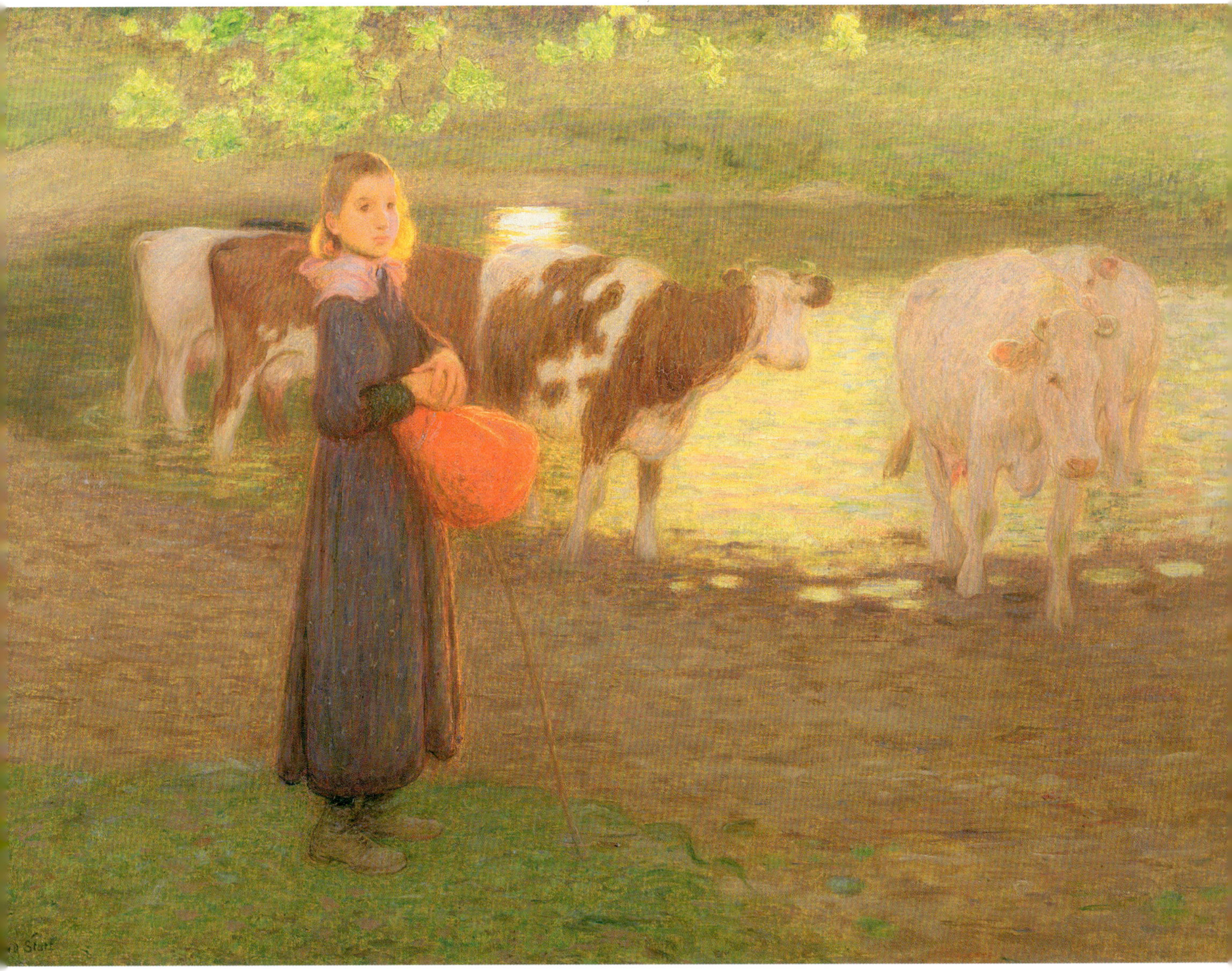

The anonymous critic also described the painting as a 'little picture of cows at a pond, with a girl in the foreground who is about to take them home; a golden afternoon light is falling upon the water, the trees, and the cattle.'[249] As this description accords with the later version being discussed, a dating of circa 1898 is feasible.

The final painting in this series, *Changing Pastures* (1893), presents an evening scene whereby the young herder is moving her cows from one grazing field to another. The colours of the earth, including the girl's clothing, are deeper toned to truthfully reflect the lateness of the hour. However, the drabness of the scene is relieved by the bright yellow-orange orb of the setting sun, and the pink aura surrounding it which has the effect of turning the sky multi-coloured. This reveals Stott's fluency and imagination in creating atmosphere through his knowledge of tones and hues, and by these aesthetic means he can turn the ordinary and the commonplace into a scene imbued with visual beauty.

PAINTINGS OF SHEPHERDS AND SHEPHERDESSES

32. Edward Stott, *The Watering Place*, possibly 1898. Version two. Oil on canvas, 61 x 85cm. Blackburn Museum and Art Gallery, Lancashire, UK/Bridgeman Images

Shepherds

Stott reflects the tradition of shepherding being handed down from generation to generation in *The Fold* (also known as *The Penfold*) (1895) (Fig. 33), *Peaceful Rest* (1902) and *Folding Time* (1904) (Fig. 34). In this trilogy, *Peaceful Rest* acts as a transitional work situated as it is between the young shepherd in *The Fold* and the elderly shepherd in *Folding Time*. It is in these three works where Stott's authentic approach to the subject matter can be identified, as there are factual elements which are specific to the Sussex Downs, and the particular representation of the Sussex shepherd. The colours Stott has used in *The Fold* are accurate reflections of the colours of this particular landscape at certain times of the day and at certain times of the year.[250] The clarity of the colours is due to the quality of light that covers the wide area comprising the Downs and is quite unique to that part of the country. With regards to the shepherd boy, his likeness fits the description of a young shepherd W.H. Hudson came across in his travels. In *Nature in Downland*, Hudson described meeting a shepherd boy who is standing motionless, crook in hand, with his sheepdog by his side:

> As I came close to him he made a very pretty picture, standing against the blue sky.... The young shepherd, aged about fifteen, had one of those perfectly saxon faces which you see more in Sussex than anywhere in England – a large round face, rosy brown in colour, sky blue eyes and light brown hair.... The expression, the shy yet pleased look-...was child-like and very pretty. He had loose-fitting grey clothes on and a round grey peak-less cap.[251]

Stott's painting of 1902, *Peaceful Rest*, features the next generation of shepherd. When this picture was exhibited at the Royal Academy exhibition of 1902, Frank Rinder reviewed the painting:

> *Peaceful Rest* by Mr Edward Stott, has been somewhat unkindly juxtaposed to a picture wherein are positive blues. Search Burlington House and you will find nothing more quietly beautiful, charged with more of fine personal feeling. Almost any evening in Sussex a shepherd can be seen thus lighting his pipe as the flock wander by a pool. But only an artist carries away an impression of so subtle a beauty, is able to compose that impression – to give sweep to the marginal line of that blue pool, on whose surface evening clouds are mirrored, to subdue any over-exuberance there may be in the grass, thus to introduce a few trees at the base of a chalky break in the Downs, reposefully to select from and interpret conflicting sentiments – as Mr Stott has done.[252]

In this painting the shepherd is, quite literally, taking a rest and lighting his pipe in the tranquil surroundings of the chalk hills of the Sussex Downs, whilst his sheepdog

33. Edward Stott, *The Fold* (also known as *The Penfold*), 1895. Oil on canvas, 60 x 55.5cm. © Touchstones Rochdale

keeps watch. Irrespective of how beautiful in colouring and tender in sentiment Stott's painting is, it should be remembered that the working life of a shepherd entailed being out in all weathers and at all times of the day, particularly during the lambing season. In *A Shepherd's Life: Impressions of the South Wiltshire Downs*, W.H. Hudson investigated the life of shepherds and made a case study out of a shepherd called Caleb Bawcombe who was forced to retire early due to poor health, but not before he had worked at least 50 years as a shepherd.[253] Bawcombe's father, Isaac, had also been a shepherd and he, too, had begun following the flock as a boy and had worked on the same farm until he was 60-years-old. He never earned more than 7 shillings a week and would not ask for a rise.[254] Whereas Rinder may have read *Peaceful Rest* as an idyllic pastoral, the painting possibly has a subtext which shows that Stott was well aware of what being a shepherd really entailed. As Anne Dinnage remarked, 'He took an interest in the shepherds and stockmen, often visiting the shepherds.'[255] In aesthetic terms, Stott has chosen 'soft' colours which has created a subdued tone and thus conveys, by artistic means, the humble life of a shepherd. The painting lacks the visual clarity of *The Fold*, discussed earlier, and the atmospheric and sombre beauty of such works as *Folding Time* (1904) and *Lambing Time* (1906).

Folding Time and *Lambing Time* focus on the third generation of shepherd, depicting elderly shepherds at evening time. In both, an atmosphere imbued with solemnity, and painted in the dark tones of the night, prevails. It is in these two paintings that Stott's ability to capture the essence of a scene combined with human interest comes to the fore. *Folding Time* clearly refers back to the work of Millet and Le Sidaner, whose paintings were influenced by the 'atmospheric veilings' of Millet.[256] Nevertheless, the expressive colouring, together with the gathering shadows and shades of the evening, is indisputably Stott. The critic for *The Observer* recognized this when reviewing the painting at the New Gallery exhibition, describing it as being:

> ...filled...with vaporous atmosphere impregnated with the pink pearliness of a full moon well up, but before the blackest shades of night descends. A close pack of sheep are entering a farmyard, against whose shadowed white walls the rose and red of two women's costumes show in lowered tones, and in the foreground an aged man watches the folding. Such facts might be the prose of the prosiest, but as Mr Stott recounts them they are poetry![257]

The glowing pink-red of the full moon, positioned high up in the centre of the scene, captures the lateness of the hour and draws our attention to the central figure of the young girl who is flanked by the older woman who is holding a toddler. This small group comprises three generations of females who stand by as the ewes and their lambs file into the secure and warm interior of the thatched barn. To the right of the foreground, and set slightly apart from the flock, is the elderly shepherd who is watching over the proceedings with the ubiquitous sheepdog by his side.

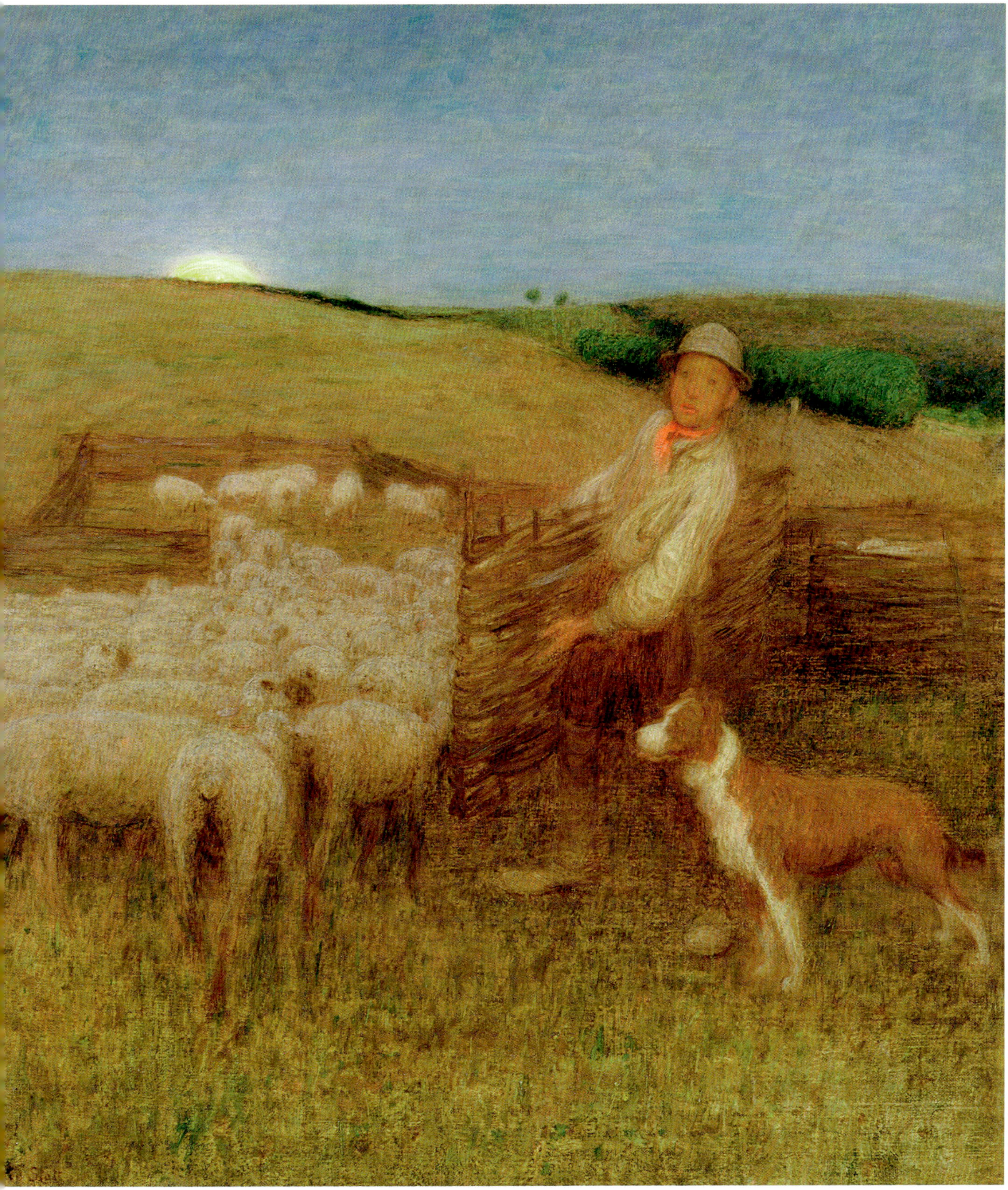

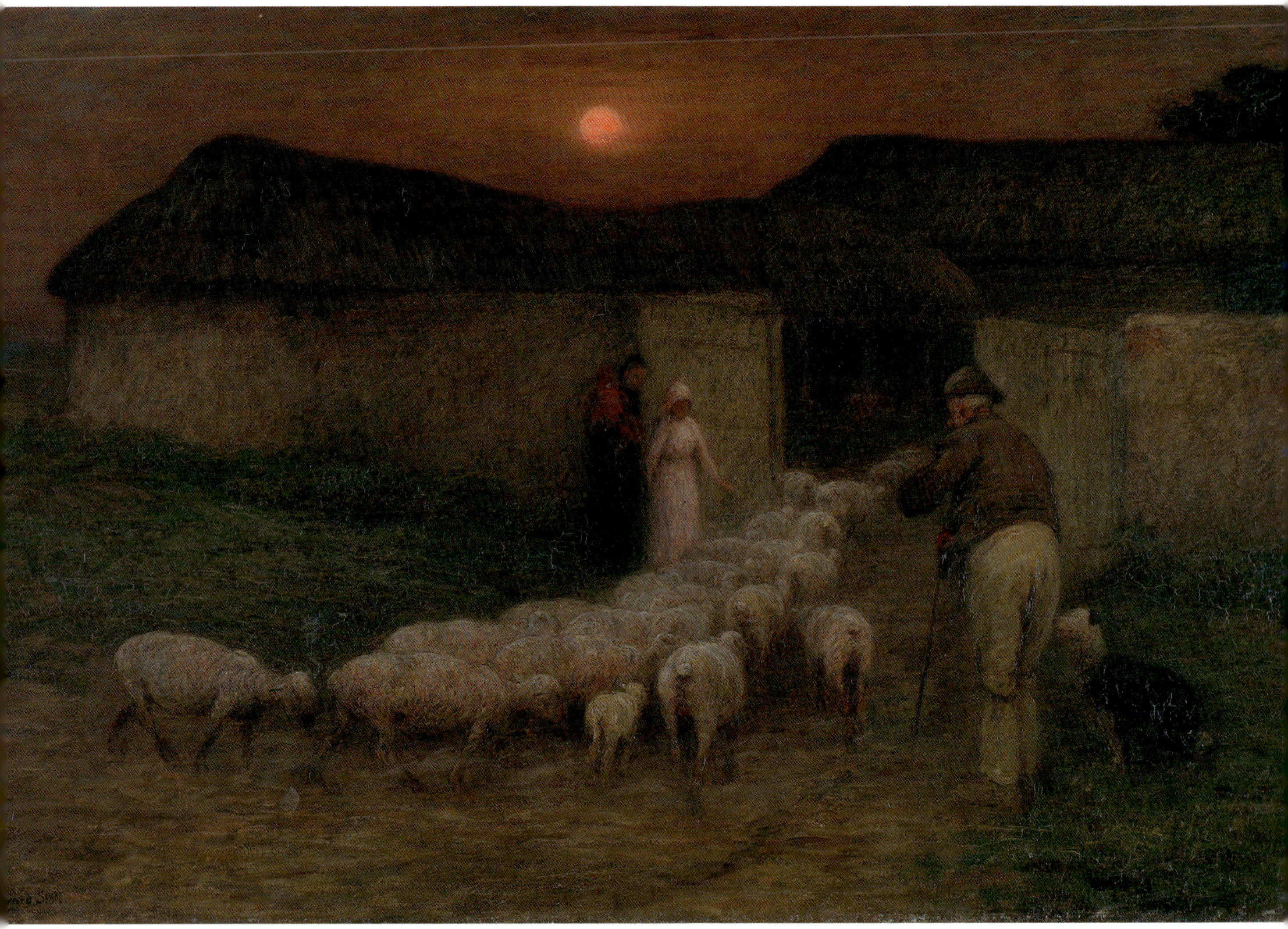

The subject matter of this painting could be read on a metaphorical level in that there is an element of protective paternalistic responsibility involved in being a shepherd.[258] This idea is reinforced if we consider that the small group of females are in such close proximity to the flock of sheep, that they could almost be part of the flock and also possibly the shepherd's responsibility.

This idea of 'paternalistic' responsibility also occurs in *Lambing Time*, and reflects that part of a shepherd's work that cannot end until all the lambs have been safely born. The seated shepherd, with pipe and ever-vigilant sheepdog, watches patiently over the proceedings. The theme of survival also underpins this painting with its association of life and death and can also be interpreted on another level – that of a shepherd's livelihood. The lambs would become the next flock and so it was essential that as many of them survived as possible. Furthermore, a shepherd who worked for someone else was often allowed to keep a number of lambs for himself by way of a bonus on top of his wages. This would depend, of course, on the survival rate of the lambs. As Caleb Bawcombe recalled, one year there was no extra money from lambs due to foxes which amounted to a personal financial loss valued at between £3 and £6.[259]

34. Edward Stott, *Folding Time*, 1904. Oil on canvas, 56.5 x 87cm. Ferens Art Gallery, Hull Museums, UK/Bridgeman Images

This group of shepherd paintings tells the story of a shepherd's life from the early days as a young shepherd to that of the older shepherd, and of the routines, responsibilities, and long working hours. What Stott has truthfully conveyed is the seasonal and daily structures of shepherding and is a true reflection of the working life of shepherds. Ditchfield made a study of this and it is apposite to quote him at length, because what he has put into words Stott has translated into image:

> [the] management of sheep in fields and on arable land differs greatly from that on the hills and downs. In the former they are penned in folds and eat root crops, and when they have finished a portion of the field the shepherd sets up hurdles around another square into which he drives his flock. In the lambing season which often occurs when the snow lies deep, he covers shelters with thatch to protect the lambs, and it is a hard and difficult time for the shepherd who lives in his van and is always in attendance upon his flock. But the Downs shepherd is a different being. He is usually found motionless, just leaning on his crook...and his dog at his feet.... Not a young man – but of an age not easy to fix, and having on his weather-beaten face an expression moulded by generations of men (for Downs shepherds, as a rule, descend from father to son) who have looked daily upon the same scene, the sky, the sea, and Down, and with the same object in view – to feed that flock and renew it from year to year.[260]

Thus, Stott has accurately portrayed the working life of shepherds, and included just enough human interest to lift these paintings out of the ordinary and into the poetic through their atmospheric qualities, colouristic beauty, expressiveness, and the tender sentiments conveyed.

Shepherdesses

Stott's paintings of shepherdesses take us into the subjective realm of the poetic rather than the objective realm of the 'real'. In *The Sheep Pool* (1889) (Fig. 35) the chalk hills of the Sussex Downs lend a factual topographical aspect to the scene, but his choice of soft pastel colours raises it into the poetic realm and are appropriate for a painting of a dainty 'Bo Peepesque' shepherdess. Stott produced two versions of this work: one executed in oil, the other in pastel. The oil was exhibited at the New Gallery in 1889, along with *Nature's Mirror*, *Through a Stubble Field* and *Snow on the Hills*. As the black and white illustrations at the back of the exhibition catalogue show, *Nature's Mirror* was something of a fantasy scene portraying three figures in a barren landscape at the side of a lake, with a crescent moon reflected in the water,

35. Edward Stott, *A Study for 'The Sheep Pool'*, 1889. Oil on canvas, 31 x 46.5cm. Private Collection/Bourne Gallery, Reigate, Surrey/ Bridgeman Images

whilst *Through a Stubble Field* consisted of a flock of geese being herded by a young boy.[261] The critic writing for *The Saturday Review* felt that *The Sheep Pool* was 'within its limitations admirably faithful, and even beautiful,' and that 'Mr Stott has so much talent that all we can wish for him is a little judgement.'[262] It is not clear what the critic meant by this, but it might have been a reference to the painting's poetic effect or choice of colours rather than it being a realistic portrayal which was often preferred by those art critics who favoured traditional work. This possibly explains why the same critic preferred *Through a Stubble Field* because it was 'far more true to nature', whilst the fantasy of *Nature's Mirror*, which was painted in similar colours to *The Sheep Pool*, was considered to be a 'failure' and 'daring'.[263] The critic further stated that 'Mr Edward Stott assaults the eye with some of his startling experiments.'[264] Stott's interest was not so much in producing a work that was reflective of truth (and according to Hudson shepherdesses were a rare sight), but rather in exploring the potentiality of colour in order to convey a particular emotion or idea. Unlike his paintings of male shepherds where his choice of palette had more veracity appropriate for the realistic scene being portrayed, with *The Sheep Pool* Stott's aim was to depict a shepherdess with feminine qualities who clearly was waiting for the rest of her flock to amble down the hill to the pond.

With the later (second) version of *Trees Old and Young, Sprouting a Shady Boon for Simple Sheep* (1899), Stott has replaced the open-air of the Sussex Downs with a secluded and shady bower. Gone too are the confectionary tones used for *The Sheep Pool* and, in their place, he has used a rich and heady palette of deep colours which range from the red of the shepherdess' dress to the striking blue of the water. This painting was well received by the critics when it was exhibited at the New Gallery in 1899. Commended for its beauty, colour and poetic vision, the critic for *The Guardian* wrote that:

> Edward Stott is still...preoccupied with problems of light dappling under the shade of foliage. In his *Trees Old and Young*, we see the figure of a girl seated by a pool over which prevails the shadow of a tree whose boughs do not come within the canvas. The stinging blue of the sky is only told to us by its reflection upon the water, to which sheep are huddling to drink. Over the shadow on the ground the sunlight has spilled itself in splashes of gold, and the girl's face and the fleeces of the sheep are lit with its warm flakes. The almost featureless bank of field behind is touched everywhere with the interest of the true painter-like feeling by which the artist works. How few of our artists who rank higher in popular estimation have the gift of lucent colouring which makes the homely subject of Mr Stott so living and lovely.'[265]

The critic for the *Daily News* remarked that certain landscapes at the New Gallery had a 'quiet power and beauty through colour and poetry', and singled out Stott's paintings for their 'feeling of colour and the beauty of it [which] is what characterizes the

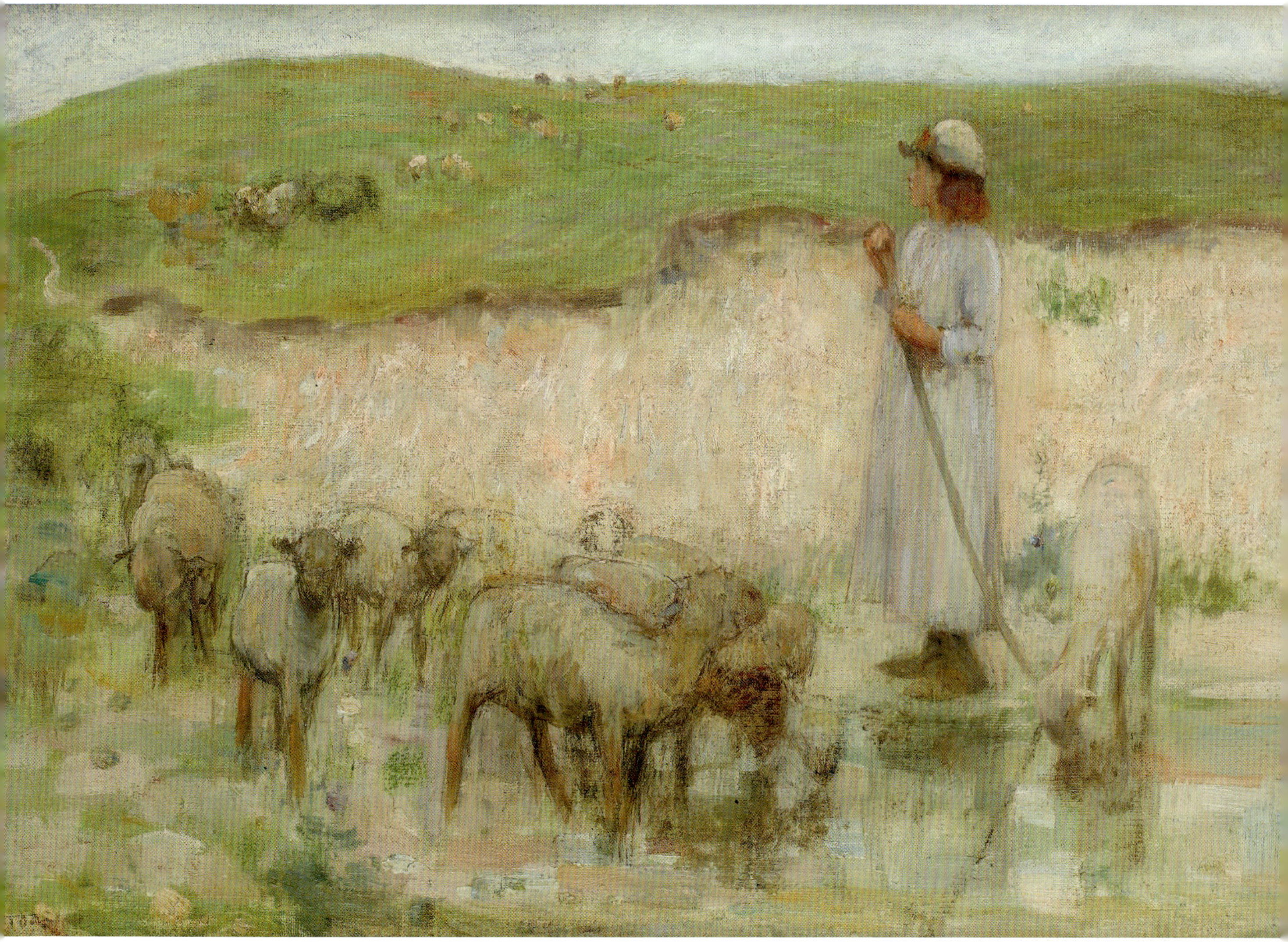

work of Mr Edward Stott; the painter sees what the ordinary man would never see, and his art enables him to show it to us. This suffusion of colour, colour that is at once full and tender gives the charm of feeling to his work.'[266] The critic for *The Times* described the painting as 'pure poetry', although the extreme brilliancy of the pool was disliked because it was felt not to be reflective of truth.[267] The most descriptive piece of criticism appeared in *The Art Journal* in which the critic conjured up the idea of a poetic idyll – 'Golden crowns of sunlight come through the overhanging trees and gild the nibbling flock. Beyond this symphony of colour, and past the gnarled roots of the shady canopy, the landscape melts away.'[268] The poetic tone used by the critic is apposite because, as mentioned in Chapter Three when discussing the earlier example, the title Stott gave this work came directly from Keats' poem *Endymion.* Thus, this painting of a young shepherdess resides in the poetic world where she passively sits whilst her sheep take a drink. Similarly, in *The Sheep Pool*, the shepherdess stands patiently by waiting for her flock, unlike the open-legged stance of the boy in *The Fold* who is actively holding open the sheep pen. To depict a shepherdess in this unladylike way, and any suggestion of strength, would be inappropriate. This idea of rustic innocence and femininity comes to the fore in Stott's paintings of country maids who are depicted in orchard settings where they are either feeding fowl or picking fruit.

PAINTINGS OF COUNTRY MAIDS IN ORCHARD SETTINGS

STOTT PRODUCED THREE PAINTINGS WHICH focussed on the theme of country maids in orchard settings: *In an Orchard – An Early Summer Morning* (1892) (Fig. 20), *The Year's Youth* (c.1898-1901), and *The Apple Gatherer* (1900). Attached to a house or smallholding, and usually enclosed within a boundary wall or fence, orchards can be classed as semi-private spaces. Much has been written on the issue of gendered space and its relationship to the public versus private world. Howkins extended the discourse to include farming communities where the spatial boundaries of public and private/male and female become blurred. Using dairymaids as an example, Howkins differentiates between the 'indoor' work of the dairymaid which was deemed to be more respectable than the 'outdoor' work of the female fieldworker owing to the fact that the dairymaid was out of public view. An example of this can be found in Stott's painting of 1895, *Milking Time – Early Morn* (Fig. 18), which shows a young milkmaid in a cowshed. As Howkins states, the 'work of a dairymaid was acceptable…the fieldworker was usually not. The very difference in name is significant – the dairy*maid* and the field*woman*, the one with its stress on innocence and the rural idyll, the other with its connotations of experience and harshness.'[269] Parliamentary papers also revealed that there was an implicit association made between female field workers and a perceived lack of respectability, with the implication that the transition from the outside world of field work to the domestic sphere of motherhood and wifehood was virtually impossible. This was certainly the conclusion reached by the Honourable E.B. Portman in his second report to the Royal Commission on the employment of children, young persons and women in agriculture, in 1867-8:

> There can be no doubt as to the moral effects of field work on the girls. From an early age they become accustomed to the use of foul language, such sense of decency as they may have when they first go out is entirely broke down, and a roughness of manner and a dislike of restraint are engendered which entirely unfits them for domestic service or for their duties in the future as wives and mothers.[270]

Following on from Portman's report, the concern over certain female employments in the farming industry was continued in the writings of Richard Jefferies in the 1870s. Jefferies concentrated on the unnaturalness and oddity of the female field worker who was dressed in a mixture of male and female clothes, and had a rough weathered appearance.[271] In his description of the field woman, Jefferies could almost be describing Clausen's field women as they appeared in his paintings; in particular, one of his preferred models who has been identified by Gruetzner Robins as Susan Chapman.[272]

The country maids in Stott's works, who are situated within the semi-private space of the orchard, encapsulate and perpetuate the idea of rustic innocence and simplicity. The features of the young girl in Stott's painting *In an Orchard – An Early Summer Morning*, are obscured beneath her pale pink bonnet, which not only protects her head from the sunlight, but also prevents her skin from getting brown and weathered. Furthermore, the bonnet shields her face from the viewer's gaze, and her demeanour is one of shyness as she looks down at the group of small hens and birds she is feeding. Similarly, in *The Year's Youth*, the girl is in profile and her slight frame covered by a long blue dress. Placed within a pretty orchard where white (possibly cherry) blossom dots the trees, she reaches up to the branches, whilst yellow ducklings peck at the ground around her. The third of these 'orchard' paintings is a work of 1900, *The Apple Gatherer*, and in this work a presentational shift has occurred. The young woman's bodily presence is such that it dominates the foreground to the extent that it fills the space, and the vibrant red of her clothing reinforces her visual presence. This is in complete contrast to the depiction of Stott's other two country girls. In her literal 'forwardness', although this does not imply a loss of innocence, she has lost the delicate femininity that is present in the other two maids. It is in this painting that a connection with specific works by Clausen and La Thangue can be made. Not only did they paint similar subject matter, but depicted their young 'apple gatherers' and 'poultry maids' with a physical presence and sturdiness. This is evident in an early painting by Clausen of 1882 called *Springtime*, and *In the Orchard, 'Haylands', Graffham* (c1898), by La Thangue. In Clausen's painting, not only does the young woman have bodily presence, so do the cockerel and hen which are in contrast to the small dainty birds in Stott's two examples. Kenneth McConkey, writing specifically about La Thangue's child workers, which can also be applied to Clausen's work, states that these children with 'Ruddy complexions and strong hands reveal that they were born to outdoor toil. For the painter, the country child embodies the health, strength, resourcefulness of self-reliance lacking in contemporaries.'[273] In La Thangue's painting, the strength of the young apple-gatherer is conveyed by the way in which she carries the full basket of applies, with fully extended arms, to suggest the weight of the basket. Furthermore, the forward sweep of her arms is mirrored in the forwards movement of her dress and pinafore, which gives the impression of a breezy day. As suggested by the volume of apples that have been

36. Edward Stott, *The Bird Cage*, 1905. Oil on canvas, 76.6 x 52cm. Manchester Art Gallery

picked, these will be used for large-scale cider making which was a labour-intensive activity often carried out by wives and children.[274] In contrast, the young country girl in Stott's painting, *The Year's Youth*, holds a small blue plate under her arm which suggests she is only picking a small amount of fruit for domestic purposes. Similarly, in *The Apple Gatherer*, the young woman is picking apples and placing them in the fold of her dress suggesting their use is for domestic purposes only. Stott did, however, produce some preliminary studies (Fig. 4) for a work called the *Cider Press* and later completed a painting called *The Cider Harvest*.[275]

The aesthetic appeal of Clausen's and La Thangue's paintings lies in the visual power these works have, whether it is due to the natural healthiness of their country girls, the rich immediacy of the artists' chosen palettes, or the assured masculine handling of the brushwork. In Stott's examples, the aesthetic impact is not as pronounced but they nonetheless have a subtle power. This has been achieved through the delicate handling of the brushwork, the tender way in which the scenes have been presented, and the beauty of Stott's chosen colours. For *In An Orchard – Early Summer Morning*, Stott has used restful muted tones of grey, green and pink. However, in *The Year's Youth*, his choice of bright blue, green and acid yellow, all of which are offset by the white blossom, make more of a visual impact. In *The Apple Gatherer*, the bold red of the girl's dress dominates which, as well as making her central to the scene, somewhat detracts from the 'sketchy' unfinished-looking background. Stott produced a fourth painting, *The Bird Cage* (1905) (Fig. 36), which presents a close-up of a child who is reaching up to the branches from which a bird in a cage is suspended. Her looped plaits reveal her to be Peggy, one of Stott's favourite models. Although her exact identity is unknown, she also appears in *The Gleaners* (1903) and in an undated sketch by Stott of a young girl knitting. Like the young woman in *The Year's Youth*, she holds a brightly coloured circular plate under her arm. Overall, the colours Stott has used are uplifting and jewel-like in their richness.

The way that Stott has chosen to portray his country maids reinforces the idea of rustic innocence. In fact, taking his paintings of girls and young women generally, there is not a hint of impropriety nor even the potential for it, and he seems unable (or unwilling) to paint anything that is remotely indelicate or unladylike. Even in his paintings of female field workers such as *The Gleaners* (1903) and *Harvesters* (undated) (Fig. 30), there is an inherent delicacy and femininity about his young workers.[276] In *The Gleaners*, Stott focusses on the child in the foreground. With her round girlish face, and hair in looped plaits, she epitomizes childlike innocence. Behind this girl, there is a figure of a young woman who also has a certain grace. Both figures are holding freshly gleaned bundles of wheat rather than being shown in the active physical process of gleaning, which is taking place in the background. In this sense, Stott could perhaps be accused of idealising these scenes as clearly the images do not accord with the earlier findings of Jefferies and other commentators at the time.

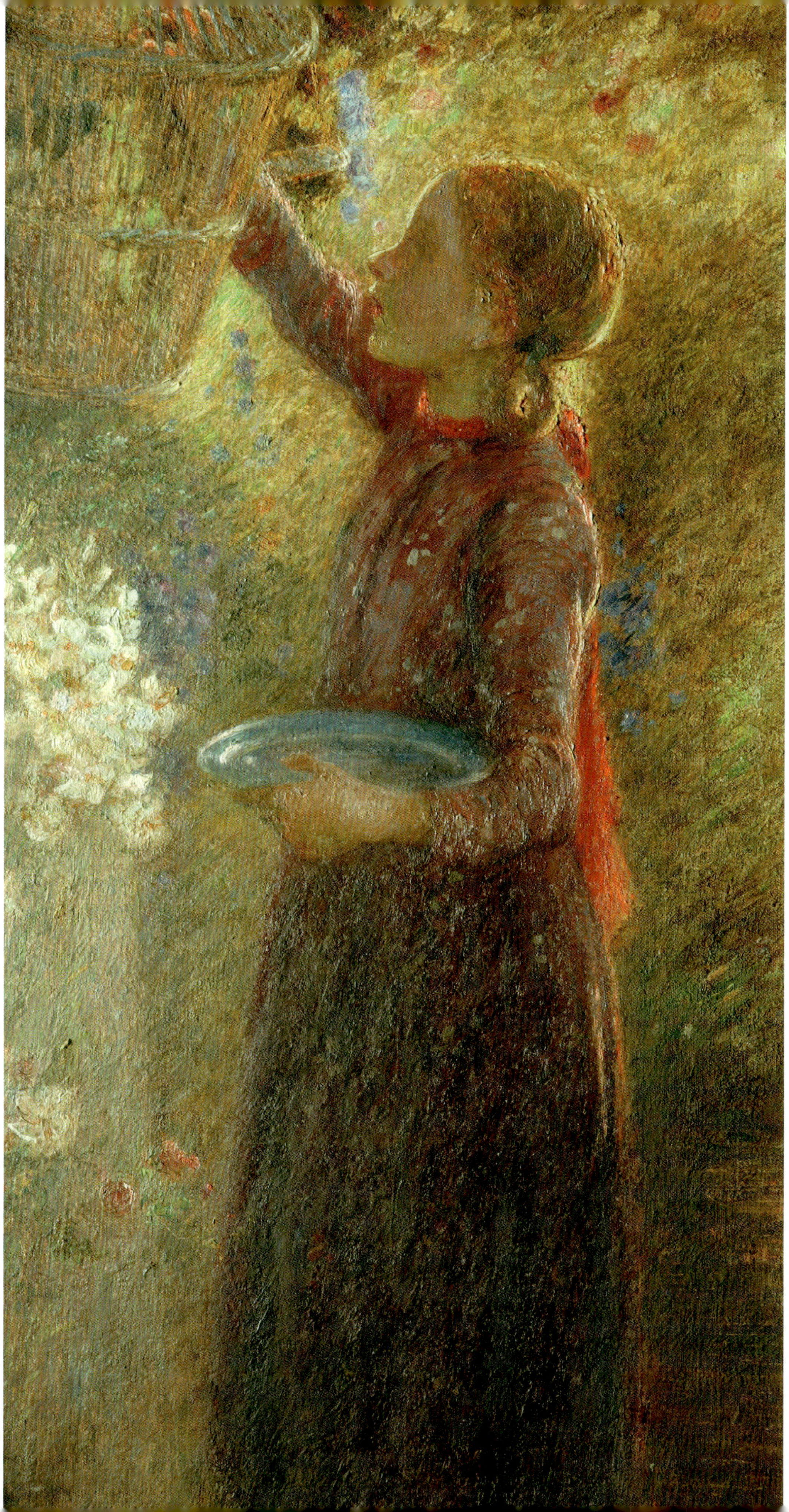

37. Edward Stott, *Home by the Ferry*, c.1891. Oil on canvas, 71.1 x 92.1cm. Private Collection/Bonhams London

AMBERLEY 'AFTER HOURS'

IN ANOTHER SERIES OF PAINTINGS, Stott focusses on scenes of Amberley village. He presents families and workers returning home by ferry or on foot, intimate village snapshots of children sitting outside having supper or playing cricket in the street, or boys with their horses at the close of day. In the street scenes, a suggestion of warm and inviting cosy interiors is conveyed by the bright squares or rectangles of light shining through a window or open door, and anticipate Stott's paintings of interiors which are discussed in Chapter Five.

Paintings of families and workers returning home

This group of paintings, which is by no means exhaustive, includes *Home by the Ferry* (c.1891) (Fig. 37), *The Landing Place – Late Evening* (1895), and a possible reworking of this painting called *Returning Home* (c.1910), *The Harvester's Return* (1899), and *Saturday Night* (1900) (Fig. 38).[277] A further work, of which only a full study was ever completed and not exhibited, was *The Footbridge.*[278]

In *Home by the Ferry*, Stott has continued his early interest in subject matter of this kind which resulted in his final *plein air* painting of 1887, *The Ferry Boat* (see Chapter Two). In the later example, which shows the oncoming of night time, our attention is drawn to the three young girls who stand back from the river bank. The bright pink bonnet of the eldest girl focusses our attention on this group, whilst at the edge of the bank a young boy calls for the ferryman. Although this painting was exhibited at the Royal Academy in 1891, and despite its aesthetic appeal and the human story it is telling, the painting appeared not to have attracted any press notice. From an art historical viewpoint, this work is interesting because it provides clear evidence that Stott was building up his own personal repertoire of poses, and his trademark colours of pink, grey and ruby red; the latter being a colour particularly favoured by Stott and which he repeated in many of his paintings. He had also, by this time, perfected his 'signature' style which consisted of methodically and painstakingly applied short brushstrokes coated with sufficient oil paint to produce a tangible surface that created overall texture rather than the appearance of an 'academically' smooth surface. Stott repeated the theme of *Home by the Ferry* with the first version of *The Landing Place – Late Evening* which was exhibited at the New Gallery, where it was praised by the critic for the *Daily News* for its 'truth of colour.'[279] The critic also described the scene as 'the closing in of a summer's evening, when in the twilight, colour deepens and seems actually intensified as the darkness comes on.'[280] Although there is no extant image, a brief description appeared in the New Gallery exhibition catalogue where the subject matter was described as a picture of a girl holding a baby, with a young boy by her side, having just been dropped off by the ferryman, with a 'bright patch of reflected moonlight' behind them.[281] Based on this description, it looks as if this painting was reworked by Stott which subsequently evolved into a later work of circa 1910, this time with the title of *Returning Home.*[282]

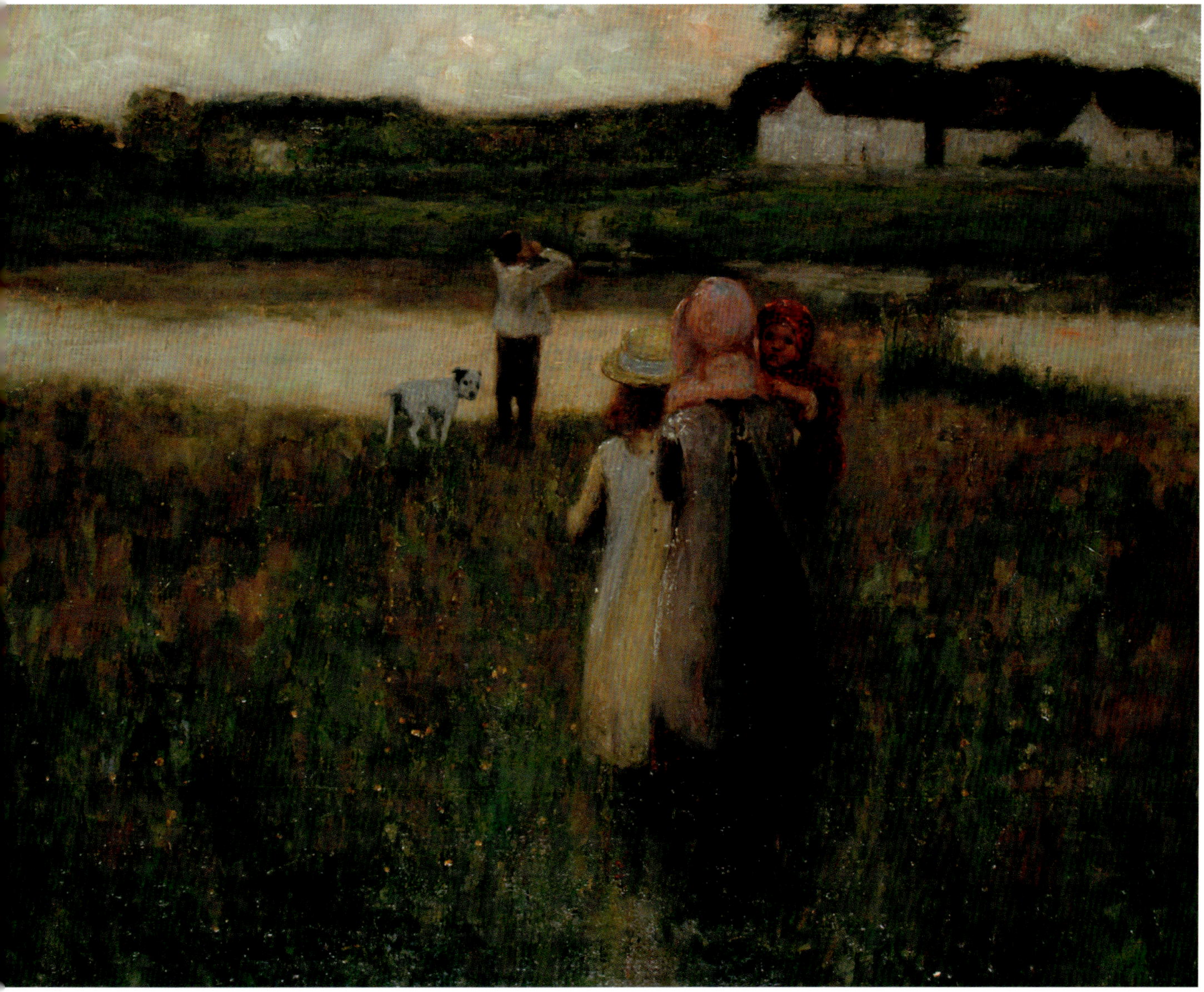

These paintings are also of social and local historical interest as they speak of the dying trade of ferrying. The work of a ferryman carried with it great responsibility, and the necessity of having in-depth knowledge of a river's currents. With specific reference to the River Arun, it was a fast-flowing river and could be treacherous.[283] In Stott's time, there were at least three recorded fatalities: Edward Gosden, age 6, drowned in 1890, followed by the drowning of Leonard Helyer, age 16, also in 1890. In 1896, William Lee, age 35, met his death whilst boating.[284] Thus, these paintings by Stott that show the crossing of a river by way of a ferry have nostalgic overtones as, with the building of footbridges (see Stott's study *The Footbridge*), the job of a ferryman was under threat. Perhaps, in a rare resigned moment of acceptance, it appears that Stott has subtly commented on the encroachment of modernity into rural life.

Two of Stott's paintings focus upon the theme of families or workers returning home on foot at the end of the day – *The Harvester's Return* and *Saturday Night* (1900). The former portrays two male harvesters (a man and a boy) who are leaving a

38. Edward Stott, *Saturday Night*, 1900. Oil on canvas, 66 x 82.5cm. © Towner Art Gallery, Eastbourne

newly-reaped field, with female gleaners still working away in the distance. The tranquility of the scene, combined with the atmosphere of a late summer evening, and the golden yellow shocks of wheat standing in neat rows, belies the arduous and labour-intensive nature of harvesting. As Christiana Payne found in her study of agricultural farming, the hours were long and, with specific reference to harvesting, the process required constant bending in the tasks of reaping, binding, setting up the sheaves and gleaning.[285] Tim Barringer, speaking of John Linnell's paintings of this kind, and Linnell's *Harvest Moon* (1855) is an example, states that this painting 'evokes the atmosphere of the late summer evening, depicting a line of field workers and gleaners returning from the harvest field…. In the distance…a row of three reapers [are] still at work.'[286] Barringer further notes that paintings such as these focus on the 'idyllic aspects of the landscape – the poetic image of nature capturing the last rays of the setting sun' whilst simultaneously suggesting the 'hard labour that exists within it.'[287] This suggests a shared sentiment between Linnell and Stott. Whereas elements of *The Harvester's Return* by Stott may recapitulate the influence of Clausen and French rustic naturalism, particularly in the presentation of the male figures, it also samples aspects of the English tradition through, say, an artist such as Linnell. This occurs in the women gleaners in Stott's painting who are mere specks in the distance, carrying out the repetitive and intensive process of gleaning after the male harvesters after finished their work.[288]

Saturday Night tells of a family returning to their home, which is some way in the distance, late at night. It attracted a lengthy review in the *Daily News*, and Stott received the recognition he was due.[289] Stott has accurately and succinctly captured the feeling of the long and tiring trudge home through the use of perspective, as the immediacy of the broad path in the foreground diminishes into a long curving line. The distance is further emphasized by the white speck of paint that denotes a cart and horses traveling along the lane. The family group, halted in their progress, look towards the distance they still need to travel, with each member caught in a moment of action; the toddler peeping over her mother's shoulder, the young boy halted in his walk, and the young girl who is carrying a heavy red sack looking back at the unseen person following them. The structure of this work has a formal simplicity, which was commented upon by the critic for the *Daily News* who described the landscape as 'broadened and simplified and impressive.'[290] In the formal structuring of the landscape in this way, whereby the fields are contained within curving bands of hedgerow or a line of trees, *Saturday Night* arguably pre-empts those highly formalistic and brightly coloured modernist landscapes of, say, Spencer Gore. Although the painting appears to have darkened somewhat over time, the original would have seen Stott choosing saturated jewel-like colours such as deep aquamarine, emerald, ruby red and amber. This prompted the critic for the *Daily News* to speak of the 'feeling of beauty, of deep suffused colour…the delicately appreciated gradation of tones, all in the low key of evening light.'[291] Frank Rinder wrote of the 'rare beauty

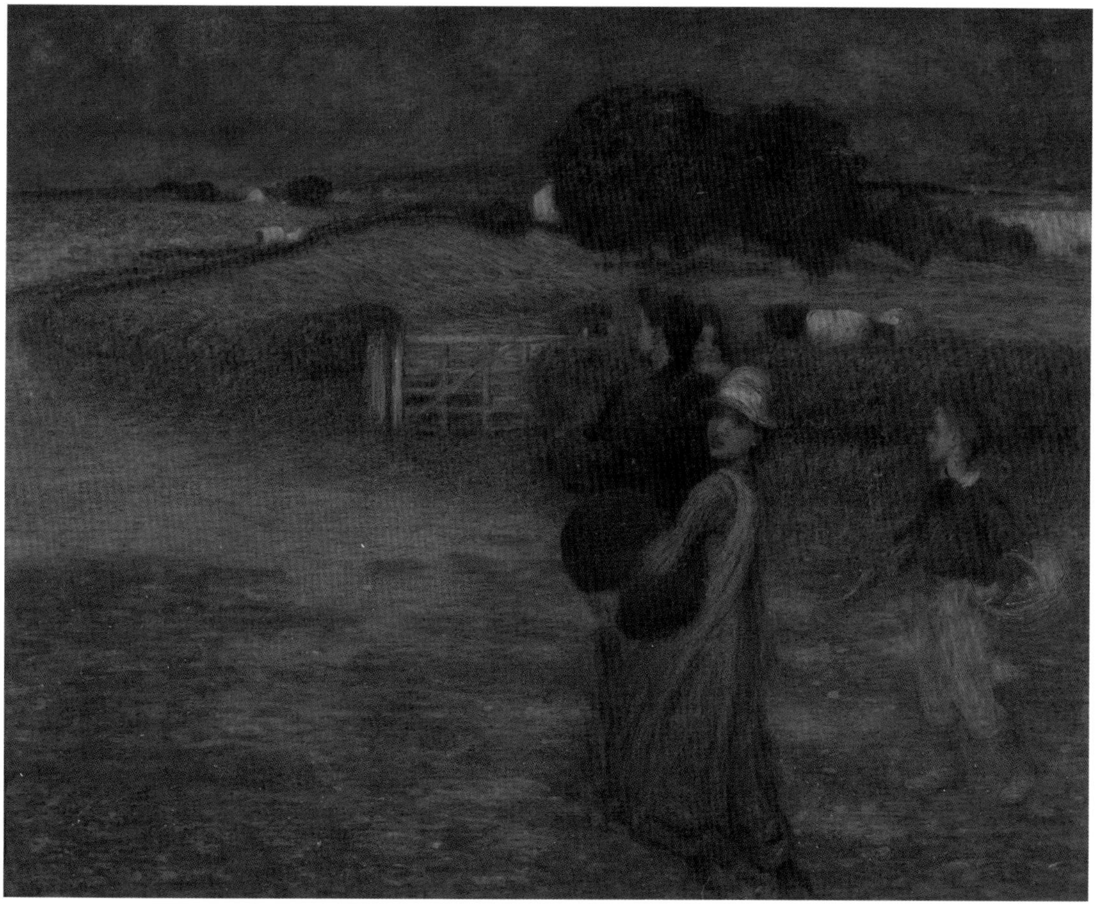

[of] this landscape…[which] expressed among other things that real…link which binds the peasant to his environment, the subtle correspondence between human life and nature.'[292] In the critics' minds, this painting also served to differentiate Stott's work from that of Clausen and La Thangue when all three artists had their paintings exhibited at the Royal Academy exhibition of 1900. *The Guardian* critic described La Thangue's painting, *The Ploughboy* (1900), as a typical example of the artist's 'strong, cold power of illumination.'[293] Speaking of La Thangue's choice of colour, the critic viewed it as the opposite of prismatic and in its 'blank, economic fashion' it showed a 'radical difference between [his] methods and those of Mr Stott, or even Mr Clausen, the artist whose work lies nearest to his.'[294] The critic then turned attention to Clausen's contribution, *Making a Rick*, which showed that Clausen had moved away from the influence of rustic naturalism and had 'struck a new and very delicate harmony', where the handling was 'prettier, more suave and fluent, than that to which the artist has accustomed us.'[295] Clausen's painting was hung opposite Stott's *Saturday Night* which was praised for its 'rich jewel-like note [that] makes it almost a decorative work by contrast to the open-air play of Mr Clausen's brush.'[296] When comparing Stott's painting alongside those exhibited by his two contemporaries, it is not difficult to imagine just how palpably different his painting would have presented itself both in terms of handling, atmosphere and colour.

39. Edward Stott, *The Village Street*, 1894. Oil on canvas, 39 x 78cm. Bradford Art Galleries and Museums, West Yorkshire, UK/Bridgeman Images

SCENES OF LEISURE

Courtship

Towards the end of the nineteenth century and beginning of the twentieth century, Stott tentatively explored the theme of courtship in at least three paintings: *Love's Twilight* (c.1897-1901), *A Moonlight Idyll* (1902), and *The Reaper and the Maid* (c.1907). It would be fair to say that these works are the least successful in Stott's oeuvre and have none of the usual vibrancy and joyousness that informed much of his work. However, they show that Stott was aware of this aspect of village life even if it appeared to hold little personal interest for him, as well as raising awareness of these little-known paintings and thus add to the knowledge of his overall oeuvre. One painting, *Love's Twilight*, was the subject of correspondence between Stott and the painting's owner, and reveals how Stott worried over his work and was protective of its reputation.

Love's Twilight features a young maid standing by an open gate talking to a man on horseback, who is wooing her. The setting for the scene is an Amberley street where ducks or geese wander down the road and cottages are visible on either side. Stott painted the work in 1897, but did not exhibit it until 1901 at the New Gallery. The painting was purchased by David Croal Thomson in 1912, and as correspondence between Stott and Thomson reveals, Stott maintained an interest in what happened to his paintings.[297] On 26th April 1912, Stott wrote 'It interests me very much to hear that you are now the owner of my little picture *Gossiping*. This though is a new title – I called the picture *Love's Twilight*'.[298] In a further letter, he asks for the painting to be returned to him so that he could work on it to 'its advantage.'[299] Thomson duly sent the painting to Stott who wrote:

> What is necessary will take some time to do – parts having to be scraped down and reprepared and left to thoroughly dry before the final touches are superimposed. I'm afraid you will have to let me have the picture here for <u>two to three</u> months. In a general way the picture is a better one than I anticipated. It is always trying to me to see one of my pictures painted so long ago. Still as I say there is a great deal about this one that I quite like and the rest I feel can be much improved.[300]

Stott also complained that Thomson had not sent the frame, and asked to have it sent on. The saga of *Love's Twilight* continued once Stott had received the frame, and he was clearly not happy:

> 'The <u>tone</u> of the gilt frame…is very offensive. I assure you it was not like this when the picture left me some years ago. The last owner – a man at Southport might be the guilty one. Do you mind if I get Taylor my frame maker to modify the colour of the gilt and also to fit a <u>glass</u> in the frame. Both will benefit the appearance of the picture very much.[301]

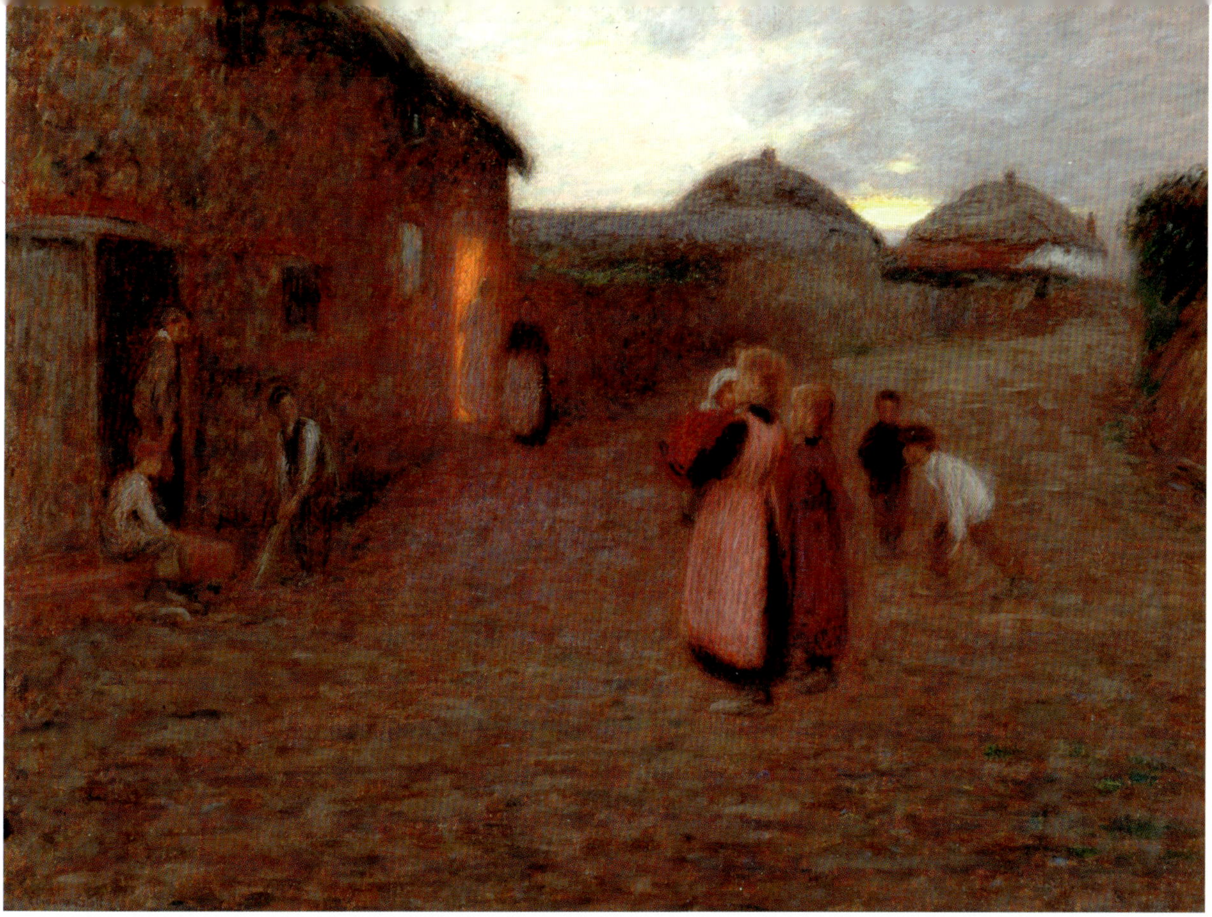

The painting and frame were returned to Thomson in December 1913, both having been significantly worked on. Stott thanked Thomson for the sum of £25 that he had sent and stated 'I'm glad I worked on it again. I feel now that I shall not be ashamed to meet it again…. I believe the picture has now some value, so I feel perhaps I have really earned the money & tender you my grateful thanks.'[302]

Stott continued the theme with *A Moonlight Idyll*, which was exhibited at the New Gallery in 1902. From a description given in the catalogue, the painting depicted two 'rustic lovers': a girl sitting on a fence, with a man standing by. A field of cabbages, and two or three white-fronted cottages, provided the backdrop. (This painting was purchased by C.T. Harris, and subsequently purchased by W.W. Sampson on 28th November 1913 when it came up for sale at Christie, Manson and Woods following Harris' death. Its current whereabouts is unknown.) The scene of the final 'courtship' painting – *The Reaper and the Maid* (1907) – is a landscape in which a young maid is being shown solicitous attention by a reaper, possibly when the working day has ended. The oil version, which was exhibited at the Royal Academy in 1907, has disappeared. However, the image for a study in coloured chalks has survived where it appears that Stott would have used low-key earth tones for the finished work. The act of courtship in this painting accords very closely with a painting by George Heming Mason of 1872, *The Harvest Moon*, which also contains a scene of courtship with compositional similarity.

40. Edward Stott,
The Old Gate, 1895.
Oil on canvas,
81.6 x 97.6cm.
Manchester Art Gallery,
UK/Bridgeman Images

Children at Leisure

With this series of paintings, Stott had more critical success and gained something of an international reputation. Whether it is quiet scenes of boys fishing such as those featured in *November Twilight* (1893), children sitting outside their cottage having an evening meal, or playing games in the street, Stott seems to have been at his happiest when capturing their youthful innocence and care-free existence. Two such paintings are *The Labourer's Cottage – Suppertime* (1893) and *The Village Street* (1894) (Fig. 39). What is immediately apparent is Stott's choice of palette. Whereas in the former painting he has used cool grey-green tones to reflect that the sun has set, in the latter work he has chosen warm orange-pink and earth tones to convey the setting of the sun. Both paintings, then, display sincere colouristic and truthful concern with the capturing of the deepening shades of evening time. Furthermore, both paintings incorporate Stott's leitmotif of a welcoming bright light shining through a window or open door, which suggest the lure of domesticity. In *The Labourer's Cottage – Suppertime,* this is achieved by way of a bright yellow square of window, whilst in *The Village Street* the light is suggested by the bright orange rectangular door, on the threshold of which stand two women. Both paintings also centre on children. In the former painting, three children sit outside a thatched cottage having their supper in the cool light of evening. The young boy is holding a bowl and spoon which is a repeat of the motif that Stott used in *As Happy as a King* (1884) (see Chapter Two). The atmosphere in this painting is one of absolute quiet and stillness, whereas *The Village Street* depicts a livelier scenario. Two young girls, one of whom is holding a baby, stand by whilst a group of boys play cricket. Whilst the subject matter of both works is prosaic, their poetry comes through in Stott's use of colour and atmosphere, which attracted the attention of the critics. When the *Birmingham Daily Post* reviewed *The Village Street,* the critic remarked that Stott 'has made a poem out of a village scene, that divested of the sentiment and feeling which has been his inspiration, would have been as prosaic as the multiplication table.'[303] Attention was also drawn to the colours, in particular the 'ruddy gold firelight which streams from the open door', and the purple and grey sky with a contrasting streak of pale orange which disappears just behind the cottage roofs.[304]

Three paintings in which boys on horseback feature – *The Ferry Boat* (1887) (Fig. 15), *The Old Gate* (1895) (Fig. 40) and *The River Bank* (1901) (Fig. 41) – all have an international connection. *The Ferry Boat* (see Chapter Three) was exhibited at the Munich *Genossenschaft* (co-operative) exhibition of 1890.[305] The *Genossenschaft* exhibitions showed work that leaned towards tradition and conservatism, and Stott's painting would have fitted into the ethos of the exhibition due to its sentimental treatment of the subject, and the solemnity of the occasion as the boy on horseback watches the departing party. It also reflected the civilising values of support and responsibility, and perpetuated the idea that rural life was stable and centred around order and routine. In this sense, Stott's painting appeared to reinforce the

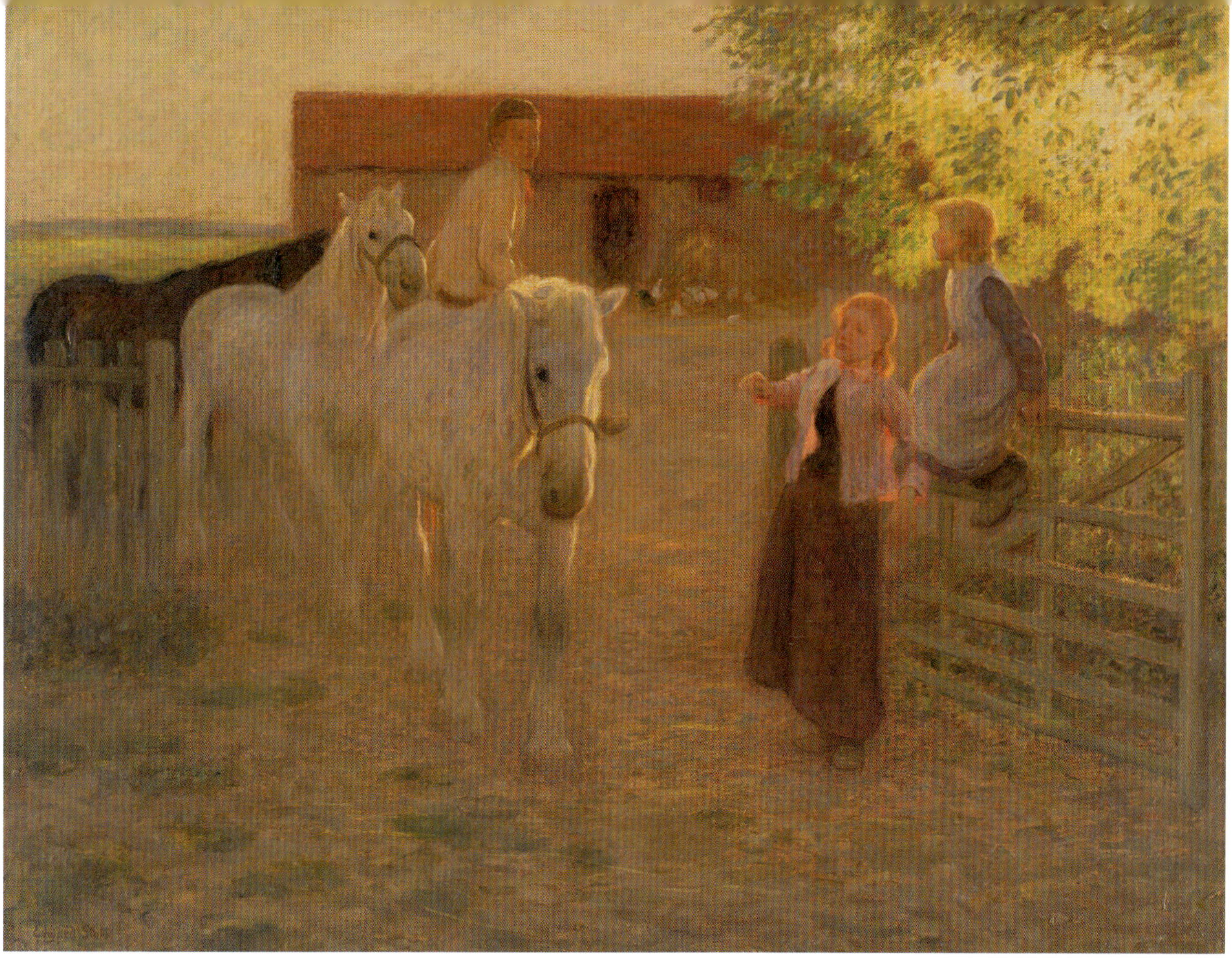

social, cultural and political values of Kaiser Wilhem II.[306] Stott also achieved international success with *The Old Gate* when it was chosen to appear in Munich in 1895 at the (possibly) *Genossenschaft* exhibition.[307] In terms of subject matter, Stott presents an idyllic scene of a young boy and his team of horses returning home on a late summer's evening, where he is welcomed back by two girls at the open gate. This kind of imagery would have appealed to the traditional *Genossenschaft* salon where the slow clip-clop of the horses' hooves on the ground, and the rhythmic swaying of the boy and horse as they pass through the open gate, conjures up the impression of an unhurried existence within an idyllic country setting. When this painting was exhibited at the New Gallery in 1896, the critic for *The Guardian* described it as a 'Very beautiful and poetic rendering of a farmyard...touched by the last rays of the declining sun. The whole scene swims in a soft warm shadow, except where the direct beams glint on an edge or face or limbs or traverse a pink jacket, or cast an aureole of light around a golden head.'[308] The painting was subsequently exhibited at the Brussels Exposition of 1897, and the Paris Exposition Universelle of 1900, for which Stott was awarded a Bronze Medal.[309] The inclusion of the painting in Paris was possibly as a result of Isidore Spielmann who was a friend of Stott (see Fig. 42). Stott had, in fact, written to Sir Edward Poynter in 1899 asking if he would be receiving an invitation to exhibit at the Salon.[310] It is not known if Poynter replied,

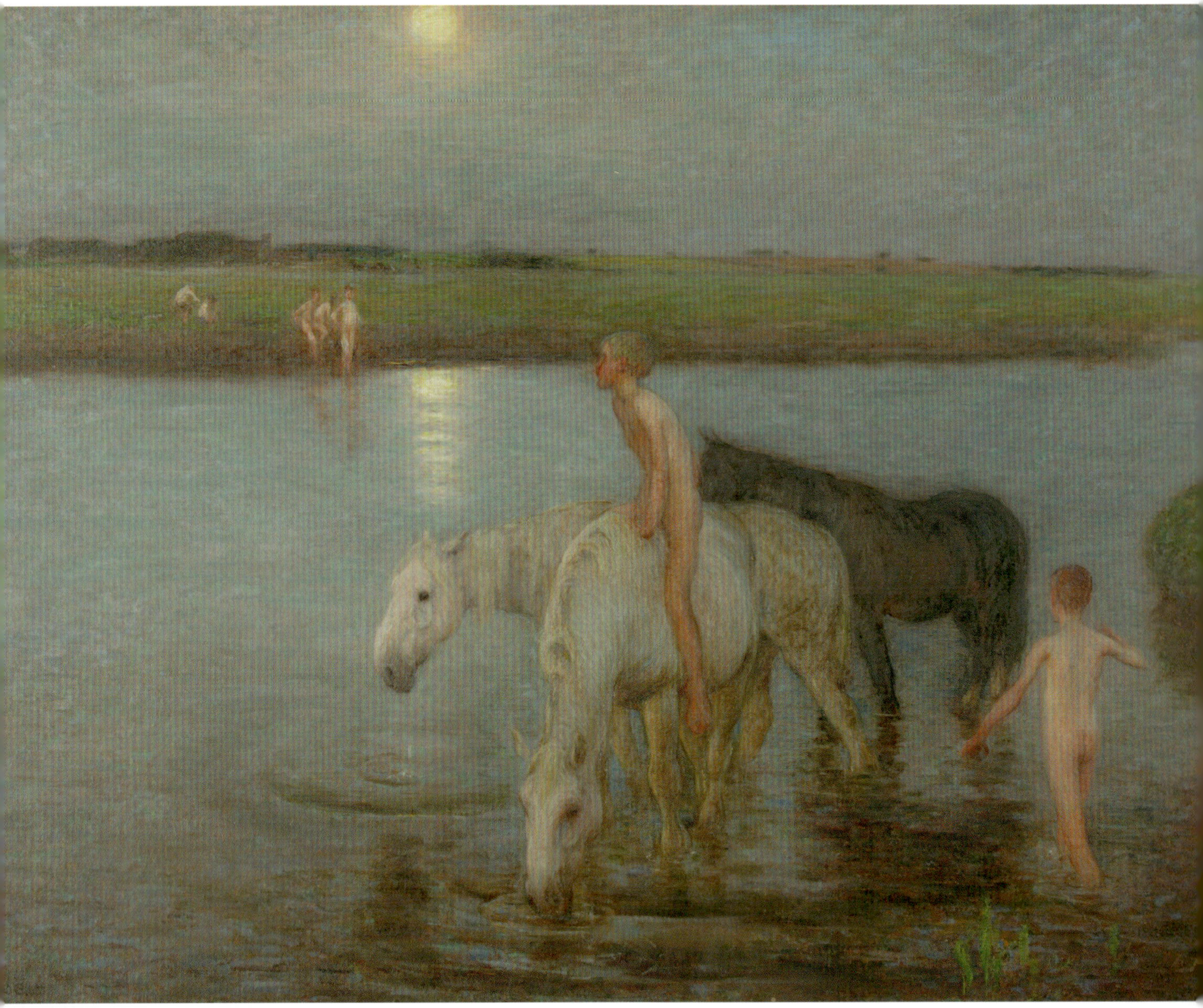

but Spielmann – in his capacity as secretary and delegate of the British Fine Art section – wrote to Stott on the 6th February 1900 enquiring as to the French title of *The Old Gate.* Stott replied on the 8th February with two suggestions – *L'Entre de cour de Ferme* and *La Vieille Porte Cochère* – with the first title being preferred.[311]

With respect to the final painting, *The River Bank,* it is possible that this was a reworked painting of 1894 called *A Summer Evening* (now lost). This earlier work was exhibited at the New Gallery where the critic writing for *The Guardian* commented on 'Mr Stott's love with the dusk when it is still full of light, a light that trembles between rose and green. The horses go down to drink in the pond with boys astride of them.'[312] The description given accords closely with the later painting which was exhibited at the Royal Academy in 1901 where it attracted the

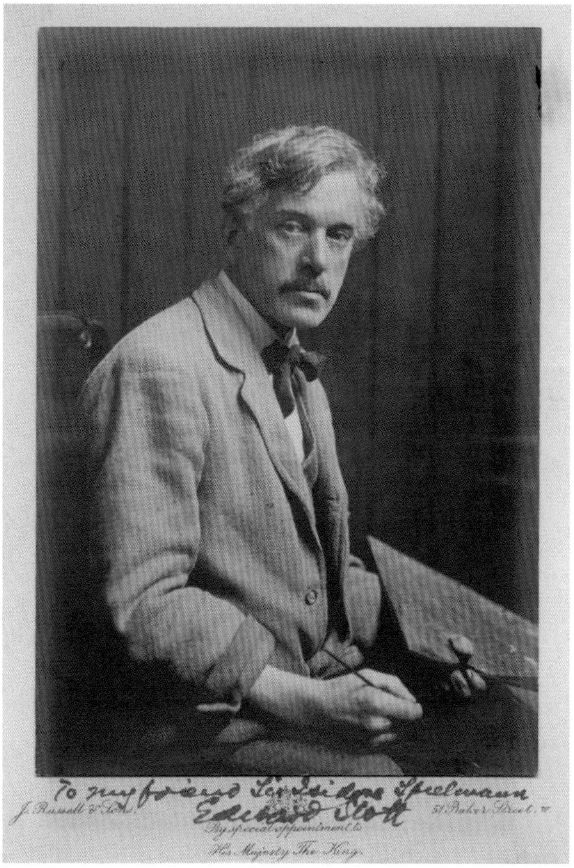

41. Edward Stott, *The River Bank*, 1901. Oil on canvas, 69.9 x 96cm. Possibly a reworked version of *A Summer Evening*, 1894. Manchester Art Gallery, UK/Bridgeman Images

42. Photograph of Edward Stott, with the inscription 'To my friend Isidore Spielmann', by James Russell & Sons, date unknown. © National Portrait Gallery, London

attention of M.H. Spielmann. Spielmann described the painting as a 'beautiful study of twilight…in which boys are bathing, while the air is alive with subdued colour.'[313] He was less than complimentary, however, when describing the horses and boys: 'The forms of the horses incline towards the ugly; the figures of the boys, mere naked clod-hoppers, have only the beauty of colour and naturalness to help them…'[314] It is a visually stunning work which has been brought about through Stott's contrasting palette of turquoise and green, a blue sky tinged with pink which casts a rosy glow over the scene, and the pale flesh tones of the naked youths. As there appears to be no precedent for this subject matter in British art, the idea is highly original.

The *River Bank* appears to display aspects of a German style of art known as 'Jugendstil' (youth style).[315] This was a specific style used by the Munich Secessionists and formed part of their interpretation of art nouveau, of which certain of their subject matter focussed on images of nude adolescents depicted in the country-side, and often on horseback. The style and subject matter was made popular in the German magazine *Jugend* which started in 1896, which was two years after Stott's original painting of 1894, *A Summer Evening*.[316] Echoes of Stott's painting can be identified in certain works by the Berlin artist, Max Liebermann, who contributed to *Jugend* and who also exhibited at the Munich Secessions. Liebermann continued the theme in Impressionist-inspired works such as *Der Reiter am Strande* (1904), and a sketch of circa 1908, *Nackter Reiter am Strande*.[317]

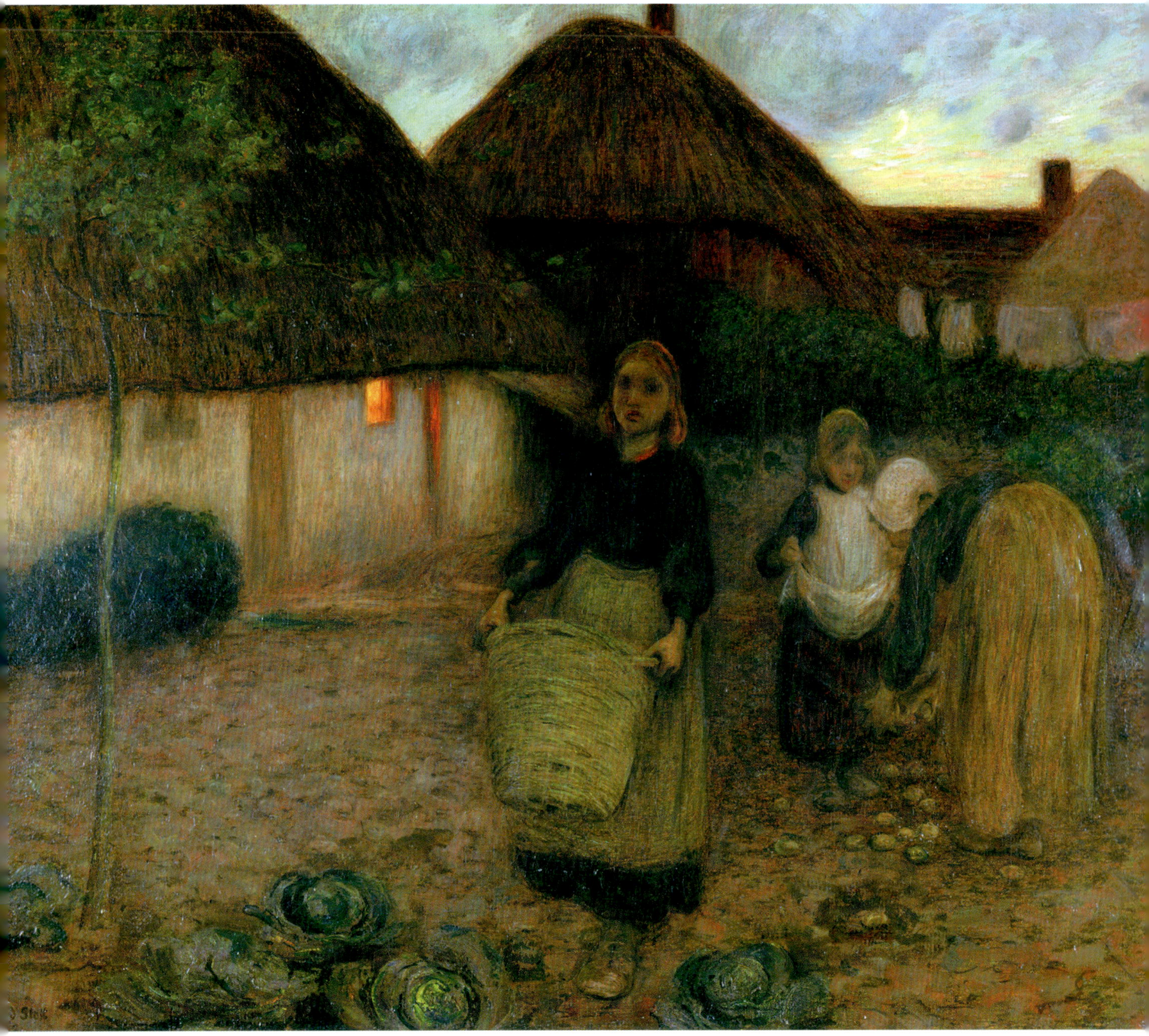

43. Edward Stott,
The Widow's Acre,
1900. Oil on canvas,
74.8 x 60.1cm.
Laing Art Gallery,
Newcastle-upon-Tyne,
UK/© Tyne & Wear
Archives & Museums/
Bridgeman Images

5

AMBERLEY INTERIORS

'Domesticity' and 'Cottage Madonnas'

FROM AROUND 1900 STOTT TURNED his attention to scenes of interiors, focussing on domestic subject matter and 'mother and child' imagery. This change of direction coincided with Stott finding domestic contentment and support when he moved in with the Dinnage family. As Stott once remarked to Anne Dinnage, his lifelong companion and helper, 'I can get lodgings anywhere, what I want is a home'.[318]

Although small in number, these paintings are significant. In socio-political terms, they were produced at a key moment in British history where they subliminally appear to address certain issues. Firstly, a change in government saw the demise of the Conservative Party and the rise to power of the Liberal Party.[319] Secondly, the Suffrage Movement was formed resulting in a challenge to the ideology of 'separate spheres'.[320] The third factor was the Boer War, where it emerged that many of the recruits were unfit to serve. Collectively, these issues contributed to the rise of the 'cult of motherhood'. In art historical terms, particularly when a social history reading is applied, Stott's rustic interiors continued the trend popular in Victorian times for paintings depicting cottage life where they often conveyed a moral, political or social message. It can be no coincidence either that the majority of Stott's paintings at this time were exhibited at the Royal Academy which was known for its 'conservative' values, and that Edward Stott was duly elected as an Associate of the Royal Academy in 1906. On a biographical level, from evidence contained in the

44. Edward Stott, *Washing Day*, 1899. Oil on canvas, 46.7 c 51.9cm. Watts Gallery Compton, Surrey, UK/© Trustees of Watts Gallery/ Bridgeman Images

Stott Archive, valuable insight can be gained into Stott's personal perspective on a woman's role in society which suggests that he was in agreement with the prescriptive policies at the time. Letters in the Getty Research Institute Library also add to the biography on Stott and disclose, in the process, that he could be temperamental and over-sensitive.

The ideology of 'separate spheres' emerged in the Victorian period and was predicated upon the association of the public world of work with the concept of the 'male breadwinner', whilst the private domestic world of the home was associated with women.[321] Of course this ideology was best suited to middle-class women who were not expected to work outside of the home. With respect to working-class women in urban and rural areas the matter is infinitely more complex and, out of sheer necessity, some of them would have had to find employment. However, those paintings by Stott clearly depict women engaged in domestic and maternal activities inside the private space of a house or garden, and thus a straightforward account of the 'separate spheres' issue is given.[322] Within the domestic sphere, the prescribed roles for women were that they should be nurturing mothers, efficient and economical in running the house (even though a sign of middle-class status was the employing of a housekeeper and servants), and supportive and compliant wives. A challenge to this somewhat socially restrictive ideology occurred in the late nineteenth century with the rise of the Suffrage Movement and first wave of feminism, which began by attacking the institution of marriage and also the laws that, making women the property of men, permitted and even encouraged abuse against women.[323] Arising out of this was the emergence of a 'new' type of woman in the 1880s and 1890s who was educated, independent, active, and assertive, and who represented a dramatic departure from the model of femininity which had defined women in the previous decades.[324]

Another issue that gave cause for concern at the end of the nineteenth century was the Boer War, which indirectly had repercussions for women. The British army had suffered humiliating military defeats in the first few months and, although by 1900 the situation had improved, the defeat of 45,000 Afrikaner guerrilla soldiers had taken an additional 18 months and 450,000 British soldiers.[325] One of the major problems was due to the poor health of the enlisters, many of whom did not get through the selection process. Those that were successful either could not stand the rigours of physical training or had to leave when their health failed. What ensued was a panic about racial and physical degeneration amongst the male species, particularly the working-class male. The blame for this was laid at the door of working-class mothers. Major General Frederick Maurice, writing in the *Contemporary Review*, stated that 'Whatever the primary cause, the young man of 16 or 18 years of age is what he is because of the training through which he has passed during his infancy and childhood.... Therefore it is to be the condition, mental, moral, and physical, of the women and children that we must look if we have regard to the future of our land.'[326] As Anna Davin has stated, 'Middle-class convention of the time took for granted

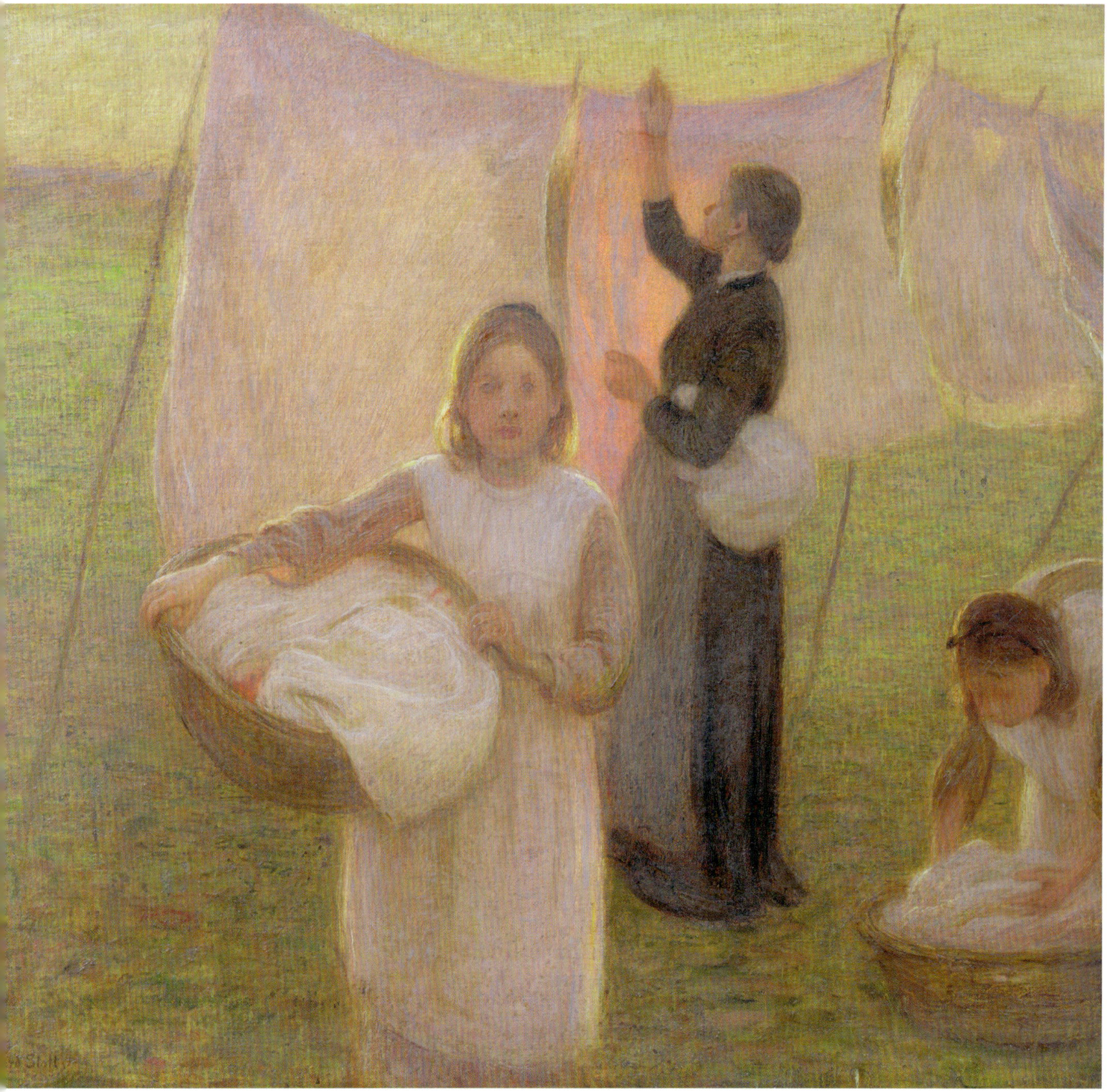

that the proper context of childhood was the family, and the person most responsible the mother.... Thus the solution to a national problem of public health and of politics was looked for in terms of individuals, of a particular role – the mother – and a social institution – the family.'[327] Suffrage and independence for women went against everything that was deemed 'natural' in the social order and would, of course, provide a potential threat to the traditional idea of a stable family unit. Edward Stott's paintings, discussed later in this chapter, would appear to reinforce this view.

45. Edward Stott, *Washing Day*, 1906. Oil on canvas, dimensions unknown. Private Collection/Photo © The Fine Art Society, London, UK/Bridgeman Images

These prescriptive ideologies have a parallel in subject matter found in paintings of rustic interiors which were prevalent in the Victorian period. Christiana Payne, in her study of paintings of cottage life in the nineteenth century, found that this genre was very popular with Victorian artists such as David Wilkie, Frederick Daniel Hardy, and Thomas Faed.[328] The genre proved to be a perfect vehicle for those artists whose paintings took on a prescriptive and didactic role in order to convey messages that usually had a moral, political or social message. These kinds of paintings, as Payne has stated, can be linked to the artistic tradition of the time and to the particular needs of Victorian society.[329] The subject matter focussed upon the rural working class who led a virtuous life which was conducive to the social order and might be considered as setting a good example to the urban working class.[330] In this regard 'paintings of cottage interiors could demonstrate the virtues and good character of the rural poor – and by extension, of the nation as a whole.'[331] It could have been Stott's intention to reflect the ideology of the Edwardian period, or as the majority of the paintings were exhibited at the Royal Academy – where he was in the running for an Associateship – a tactical move.[332] What is apparent, however, is that his paintings fitted very well into the genre and appear to hint at the didacticism of those earlier examples.

That a woman's place was in the home, and that Stott clearly valued the support and stability of home life, becomes apparent when considering biographical information. As mentioned earlier, at some point, Stott went to live with the Dinnage family when they moved from Houghton to Amberley. The Census Records show that in 1901, the Dinnage family were living in Hope Cottage.[333] Stott, however, appeared to be between locations as the Census for 1901 recorded him as being a 'boarder' at 42 Bark Place, Paddington, and thereafter at Hope Cottage. As Anne Dinnage recollected, the family was pleased but 'on the other hand, I realized that when he came to us, he would be a great responsibility, and of course I did find him so, as he was no ordinary man, but a man of many moods and never the same in the morning as in the evening. He was very difficult for ordinary people to understand.'[334] Nevertheless, Stott became one of the family and was also accepted into village life. As Anne Dinnage recalled, when Stott was elected an Associate of the Royal Academy in 1906, a telegram arrived from (possibly) Minnie Dinnage saying 'Hearty congratulations'. Stott ran down to Mrs Dinnage saying 'Mrs Dinnage, Mrs Dinnage, I'm in' and he began to shake hands 'with us all. Even the dog jumped onto his lap, a thing he much objected to; but the dog was allowed to remain on this occasion [and] the band played in front of his house that evening, and he had one or two friends to supper.'[335] When Hope Cottage was taken back by the owner, they all went to live in what is now called 'Stott's Cottage'.

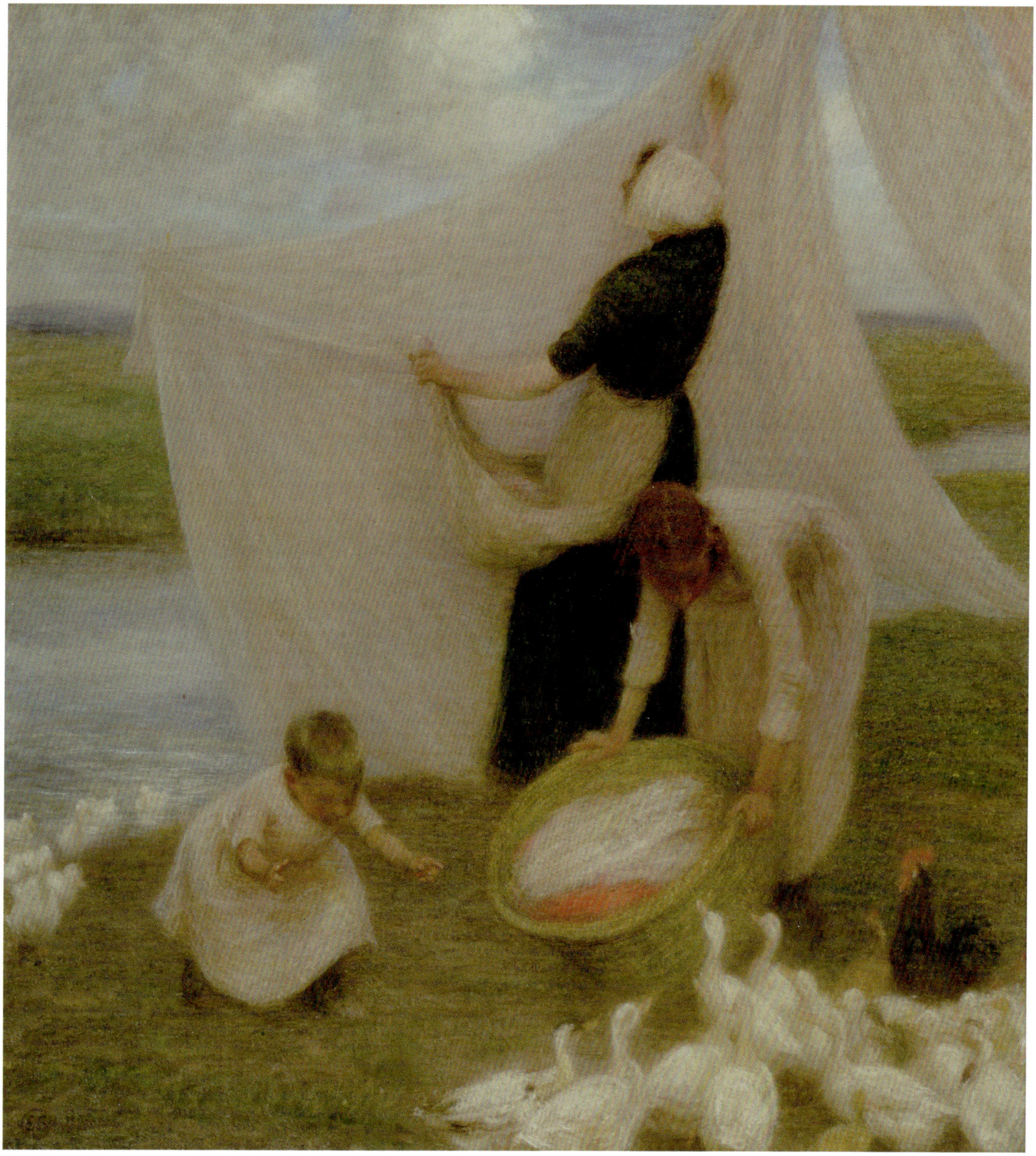

Letters in the Stott Archive, together with Anne Dinnage's undated Diary entries and 'Reminiscences', provide valuable information on Stott's time in Amberley and also give some access to his personal thoughts. Certain statements suggest that he was aware of the visual significance of the subject matter that he was depicting, and his subsequent endorsement of the political ideology underpinning it. Anne Dinnage revealed that Stott was against marriage because he thought it resulted in the end of an artist's work, and also because he had witnessed many disastrous marriages among his colleagues.[336] In a broad sense, according to Dinnage, Stott disapproved of women and was firmly against the Suffragist movement, exclaiming one day to her '"See what your sex has been doing!".'[337] Laurence Housman, artist and art critic, and who had once been Stott's friend, was pro-suffrage. Housman wrote to Dinnage on the 7th July 1912:

> Dear 'Annie of Amberley'.... I have often wondered whether you and your sisters have become interested in the suffrage movement for the success of which I am giving all the time I can spare; if you are not it only means that it hasn't been brought home to you in the right way. You ought to take in one of the Suffrage papers-.... The one I write most for is 'Votes for Women'. I send you with this, two of my pamphlets...[338]

Needless to say, this encouragement by Housman for Anne Dinnage to become independent and empowered would not have met with Stott's approval in view of the lifelong and devoted assistance she gave to Stott, even to the extent of putting her own artistic talents to one side.[339] It is worth a brief digression here to discuss the subject of Stott's and Housman's loss of friendship. The usual reason given for the disagreement was due to the fact that Stott liked to give his friends and visitors to his studio in Amberley and London, 'private views'. Housman, in his role as art critic, preferred to view the work for the first time hanging in an exhibition, and consequently stopped visiting Stott who took offence and the friendship ended. There are suggestions that Stott could be 'prickly' and perhaps high-minded. In a lengthy letter Stott wrote to his friend James Little on 10th October 1893, it transpires that Little was attempting to get David Croal Thomson to publish an article on Stott in the *Art Journal*, but Stott was offended because Thomson had not approached him directly. He writes:

> I am glad to think that you will not press Thomson any more in regard to my Art Journal article.... I feel sure that he wd [sic] conclude that you were pressing him at my instigation and that he wd [sic] try to crush a supposed self seeker. To have my work appreciated and even spoke of to me is always gratifying but I wd [sic] never ask to have things said about me – if either the work or its author is worth anything saying of in his Journal let him ask for it.... I do not fear for many a nice word of recognition from even better papers than the *Art Journal*.

What is not done graciously is not worth having.... But what I have said is of course strictly between ourselves – if in the future D.C.T should think that such an article wd [sic] not soil the pages of his Journal and wishes for it – then I shall be his man.[340]

Two months later, Stott tells Little that he saw Thomson who 'was most gushing. Indeed he went out of his way to make himself agreeable and spoke of how much he liked my work at the spring shows.'[341] What differences may have existed between Stott and Thomson were resolved by 1897. Stott and Little enjoyed a long friendship, but even that could be strained at times. In an undated letter, Stott writes 'I have been greatly troubled since I received yr [sic] last letter. It will be an inexpressible grief to me should our long friendship be hurt or in any way affected by what I said in my last letter in regard to West Sussex criticism.'[342] This may refer to an article Little wrote in 1892, where he had critically reviewed paintings by artists who were working in the Weald area which had been shown in the London Summer exhibitions. In his article, which made reference to Stott and some of his contemporaries, he had lamented the fact that not one of the artists came from the area and were essentially outsiders, which Stott may have taken exception to.[343] In a second undated letter to Little, Stott writes 'Why do you get such silly ideas into yr [sic] head? Just as if I should take what you say in yr [sic] artistic criticisms with consideration in our private life and friendship![344]

Returning to the question of why Stott appeared to generally disapprove of women or, at least, of the 'new' woman, and in spite of being against marriage, he nevertheless wanted the creature comforts of a stable and smooth-running home life but obviously without the responsibilities and distractions that having a wife and children would bring. As for his views on 'disastrous marriages', as recalled by Anne Dinnage, this did not prevent Stott from partaking of family hospitality when offered. As he wrote to J. Stanley Little on the 9th December 1893, 'I shall spend Christmas again with the Estalls which will make the sixth we have spent together.'[345] In a further letter to Little, dated 20th June 1900, by which time Mrs Little had given birth to a baby girl, Stott appeared ready to accommodate them – 'I hope you will be coming this way again soon and that you will be able to stay a night or two at Amberley. I really don't see why there should be any difficulty about the baby. We should be able to look after it between us.'[346]

In 1910, the Dinnage family and Stott had to leave Hope Cottage. By this time, Stott had already bought his studio, the paddock it stood in, and the two adjoining cottages. Although Stott did not like to take the cottages away from the families living in them, as he and the Dinnage family were about to become homeless, the two cottages were turned into one dwelling and became a home for himself and the Dinnages.[347] With the Dinnages, Stott found his surrogate family and it was an arrangement that was to last until his death in 1918.

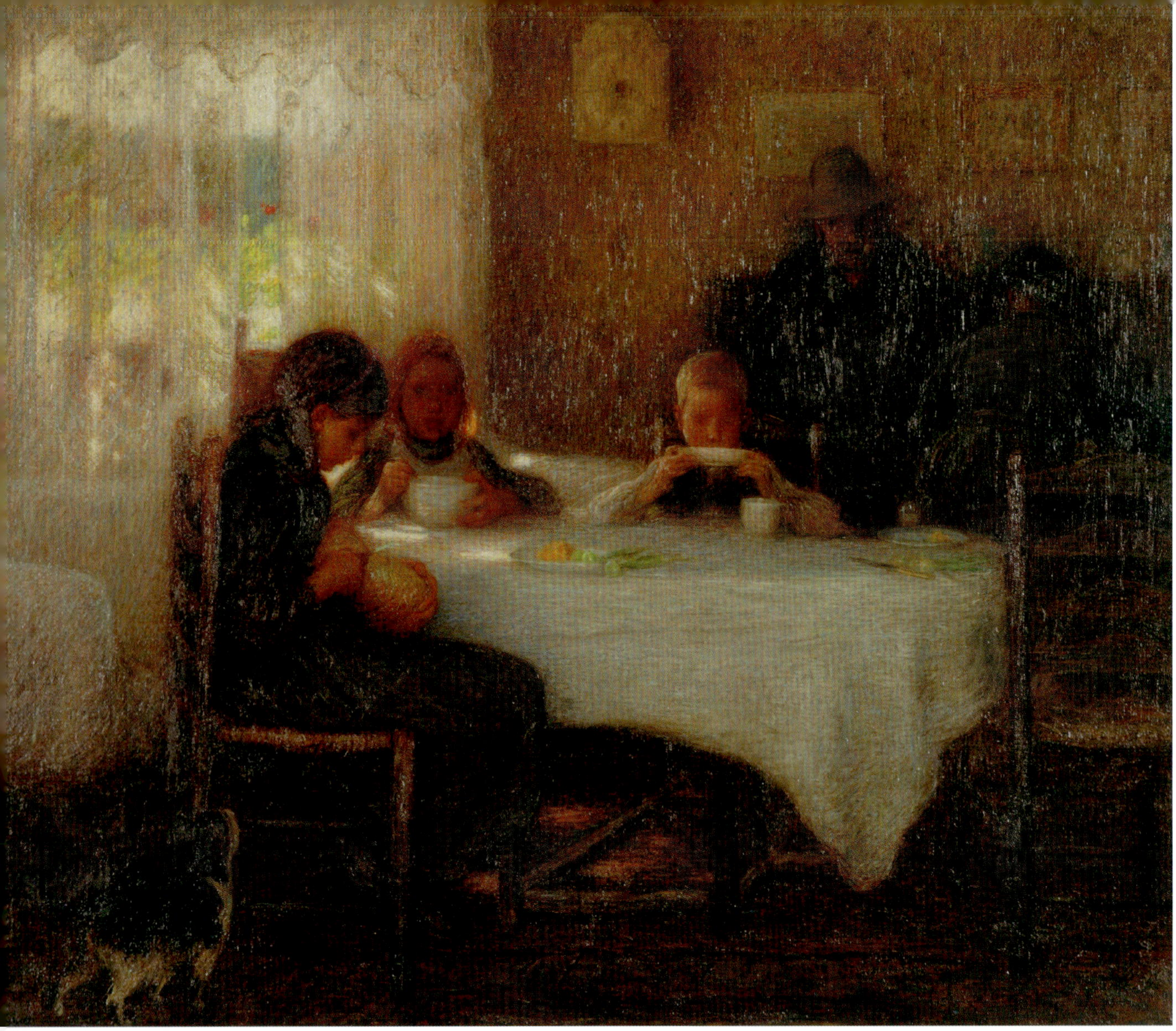

IMAGES OF DOMESTICITY

STOTT PRODUCED A SELECTION OF paintings which reinforce the idea of 'separate spheres', as they all depict women (and children) either within the domestic space of a cottage interior, or in private garden settings. In three of the examples, the idea of female generational support, coupled with the handing down of female-centred tasks from mother to daughter, is at the forefront. *The Widow's Acre* (1900) (Fig. 43) conveys the notion of self-sufficiency as the 'widow's acre' is given over to the growing of vegetables.[348] The task of picking and carrying the vegetables is undertaken by three generations of females, and emphasises the importance of team work. The pale yellow of the sky, together with the golden glow emanating from the interior which casts glints on the elder girl's hair, suggests the oncoming of evening and that a woman's work is never done. A sense of neighbourhood is conjured up by the thatched cottages adjacent to each other, with female domestic life simply conveyed by the line of washing glimpsed in the garden next door, with privacy preserved by the hedge. The theme of laundry day also inspired Stott to paint two works with the same title of *Washing Day* (1899 and 1906) (Fig. 44 and Fig. 45). Not only do they show how Stott's mastery of colour could capture contrasting atmospheric conditions – one on a sunny day, and the other on a cloudy day – but they also continue the theme of 'women's work'. Both paintings focus on the female-orientated task of hanging out and taking down washing. The mother is helped by her daughters and, in the later version, a toddler plays on the ground surrounded by geese. These two examples thus reinforce the domestic ideology where the female role was to be supportive and nurturing. It is interesting that Stott has reprised the subject of generational support which informed his earlier work, such as *The Helping Hand of a Small Friend* (1882).

46. Edward Stott, *Sunday Morning*, 1901. Oil on canvas, 88 x 101.8cm. Manchester Art Gallery, UK/Bridgeman Images

Stott's first dated painting of a domestic interior was *Sunday Morning* (1901) (Fig. 46), which focusses on three children sitting at a table, with the parents occupying a shadowy presence in the background. This was a new subject for Stott and one he was excited about painting. Writing to Little on the 20th June 1900, he stated 'I'm now very busy again with my work and have two things in mind which are entirely different to anything I have done before…a cottage interior (with figures).… I'm most awfully keen on it. It's so frantically interesting and new to me. Should you like to see it?'[349] This painting was exhibited at the Royal Academy in 1901, where M.H. Spielmann described it as 'charming' and 'subtle'. He further commented that 'The degree of obscurity seems a little too accentuated for the outside light that must enter the room; but the problem is beautifully solved whether as to light or colour.'[350] When the painting was chosen for inclusion in the British Section of the St. Louis International Exhibition in 1904, Stott explained what inspired him:

> In painting this picture, it was the delicate beauty of the light coming through the window and modified and diffused through the open door that charmed me most. And after this the charm of all the family assembled together, which was on a Sunday morning, but it was above all the play of light round the children that fascinated me, and led up to the picture and its title.[351]

Although for Stott it was the painting's aesthetic qualities he was interested in, this picture serves as a good example of a representation of an ideal nuclear family. The parents, in a nurturing role, watch over their children who are sitting obediently at the table. The two younger children, one of whom has been identified as Alice Kennard, are eating their breakfast.[352] Once again, Stott has included his motif of the bowl and spoon which had come to symbolise sustenance. The older girl is responsible for peeling a large squash, a domestic task handed down to her by her mother. The table is neat and uncluttered and the interior appears to be simply furnished, with a clock and picture on the back wall. There is even a family pet in

47. Edward Stott, *A Cottage Madonna*, 1907. Oil on canvas, 74 x 61cm. Harris Museum and Art Gallery, Preston, Lancashire, UK/Bridgeman Images

the form of the black and white cat who is looking up to the eldest girl. In the painting's subject matter, it conforms to the genre of rustic interiors where the values of domesticity and well-ordered family groups is reinforced. Furthermore, whilst the parents offer shelter and nourishment to the children, who are the focus of the scene, they play a secondary role (in the shadows) within the painting. The idea of generational support is once again at the forefront of this work; it was usually the case that if the parents looked after the welfare of the children, the children were expected to reciprocate in the parents' old age. Stott produced three other domestic scenes (all undated): *The Evening Hymn* which focusses upon a mother and her two daughters sat at a table, *The New Curtain* featuring a mother holding up a long piece of sheer fabric, with her daughter facing her, behind which the outside can be glimpsed, and *The Kittens* which is a tender scene of a mother with a small child holding a kitten. These little-known works respectively emphasise the continuance of religious values on the younger generation, the domestic task of curtain making, and a shared tender moment between mother and child.

IMAGES OF MOTHER AND CHILD

STOTT EXECUTED AT LEAST THREE paintings with the theme of 'mother and child': *Maternity* (c.1903), the scene of which takes place in the private space of a garden, *A Cottage Madonna* (1907) (Fig. 47), and *The Kiss* (1908), which are located within the home. *Maternity* focuses on a woman of indeterminate age who is cradling a baby, with a toddler by her side. Whether or not she is the mother is open to debate, but it is clear she is 'child minding', whilst a man and woman can be seen tending the vegetable patch in the background. The stone and brick path leads directly to the open door of the cottage, which looks warm and inviting from the orange glow shining within, and the well-tended vegetable patch and flower garden create a feeling of care and welcome. This painting not only speaks of self-sufficiency, industriousness and teamwork, but also of generational support. As such, the painting presents an ideal picture of family life in the rural world. It is possible that this painting had been chosen to appear at the St. Louis Salon, but in a letter to Isidore Spielmann dated the 12th November 1903, in which Stott sent a list of paintings he would like to exhibit, he writes 'I am sorry to say that I cannot induce Mr Pullar to send *Maternity* – he does not care for the picture to be away for so long, considering that he has so recently possessed it.'[353]

Anne Dinnage was the model for Stott's 'cottage Madonna' paintings (Fig. 48). *A Cottage Madonna* is an exquisite work of a mother holding onto a large naked baby with golden curls. The baby is probably the village policeman's youngest child, George Lee, who was brother to Reggie Lee who also modelled for Stott. Anne Dinnage said of the baby that he was a 'Lovely boy with curly hair and was used

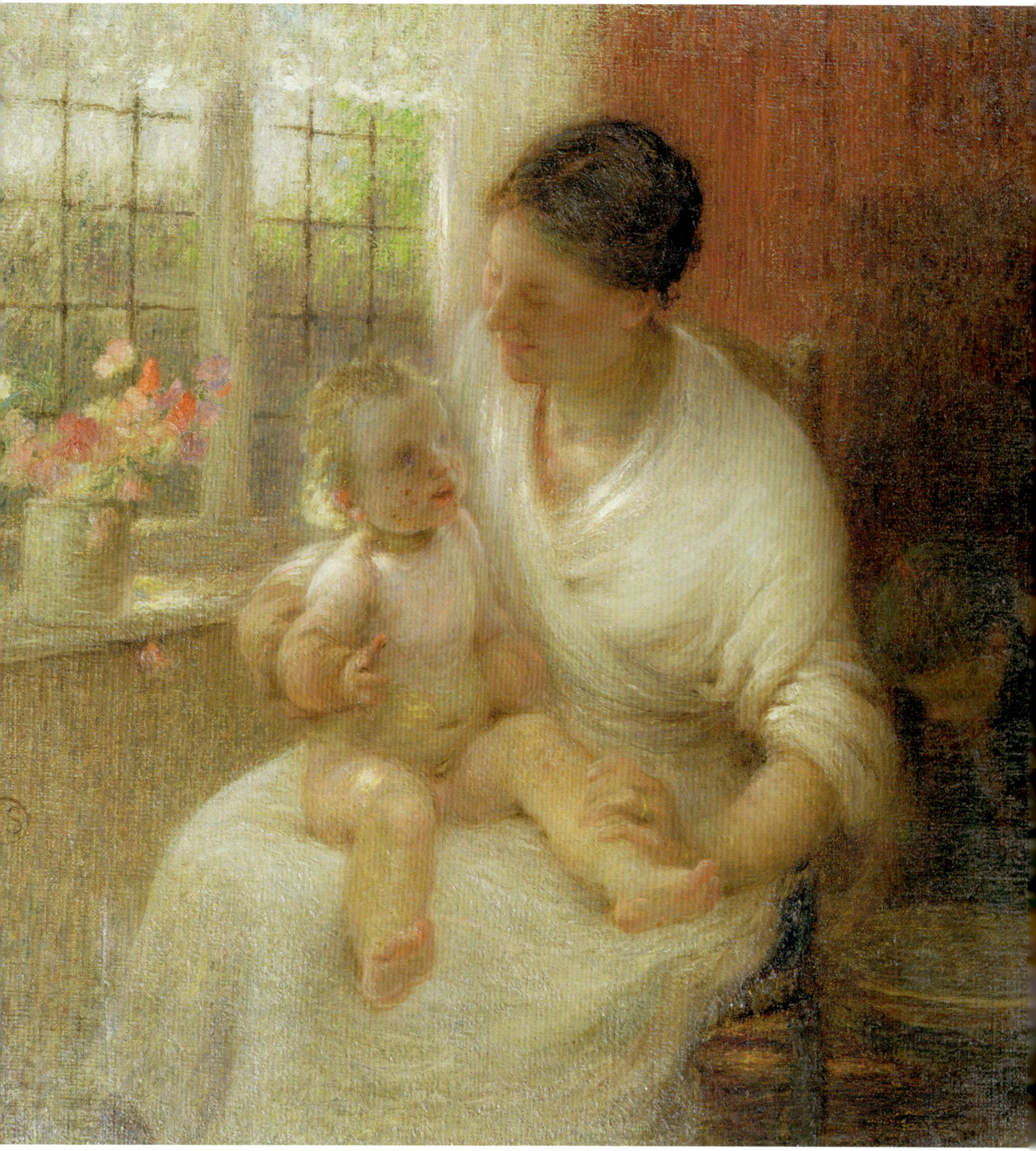

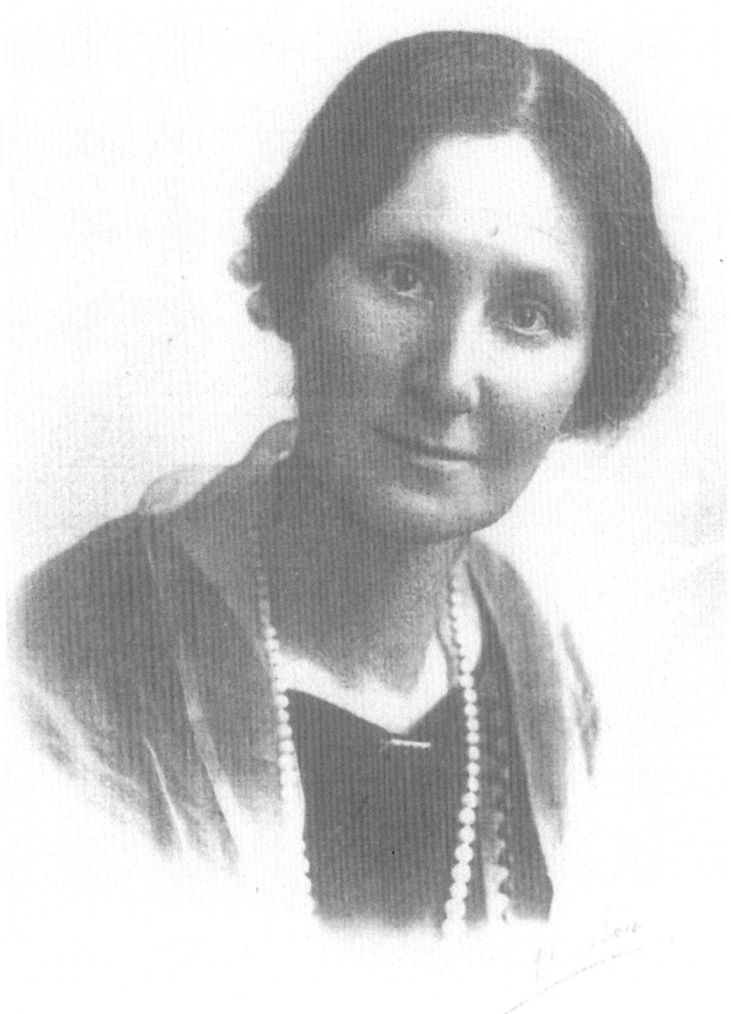

in a great number of pictures. Many studies were made of him in all sorts of positions, and utilized in *The Holy Family* and in other paintings. But this baby died quite suddenly and Stott was very grieved.'[354] The scene is full of tenderness, and the palette used is colourfully uplifting. The bright light from outside streams in through the window and lights up the forms of mother and child. In *The Kiss* (1908), Stott's choice of palette has become darker and his range of colour reduced. The background is almost black, but a colourful note by way of deep pink and pale pink flowers in the lower right-hand corner lifts the scene. However, the main focus of the painting rests on the large baby and the mother's face which are both lit up by the large moon visible through the window. As with the second version of *Washing Day* discussed earlier, *The Kiss* also marks the beginning of Stott's mature period where a seriousness of intention enters his work and prefigures his spiritual phase. This work attracted critical notice. Whilst *A Cottage Madonna* appeared not to attract any critical attention when it was exhibited at the Royal Academy in 1907, the critic for *The Times* described *The Kiss* as a 'rural Madonna and Child of the most grave and delicate beauty,...so charming in its sentiment and so delightful in colour and tone, [it] is about the most perfect thing that Mr Stott has done until now...'[355] P.G. Konody wrote of 'The Triumph of Mr Stott' in the *Observer*, describing the work as:

> ...complete in the realisation of the desired effect of light, so perfect is the modelling of human form, so tender in sentiment as *The Kiss*. The technique of the flesh-painting of the baby, whose fair curls are arranged like a vaporous halo, has something that recalls the manner of Watts, but is infinitely true to Nature. Nothing could exceed the perfection of that passage where the linear tangle of the child's legs and feet and the mother's hands and arms is lucidly explained and is given extraordinary plastic reality by the brush-work.[356]

For Stott, who was sometimes criticised for his figure drawings, this was indeed a triumph. Furthermore, the modelling of the human form which had caught Konody's attention, signalled the return of Stott to his early days in Paris as an art student where he had conscientiously worked on his drawing skills by studying the Old Masters, and which he began to explore further in his biblical and religious paintings. Added to this, of course, was the critic's reference to Watts who, incidentally, had painted a 'mother and child' scene circa 1903-4. This mention of Watts signalled the importance with which Stott was now being regarded. Furthermore, Konody's comment regarding the tenderness of the sentiments expressed, highlights the maternal bonding that is taking place in Stott's two 'cottage Madonna' paintings, which is clearly evident in the way that the mother gazes lovingly at her baby whilst her son reciprocates the obvious joy felt at being in her presence.

This small selection of 'mother and child' paintings visually encapsulates the ideology of the 'cult of motherhood'. As previously mentioned, the bringing up and nurturing of children within a domestic environment, where family values could be inculcated, was of paramount importance during this critical moment in British social and political history. Stott's paintings, in this regard, can be seen to reflect and reinforce these ideas. Furthermore, in giving one of his paintings the title of *A Cottage Madonna*, he is also clearly drawing attention to the Holy relationship between the Virgin Mary and Christ child; a theme which he continued to explore in his later paintings where his focus turned to spiritual and religious subjects. This last group of paintings also draw on his early experiences as an art student in Paris.

48. Photograph of Anne Dinnage, date unknown. Source: Stott Archive, Touchstones Rochdale

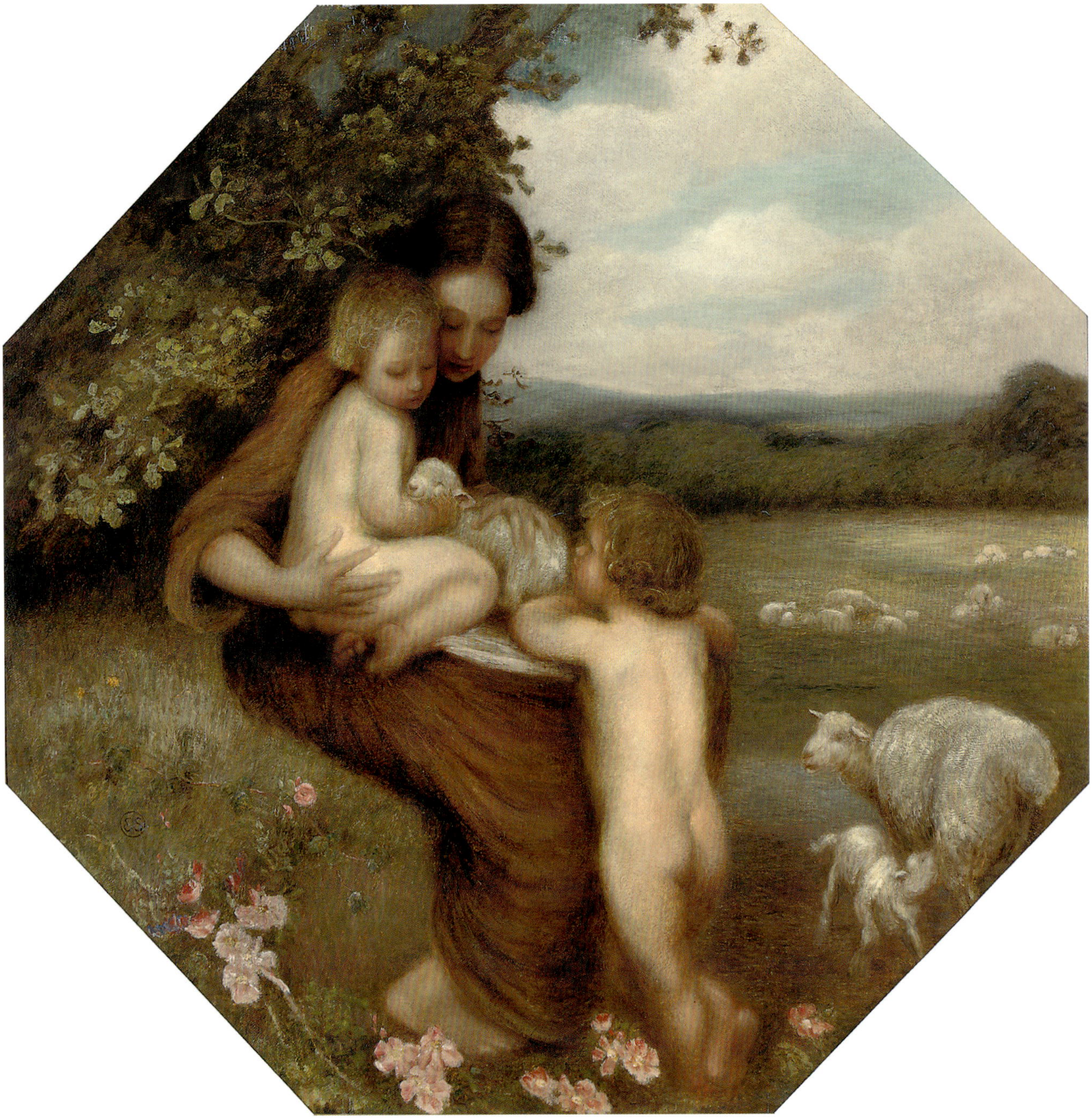

49. Edward Stott,
Two Mothers, 1909.
Oil on canvas, dimensions unknown. Private Collection/Photo © Christie's Images/ Bridgeman Images

6

AMBERLEY EXTERIORS II

Biblical and Religious Paintings

THIS FINAL CHAPTER CHARTS THE last period of Stott's artistic career. Not only does he return to the streets and landscapes of Amberley, he also refers back to his days as an art student in Paris where he studied the Old Masters to perfect his drawing and sketching skills, copied Antique casts and drew from the life model. As Marion Hepworth Dixon wrote in 1912, it was 'at the feet of the Old Masters, and...the benign auspices of the Barbizon group of painters [that] he gradually found his *metier*.'[357] In his choice of themes and subject matter, which draw inspiration from biblical and religious imagery, Stott appears to be making a visual retreat back to the ancient past whilst simultaneously maintaining a connection with the present through his reference to contemporary Amberley. As Ysanne Holt has pointed out, Stott was entering a spiritual phase 'Like Samuel Palmer at Shoreham, and later Stanley Spencer at Cookham, Edward Stott pushed a vision of an ideal community, a spiritual world where, at times, biblical scenes like *The Good Samaritan* might feasibly occur.'[358]

Stott also continued the theme of 'mother and child' imagery, but replaced the interior setting with a landscape backdrop. In this respect, he makes reference to artists of the Italian Renaissance such as the Venetian painters Giovanni Bellini, Raphael and Titian. These early influnces were recognised by the critics at the time, such as P.G. Konody who also cited the Dutch artist Rembrandt as a source of influence. He also began to pay careful attention to accurately depicting the plumpness of the baby's body, and prove his ability to grapple with the formal concerns of displaying such a body in a number of complex poses. This revived interest in draughtsmanship coincided with Stott's achievement in becoming an Associate of the Royal Academy in 1906, at a time when Edward Poynter was President (he succeeded Millais in 1896 and served as President until 1918). The Royal Academy Schools, following the tradition of the École des Beaux-Arts, also laid great store on the studying of the Old Masters and a sound knowledge of drawing. Hence, Stott was also coincidentally maintaining the traditions and principles of the Royal Academy even though he had trained elsewhere.

HOLY 'MOTHER AND CHILD' PAINTINGS

EDWARD STOTT EXHIBITED THREE OUTDOOR scenes with the theme of 'mother and child'/'Mary and Christ' at the Royal Academy over a period of eight years from 1909 to 1917: *Two Mothers* (1909) (Fig. 49), *Her Thoughts Were Her Children* (1911), which was possibly reworked and re-exhibited as *Motherhood* in 1914, and *The Holy Family* (1917). In *Two Mothers*, a number of elements come together to make the painting a success. Stott has shown technical proficiency in the depiction of the bodies of the children, correct anatomical proportion, and attention to spatial awareness in the handling of space and perspective. His three figures comprise Mary (Anne Dinnage was the model), Jesus and St. John the Baptist. The trio are placed to the left of the landscape and slightly raised up so that the space they occupy is separate from that of the natural world. The placing of the 'human' group within a raised and separate part of the landscape to that of the 'animal' group, could be viewed as a combination of 'mother nurture' and 'mother nature'. The reference to 'two mothers' in the title refers to the ewe who is being suckled by her lamb, whilst she turns to look up to Mary who is caressing a lamb. In symbolic terms, the lamb represents the Lamb of God. The tones Stott has used are low-key which enhance the tender scene being shown, and signal a move away from his usual vibrancy. This particular painting was a critical success. P.G. Konody, writing in the *Observer*, described the painting as a 'tondo', which refers to the Renaissance fashion in painting and sculptural reliefs for placing the canvas or scene within a circular form or frame. This must have been a conscious choice by Stott, as it was a form that was apposite for the theme. Konody also interestingly referred to the work as 'a modernist Madonna of the Meadows',[359] which makes a direct reference to Renaissance art; particularly, Giovanni Bellini's painting of 1505, which has the same title. However, Stott's picture is also akin to a work by Titian of about 1532, namely *The Aldobrandini Madonna*, which was purchased by the National Gallery in 1870. Compositionally, the infant St. John the Baptist, and possibly St. Catherine (without her wheel), situated on the left side of the scene and separated from the landscape beyond, has been echoed by Stott in his painting but minus the figure of St. Catherine. Similarly, like Titian's landscape, Stott's background contains sheep and a shepherd. The main difference occurs in the respective artists' use of colour.

Whilst Titian adopts a bold rich palette of red, pink and ultramarine for the Virgin's robe, which has the effect of making the holy group stand out from the lush greens of the secular landscape, Stott's colour scheme is muted and subdued, which befits the tender scene taking place. Furthermore, whilst not denying the obvious religious connotation, the colours are more apt perhaps for a secularised landscape with figures, which thus lends a modern twist to the painting. Konody also commented on 'The rhythm and balance of the design, the relation of the figures to the landscape, the sentiment of a conception that might easily have degenerated into sentimentality, place this picture almost in a class by itself.'[360] Drawing attention to the formal aspects of the painting rather than the subject matter, reveals a shift in the form of criticism from the subjective to the objective.

Stott continued to draw inspiration from Renaissance art with *Her Thoughts Were Her Children* (1911). Instead of holding a lamb in her lap, the mother/Mary holds a rabbit. This time Stott placed the mother and her two children in the centre of the foreground, with landscape as a background feature. In portraying the group in this way, he could be drawing on Giovanni Bellini's painting, *Madonna of the Meadow*, which Konody referred to. However, there is a significant difference between Stott's and Bellini's examples. In Bellini's image, the Christ child is shown sleeping in the Virgin's lap, which was a compositional device used in Renaissance painting to anticipate the *pieta*, whilst farmland, trees, buildings and hills are visible in the distance. A further departure resides in the palette used. As was typical of Bellini, the luxurious ultramarine pigment made from ground-up lapis lazuli was used for the Madonna's cloak, and a rich red-pink for her robes. In contrast, Stott's secularised 'Madonna' wears a long white dress, as if to reinforce her virginal status, with a dark coloured shawl draped around her body to add contrast. (As only a black and white image exists, and the work is in a private collection, it is not possible to say what actual colours Stott used. However, the dark and light contrast of the robe and dress is evident.) Bellini's painting was acquired by the National Gallery in 1858 and could feasibly have been seen by Stott on one of his trips to London. In a letter to Little dated 21st September 1913, Stott wrote that he would like him and Little to visit the 'National Gallery and have a look together at some of my favourites. I feel sure we would be much in accord about all the best things of the Italian Schools.'[361] Thus, it is likely that he would also have seen Raphael's painting of circa 1509-10, *The Garvagh Madonna*, which entered the Gallery's collection in 1865. Although the Virgin, Christ child and St. John the Baptist are depicted within a sparse interior with a hazy backdrop of landscape and buildings, Stott's painting seems to be more akin to Raphael's example and would certainly accord with how the critics saw Stott's painting at this time. An anonymous critic writing for the *Observer* commented on the strange title Stott had given to 'his modernised Raphaelesque Madonna with the Infant Saviour and St. John'.[362] Referring to the subject as *The Madonna of the Rabbit*, as the critic states that Stott's painting would probably have been called in Renaissance

50. Edward Stott,
The Flight Into Egypt,
1909. Oil on canvas,
81.1 x 109cm. Aberdeen
Art Gallery & Museums
Collection

times, he further comments on the 'graceful composition' and the 'open air feeling of modern art and the morbidezza of Mr Stott's characteristic technique.'[363] The only negative criticism was the flatness and lack of bony construction in the mother's head, which the critic felt was at odds with the successful modelling of the plump and dimpled figures of the two children. Stott possibly re-exhibited this painting in 1914 with the title of *Motherhood.* On this later occasion, the critic for the *Observer* once again described the painting as displaying 'Near to Raphaelesque perfection as a modern brush can carry it. The harmonious design of this English 'Madonna of the bunny rabbit' is frankly derived from Raphael, whom Mr Stott has also followed very closely in the form and modelling of the two children.'[364]

Stott's final outdoor 'mother and child' work was *The Holy Family* (1917). Using the 'tondo' device again, the formal aspects of the work bear a strong resemblance to the previous painting, although there are subtle differences with the clothing and facial features of the Madonna. As with the other examples, the painting was exhibited at the Royal Academy, and *The Times'* critic remarked that 'It reminds one faintly of the late work of Titian, but it lacks the passion which throbs so strangely in Titian's loose and misty handling.'[365] Stott's health began to fail during the painting of this work. He had been perfectly well until February 1917, and then he fell ill and went to bed with a high temperature. He was worried because he had not finished his Academy painting which was *The Holy Family.* After three days he was able to get up and return to his studio, but suffered recurring bouts of ill health.[366]

BIBLICAL AND RELIGIOUS IMAGES

EDWARD STOTT'S KNOWLEDGE OF OLD MASTERS was equally evident in his modern interpretations of other religious themes. As well as working on his 'mother and child' paintings, he was also visually translating biblical events from the New Testament and at least one scene from the Old Testament which was taken from the story of Ruth and Boaz. This is evidenced by a sketch of Ruth that Stott produced, but which did not materialise into a final painting. At the same time as he exhibited *Two Mothers* at the Royal Academy in 1909, he also showed *The Flight Into Egypt* (1909) (Fig. 50), based on the Gospel of Matthew 2:13-23.[367] Anne Dinnage's younger sister, Ruth, sat as the model for Mary, and the donkey was lent by Miss Curzon (who later became Lady Zouche).[368] There are two significant aspects in this work which reveals Stott's change in direction. The first is his handling of light sources, and the second is to do with colour. In previous paintings he had experimented with natural light sources falling onto a particular scene or area. Not only did this allow him to simultaneously convey the idea of sunlight and shadow, it also gave him the opportunity of exploring how colour changed accordingly. Both versions of *Washing Day* effectively illustrate this. In the earlier work, and as the critics drew

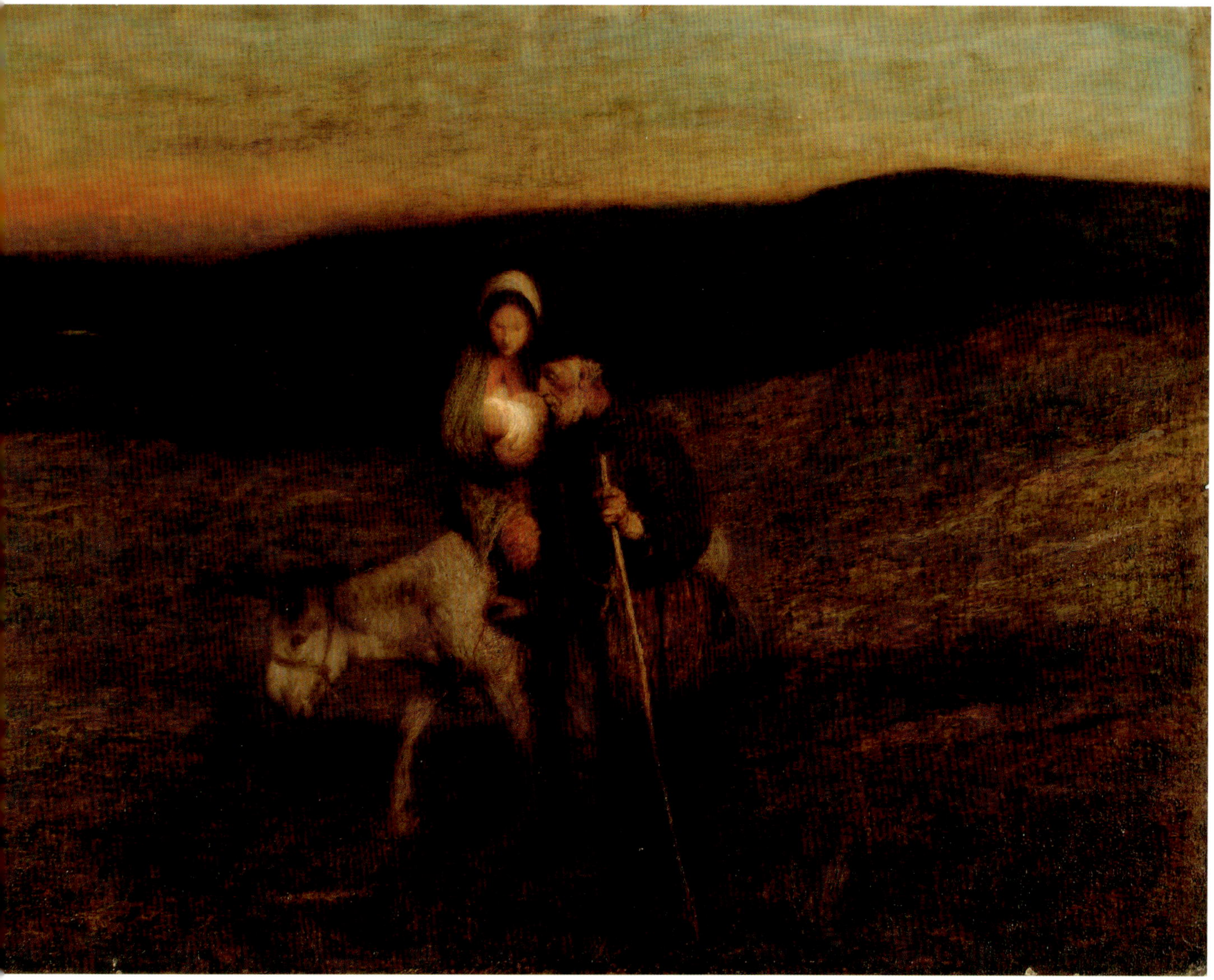

attention to, the painting showed 'the effect of sunshine through linen, and is an artistic translation of a rather ordinary scene'.[369] *The Art Journal* critic wrote that this work was Stott's 'most advanced exercise, so far, in luminosity of colour', and further remarked on the 'beautiful effect of prismatic colour produced by sunlight streaming through wet sheets as they flap in the wind.'[370] Despite the prosaic nature of the subject matter, Stott had introduced a poetic element and turned it into an experiment with colour, tone and atmosphere. Contrastingly, in the later version, the tonal qualities have undergone a dramatic transformation along with atmospheric effects. Employing subdued tones, dark clouds now float across the sky giving the sheets a greyish tinge. This change in approach is possibly indicative of Stott's maturing as an artist, and it can be no coincidence that the year of this painting coincided with his election as an Associate of the Royal Academy. Laurence Housman, writing for *The Guardian*, positively reviewed the work when it was exhibited at the Academy,

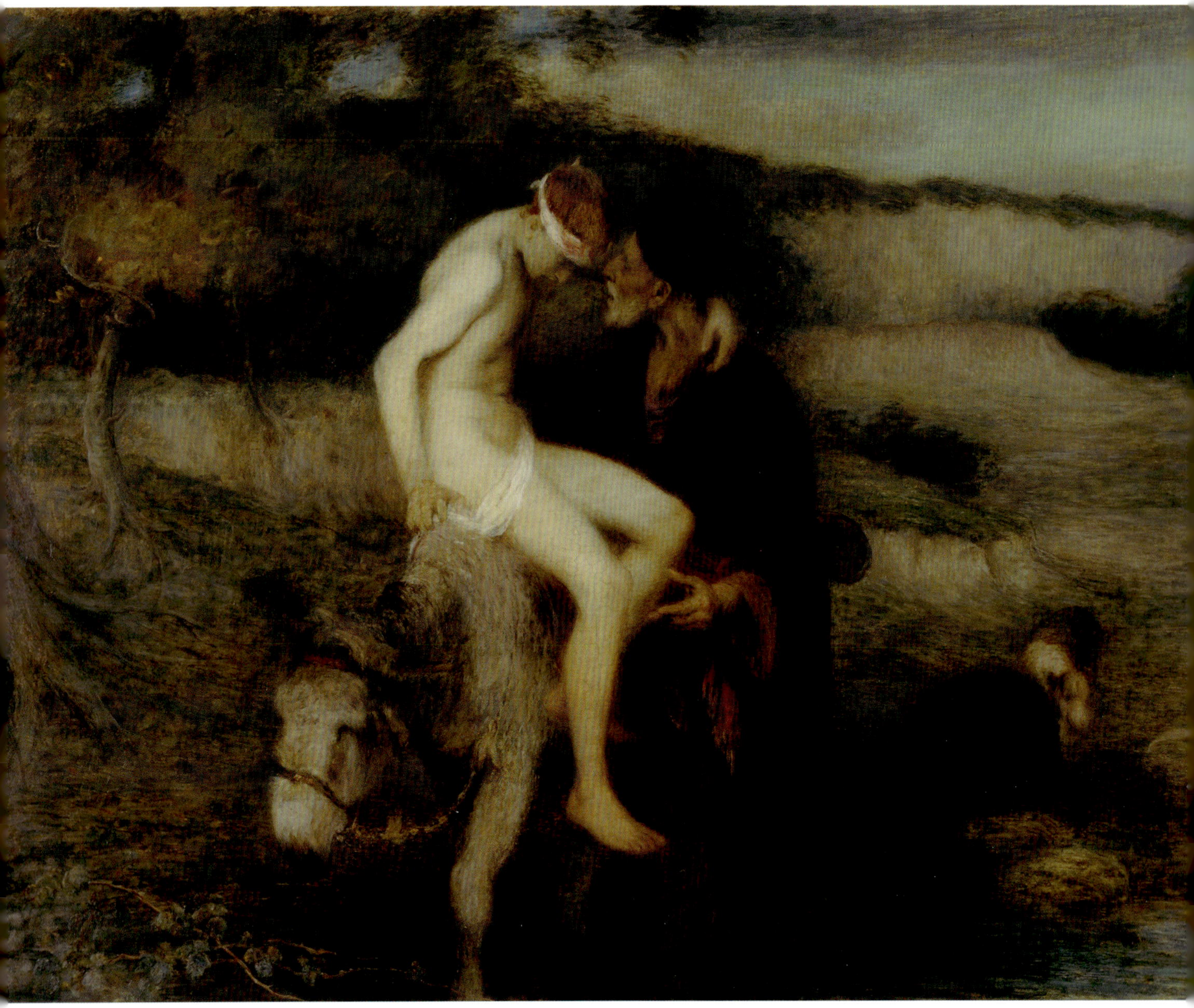

describing it as a 'delightfully peaceful little composition…sweet as it is in the poetry of its colour it is never cloying, for here, as always, the artist proves himself a true colourist.'[371]

With *The Flight into Egypt*, Stott began to use a non-natural light source by way of an artificial 'spot of light' in order to draw attention to the most significant part of the painting. In this case, the glow emanating from the baby Jesus towards the Virgin Mary. This chiaroscuro device had been used by Caravaggio in a number of paintings for dramatic effect, and also to indicate the significant action taking place. However, and somewhat typical of Stott, his light source was used to more modest and subtle effect. His use of colour also changed, becoming deeper and sombre, with the palette dominated by warm earth tones dimmed by the fading light. Reviewing this painting, Konody described the work as 'a picture conception of rare perfection.... Mr Stott's painting has a truly emotional quality.'[372] Stott's handling of the landscape and sky also needs mentioning because of the formal simplicity of its conception. Stott has conceived the background out of only three bands of earth tones, with the canvas divided up into half and then two quarters. The wider and lighter band denotes the foreground, the darker band denotes the hills in the background, and the third band is the sky with a strip of orange-yellow for the setting sun. With its lack of depth and appearance of two-dimensionality, the scene has something of the Greenbergian idea of the 'ineluctable flatness' of modernist art. Clement Greenberg had claimed that 'flatness, two-dimensionality, was the only condition painting shared with no other art, and so, modernist painting oriented itself to flatness as it did to nothing else.'[373] Whether or not Stott was consciously experimenting with creating the appearance of a two-dimensional landscape, is open to debate. Yet, certain of these works do contain proto-modernist aspects. As Holt has identified when considering Stott's paintings at this time, 'A relationship to more modernist religious compositions in France might be perceived here.'[374] Specifically citing the work of Maurice Denis, she writes that whilst Stott's paintings 'may be technically more conservative...there is no mistaking a shared intention.'[375]

In 1910, Stott sent *The Good Samaritan* (1910) (Fig. 51) to the Royal Academy. He completed many studies of the subject before finally executing it in oil for exhibition purposes. *The Times*' critic described it as 'tender and charming, with something of the sentiment of Rembrandt.'[376] The subject matter is taken from the New Testament and tells of the Parable as told by Jesus in the Gospel of Luke 10:29-37, whereby a traveller is robbed and left for dead by the roadside until an elderly Samaritan comes to his assistance. Stott's painting shows the moment the Samaritan helps the injured man onto the donkey. The Amberley chalk cliffs bring a local contemporary touch to an ancient Biblical story. There are flashes of intense colour in the painting, notably the deep maroon of the Samaritan's robe which is tied with a rose-coloured sash. A splash of turquoise reveals the edge of a pond on the right-hand side which is mirrored by the pale turquoise sky. The cream flesh tones of the semi-nude traveller are enhanced by the bright white strip of cloth laid over the lower part of his body, and the white bandage tied around his head which shows visible blood stains. Such graphic detail draws our attention to the injured man. With this work, Stott has effectively conveyed the feeling of compassion shown by the elderly man, and also the palpable weakness and near-naked vulnerability of the traveller. The painting did not attract much critical notice: the critic for the *Observer* spoke of the 'deep feeling which underlines the inception of the picture',[377] and A.C.R. Carter, writing for the *Art Journal*, briefly described the painting as 'a work of genius.'[378] Although the painting received little critical attention, it attracted significant patronage in the form of Sir Joseph Duveen (Junior) in 1911, who subsequently

51. Edward Stott,
The Good Samaritan,
1910. Oil on canvas,
81.6 x 106.2cm.
Ferens Art Gallery,
Hull Museums,
UK/Bridgeman Images

52. Edward Stott, *The Entombment*, 1915. Oil on canvas, 67.3 x 88.9cm. Williamson Art Gallery, Birkenhead

presented the work to Ferens Art Gallery in Hull in memory of his late father who started in business in Hull in the late 1860s. The Duveen dynasty were important collectors and dealers in the art world. Sir Joseph Duveen was the son of Joseph Joel Duveen who was a Jewish Dutch immigrant. Along with his brother Henry, they came to Hull in the 1860s and became leading importers of Dutch delftware and Chinese Nanking porcelain which was sought after at the time. Duveen senior went on to become a leading art dealer in New York and London. His son, Joseph Duveen, continued the business and, together with Bernard Berenson who was a key figure in the art world, rose to become one of the world's foremost art dealers.[379]

In the same year of 1910, Stott also exhibited *There was no room at the inn* (1910). Painted in dark brown tones that reflected the dim interior of a barn, his choice of palette enabled him to use the artificial light source to good effect. The light was used to illuminate the baby Jesus and Mary, and a secondary light source was provided by the lamp on the right-hand side and cast a glow on the ground beneath where the Holy group are placed. A.C.R. Carter commented on the 'beauty and completeness of [Stott's] Nativity theme.'[380] As a friend and supporter of Stott, as well as an art critic, Carter was one of the few who truly understood the essence of Stott's religious paintings when he reviewed them in *The Art Journal*:

> The paintings are not clamant vociferous sermons from a painter's pulpit, but are the reasoned yet throbbing utterances of an art steeped in knowledge and animated with the tenderest purpose. Here is a man who has actually lived the life of Millet's ideal worker.... Devoted to his calling he has made Amberley the English Barbizon... like Rembrandt he has found materials from the life around him to be transcended into pictures of mystery, of truth, and often emotion without religiosity. All his accumulated knowledge of the poetry of earth seems to have been poured into these two frames. This is the art that will endure.[381]

Stott's next submission to the Royal Academy exhibition was *Hagar and Ishmael* (1911).[382] The scene portrayed is the moment where Hagar is giving Ishmael sustenance by the side of an almost dry pond, where the skeletal remains of a sheep is visible. In terms of composition and colour, there are similarities between this painting and *The Flight Into Egypt*. Stott has used similar earth tones again, but they have been muted. It is obvious that Stott has thought deeply about the colours in this work where he has repeated certain tones throughout. At the very top of the painting is a streak of dark turquoise sky which he repeats in the sweeping shape of the hillside, and then used on the landscape and repeated in the water, albeit a few shades lighter. Similarly, the yellow deepens to orange in the sky and then suffuses the earth turning it into a multi-coloured scene. The one colour that stands out is the maroon of Hagar's robe signifying her centrality to the story being told. Compositionally, the landscape is similar to the landscape in *The Flight Into Egypt* in that it has been created out of simplified bands of colour. However, in *Hagar and Ishmael*, there is a

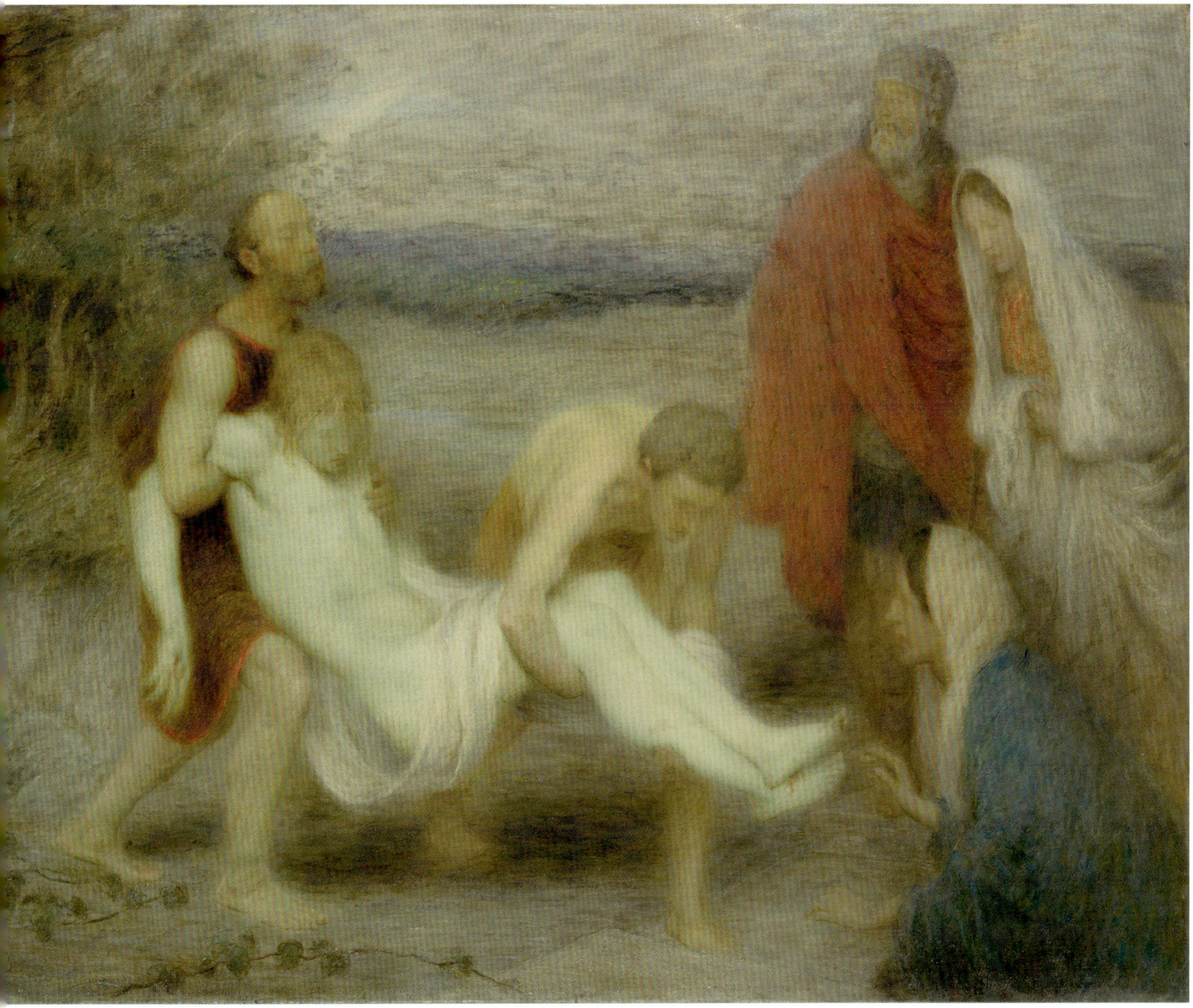

hint of perspective and depth achieved by the separation of the flat foreground from the raised edge of the field where Ishmael is sat. There is a brief mention by Marion Hepworth Dixon in her 'Appreciation' of Stott in *The Studio*, but apart from this the work failed to attract any critical notice when it was exhibited.[383]

It appears that Stott did not exhibit again until 1913, when he showed two paintings at the Royal Academy. These were two scenes from the Life of Christ: *The Carpenter's Shop* and *Adoration of the Shepherds*.[384] With the former painting, a connection can be made with a work by John Everett Millais of 1849-50, called *The Carpenter's Shop* (also known as *Christ in the House of His Parents*). Differences occur though in that the Christian typology in Millais' work, which his Victorian audience would have recognised, makes no appearance in Stott's painting – apart from the halo forming a semi-circle around the child's head – where his meaning is

53. Edward Stott, *Approaching Night*, 1917. Oil on canvas, 27.5 x 41cm. Touchstones Rochdale, Lancashire, UK/Bridgeman Images

suggested through gesture. Furthermore, the setting is very realistic. In this respect, whilst the interior in Millais' painting is clearly sacred and the faithful 'flock' have no access to the interior, in Stott's picture the space is non-sacred and where sheep freely wander in and out. Viewers of this painting, however, would have been aware of the work's religious import through its gestural signifiers. For example, the child with halo (clearly Jesus) looks down at his mother who raises her left hand and looks up to him. This gesture was typical of the conventional poses used for the Virgin Mary and Jesus in Western art. Likewise, the outstretched hand of the child points towards the carpenter (Joseph) who is very naturally about to saw through a piece of wood and who has all the tools of his trade scattered about him. These gestures take the almost triangular form of the Holy Family with Jesus' head at the apex which was a recognizable device used in Renaissance works of art. Through gesture, then, rather than symbolism, this group can be understood to represent the Holy Family. However, through the depiction of the interior as a non-sacred space, Stott is once again combining the ancient with the contemporary.

A further scene from the Life of Christ appears in the *Adoration of the Shepherds*. This scene is viewed from the outside looking into the barn which creates a feeling of being excluded or detached from the action taking place inside. Stott has used an Amberley thatched barn for the main shelter. This not only lends a local and contemporary feel to the scene, but also accentuates the humble nature of the subject. The interior is very dark, but a bright 'spiritual' light glows from the baby Jesus illuminating the figure of Mary. Konody wrote that this painting, and *The Carpenter's Shop*, was 'profoundly religious and yet essentially modern,'[385] further adding that:

> Mr Stott is an artist to whom may be applied Chardin's saying: 'Who told you that one paints with colours? – One paints with feeling'. He is the one modern artist who works with so much emotion and in such a reverent spirit that he leaves no sense of incongruity in transferring the incidents of scripture to modern times... and is akin to the early Italians and Flemings. There is no doubt about his sincerity. Both his paintings are realised with Rembrandtesque intensity.[386]

Konody's reference to Rembrandt, and Italian and Flemish art, points again to that aspect of Stott's paintings from this period where he fuses the modern with the ancient. Thus it is feasible that Stott was possibly making a retreat to the past in order to directly avoid the present. Tim Barringer's research on the anachronistic nature of Byam Shaw's work provides a useful precedent. In his study of the rationale behind Shaw's paintings, Barringer suggests that Shaw was 'wholly anachronistic in his concerns, and unable to relate to the modernity of early twentieth-century Britain.'[387] This statement could equally apply to Stott. In a letter to Little, dated December 1910, he complains that 'Artists here I believe from all I hear are having a terrible time. Pictures are out of fashion. Sentiment and poetry are all gone. Motors, Flying Machines, degeneration and philistinism are rampant.'[388] At the time Stott

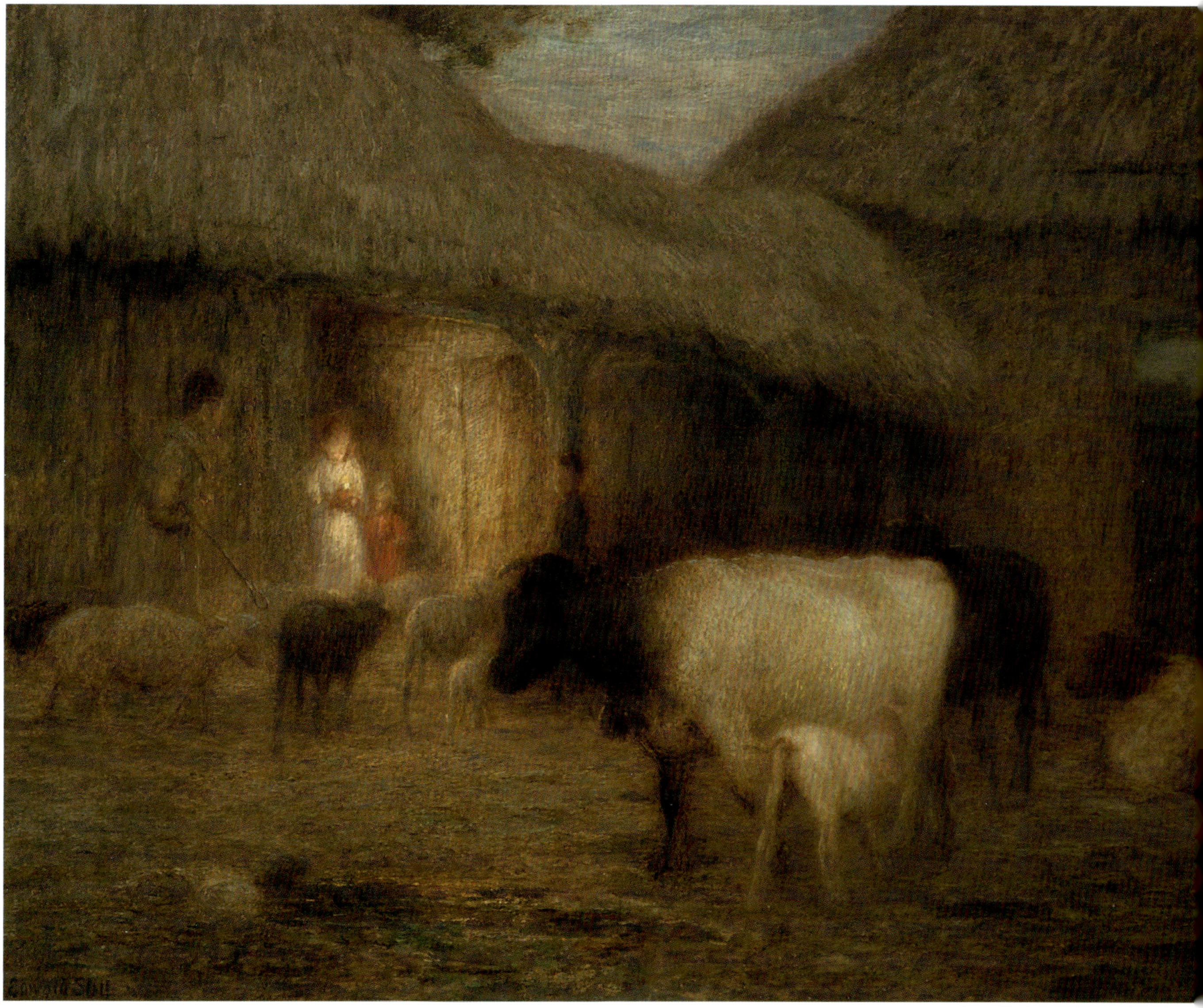

was producing these late paintings, the world was in turmoil with rumours of war rumbling throughout Europe and, closer to home, the newspapers were commenting daily on the unstable situation in Ireland regarding Home Rule.[389] Another interpretation could be the question of exile. At least two of Stott's paintings – *The Flight Into Egypt* and *Hagar and Ishmael* – centre on exiled characters, whilst a third painting called *The Prodigal's Return* is partly about the return of a son who has been in exile and is returning home.[390] It could be speculated here as to whether Stott was reflecting on his own exiled status.

Stott did not exhibit again until 1915, and spent his time working on two canvases: *The Entombment* (1915) (Fig. 52) and *The Sacred Pool* (1915), which was something of a departure in subject matter and had an 'other worldly' feel to it as discussed in Chapter Three.[391] *The Entombment* continued Stott's preoccupation with scenes from the Life of Christ. The focus of the painting is on the moment after Christ's body has been taken down from the cross and carried away for burial. Stott's choice of rich concentrated colours looks back to Venetian art. The intense azure blue of the kneeling woman's robe is repeated in the long strip of azure in the background. The dark magenta robe worn by the stern looking helmeted figure of the centurion who witnessed the execution, is continued in the tunic worn by the bearded man (Joseph of Arimathea who asked Pilate for Christ's body) carrying Christ, and repeated in the shadow beneath Christ. Elsewhere, the white pigment used for the clothing of the woman is repeated in the bodily form of Christ, which is painted in a brighter hue in order to draw attention to his lifeless figure. In symbolic terms, Stott's use of magenta could signify the blood of Christ, whilst his choice of white could symbolise purity and innocence. The opaque whiteness of Christ's lifeless form, which also has a pale greenish tinge, gives it a sculptural quality. Certain aspects in this painting, such as the repetition of colours which unify the scene, the rhythm of the lines, and Stott's symbolic use of colour, recall Roger Fry's comments on the importance of balance and unity in a work of art. In his essay on aesthetics, Fry wrote that 'unity of some kind is necessary for our restful contemplation of the work of art as a whole [which] is due to a balancing of the attractions of the eye about the central line of the picture.'[392] He then went on to list a number of 'emotional elements of design', such as the 'rhythm of the line with which the forms are delineated', and 'colour [which]...has a direct emotional effect.'[393] In Fry's usage, however, the 'emotional' should be understood in the context of something which transcends the physical earthly world, and is linked to the contemplative. In this sense, then, it transcends the moral and the social. Stott's painting would certainly seem to combine some of these 'emotional' elements, which suggests that Stott and Fry could have been like-minded individuals on matters concerning art.

The eclecticism of Stott, and his 'see-sawing' between subject matters, was evident in his work on display at the Royal Academy exhibition of 1916 where he showed three paintings: *The Prodigal's Return* (1916), which demonstrated his continuing interest in scenes from the New Testament, *The Piping Shepherd Boy* (1916), which saw a return to rustic subject matter, and *A Summer Moon* (1916) which was an exercise in atmospheric effects.[394] The critic for *The Guardian* commented on these paintings and described Stott as 'a poet full of tender lyrical feeling', where 'The vibrant touches of his brush produce a pearly shimmer, the atmospheric vagueness of which does not in any way interfere with the perfect registration of colour values or with searching treatment of the human or other form. Above all, Mr Stott is in deep sympathy with his subjects. He feels what he paints and he knows how to treat a Scriptural subject as a reality witnessed by his own eyes.'[395] The critic further added that 'He has the sincerity of the Primitives and one does not become aware of any anachronism if an English village street is made the scene of *The Prodigal's Return*.'[396]

As mentioned earlier in connection with the completion of *The Holy Family* for the Royal Academy exhibition of 1917, Stott's health at the time was poor. He recovered sufficiently to send in three paintings – *The Holy Family* (1917), *Approaching Night* (1917) (Fig. 53), and *The Patriarch* (1917) (Fig. 54). At first sight the formal and stylistic aspects of *Approaching Night* appear to repeat those used for the *Adoration of the Shepherds*. Whilst this painting had an overt Christian reference, *Approaching Night* returns to contemporary rural subject matter. Using the same image of the barn, the scene takes place outside in the yard with a glimpse of the interior which is lit by a light from a candle or lamp held by a young girl in a white dress. With all traces of the Holy Family removed, the scene portrays a flock of ewes and their lambs entering the barn at night time, whilst a large black and white cow with its calf (the same one that appeared in *Adoration of the Shepherds*) looks towards the barn. A shepherd is included, but without the biblical connotations of the earlier work. In an undated Conservation Report in the Stott Archive, the Conservator noted that the large black and white cow, when seen close up, showed flecks of turquoise, yellow, pink and green and that the brushstrokes were visible with heavy impasto and a build-up of paint. This suggests that Stott was still very much concerned with the experimental properties of paint. However, the evidence of impasto in his tangible brushstrokes, reveals a change in his handling from the delicacy and refinement of his earlier works to a facture that was rugged and masculine. In this last surge of strength, it can be speculated that this was a sign of his failing health and possibly that he was aware of his own imminent mortality.

With *The Patriarch*, Stott made a return to portraiture which was a genre he only occasionally engaged in. Arguably, his most effective portraits were those he produced in the early part of his career. With this late example, he has effectively captured and conveyed the personality of the elderly sitter who has a stern, authoritative and learned look. Whether or not the title is a reference to Abraham, the Chief Patriarch, can only be guessed at.[397] Alternatively, it could be a homage by Stott to G.F. Watts who had died in 1904, as there are similarities between the sitter and a self-portrait by Watts of 1879.[398] Certainly, as regards some of the subject matter of the paintings discussed in this chapter, Watts had also depicted similar themes – *The Good Samaritan* (1850), *The Prodigal Son* (1872-3) and *Ruth and Boaz* (1835-7) - for example. Millet had also influenced Stott and he, too, had painted *The Good Samaritan* (1846) and *Ruth and Boaz* (1850-1853). Furthermore, his former Master in Paris, Carolus-Duran, had exhibited his version of *The Entombment* at the Paris Salon of 1882. Returning to the portrait, the most striking thing about this painting is how modern it is. Posed against a dark flat background, the two-dimensionality of the elderly man's body which is clothed in plain and formally simplified garments, with subdued colours, echoes Whistler's portraits. However, there are also echoes of Renaissance portraiture where the sitters were often depicted against dark flat backgrounds.

In 1917, Stott began preparing studies for what was to be his final painting for the Royal Academy, the subject matter of which was based on the mythological

54. Edward Stott, *The Patriarch*, 1917. Oil on canvas, 103.4 x 73.26cm. © The Royal Academy of Arts, London; Photographer: Andy Johnson

character of Orpheus.[399] Anne Dinnage has told of how Stott was not an avid reader but had an interest in mythology. She began reading the story of Orpheus to Stott on a nightly basis, until he had thoroughly grasped the details sufficiently enough to commence working on the painting.[400] Stott produced a number of pastel studies of the naked youthful figure of Orpheus, such as *Study for 'Orpheus'* (c.1917-18), *Head Study for 'Orpheus'* (c.1917-18), and a chalk drawing of goats which were to be included in the painting (*Study of Goats for 'Orpheus'* (1917)). As two photographs in the Stott Archive reveal, the painting was large and in the 'tondo' form. The unfinished oil version was exhibited posthumously at the Royal Academy exhibition of 1918, as Stott had died in March.

In 1917, he had gone up to London and was joined later by Anne Dinnage. They had visited Regents Park Zoo so that Stott could sketch the goats. He had felt unwell and returned to his studio in Bayswater, where he was found to have a temperature. He recovered and returned to Amberley, where he was well all summer. On 14th February 1918, after returning from a walk at 9.00 a.m., he remarked to Anne Dinnage that he did not feel well and this, according to her, was the beginning of Stott's fatal illness.[401] He continued to worry about his painting, even though he was very ill, and wanted to go to his studio to look at it but the painting was brought to him in bed.[402] Stott descended into a 'cataleptic' state where he imagined he was painting. According to Anne Dinnage 'His hand was in the air, holding the imaginary brush, moving it this way and that and dabbing in touches here and there; he was whistling softly as he always did when painting, and his eyes were fixed on one particular spot on the wall.'[403] In his mind Stott may have finished *Orpheus.* In reality it was not the case as he passed away at 10.00 a.m. on the 19th March 1918.

In an Obituary published in the *Pall Mall Gazette* on the 22nd March, it was claimed that worry over the unfinished painting was partly responsible for his death. *Orpheus* was reviewed by Konody in the *Observer*:

> The late Edward Stott's unfinished Orpheus is of considerable interest in so far as it reveals the thinness of the structural foundations upon which he apparently built up his remarkable pictures. It is all spongy and formless. The solidity and definition of his work must have been the result of slow, painstaking building-up, touch upon touch. Mr Stott's death has robbed the Academy of one of the rare modern artists gifted with real imagination and sincerity.[404]

There is little doubt that, if Stott had lived, he would have achieved full Academician status. In 1915, a vacancy arose and it was between Stott and Joseph Farquharson with whom he had tied. Farquharson, being senior to Stott and an Associate for longer, was given the casting vote by the then President, Sir Edward Poynter. As Anne Dinnage remarked, 'At the next vacancy, he would have received full honours but there were no other vacancies for Royal Academy painters during his lifetime.'[405]

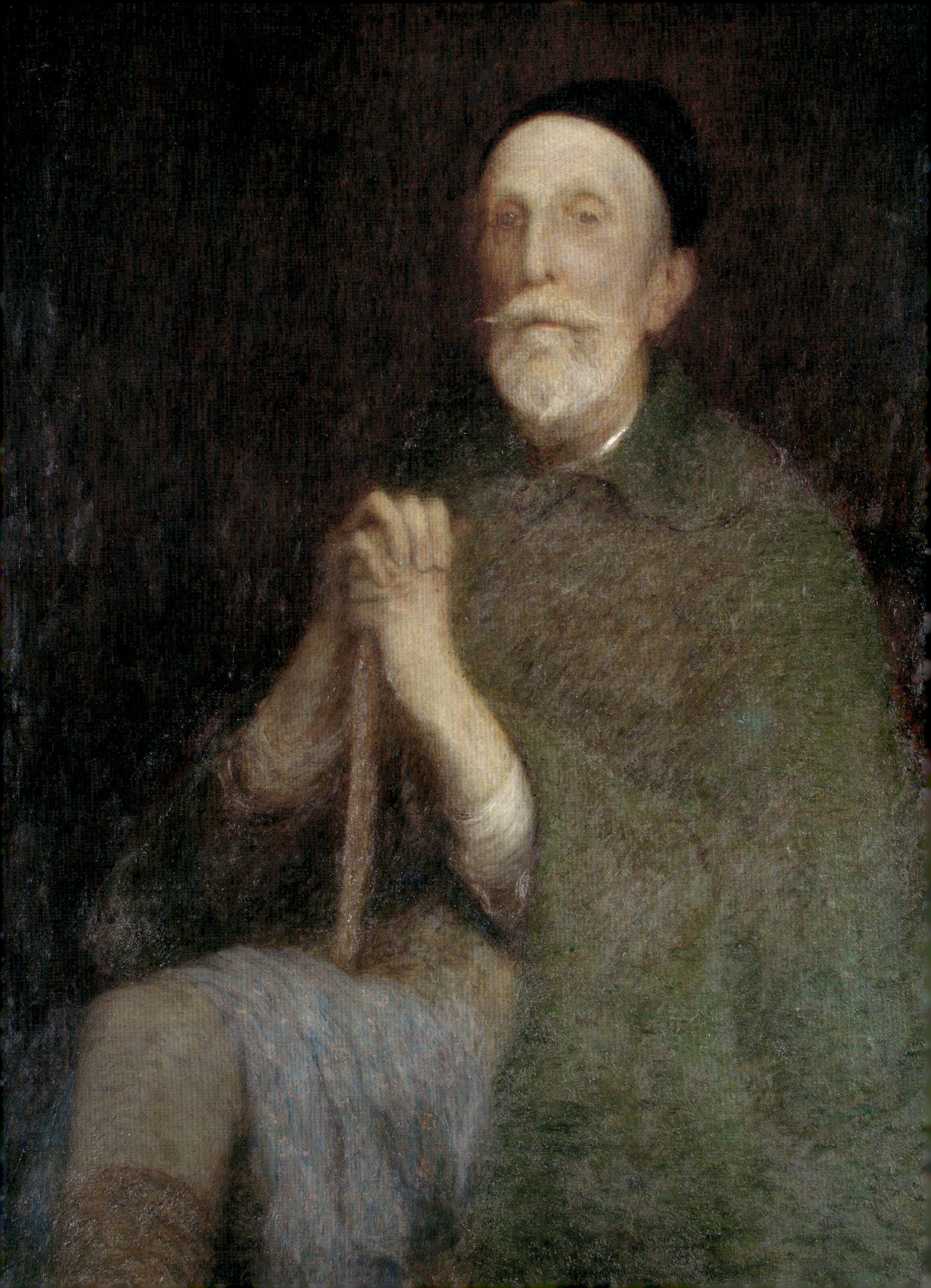

STOTT'S LEGACY

In his will Edward Stott left two legacies. To Anne Dinnage he bequeathed all his property, including furniture and household effects, and all his unsold pictures and studies . He also left her £1,500. To the Royal Academy, he left £25,000 which was to provide travelling scholarships for art students, and for the purchase of 'modern' pictures.[406] In his lifetime, it is apparent that he provided inspiration for a number of artists, including Mark Fisher, Fred Hall, William Shackleton and Fred Stratton. As Shackleton's scenes of Amberley show, he was clearly Stott's successor.[407] Nevertheless, Stott's influence has never been fully acknowledged where, in the existing historiography, he has been viewed as a follower of Bastien-Lepage and rustic naturalism, and Impressionism. Whilst his early work did indeed draw inspiration from Bastien-Lepage, and also saw him experimenting with a subtle Impressionist style, his overriding aim was to find his own 'signature' style. This came to the fore in his paintings for the New Gallery exhibitions where his controlled, but visible, brushstrokes, with just the right thickness of paint, gave a surface texture to his work. This style, together with his imaginative and knowledgeable use of colour, made his work idiosyncratic. More importantly, with the achieving of his own style, together with his wide-ranging themes and subject matters, has allowed for Stott's many contributions to the history of British landscape painting generally, and English landscape painting specifically, with a focus on rural images, to be explored.

Edward Stott was a shy man, by all accounts mercurial in his temperament, and inclined towards over sensitiveness. Above all, he was totally committed to his art. In a memorial address by Walter Butterworth, Chairman of the Manchester Whitworth Art Gallery, which took place in March 1920, Butterworth thus described Stott:

> He did not like the garish. He liked the quiet eventide – the thoughtful, quiet, idyllic, pensive mood. There was nothing humorous or joyous in his work, nothing brilliant or flashy, nothing vehement, tragic, audacious, sensational, or heroic. His effects were all tenderness and sympathy with the more gentle aspects of life. A man who was a poet in art.[408]

END NOTES

1. The paintings were exhibited with their French titles. *The Helping Hand of a Small Friend* was exhibited as *On a souvent besoin d'un plus petit du soin, The High Grasses* was exhibited as *Les Hautes Herbes*, and *The Return to the Poultry House* had the French title of *Retour au Poulailler.*
2. Kenneth McConkey, *British Impressionism* (Oxford: Phaidon, 1989); McConkey, *Impressionism in Britain* (London and New Haven: Yale University Press in association with the Barbican Art Gallery, 1999); Ysanne Holt, *British Artists and the Modernist Landscape* (Aldershot: Ashgate Publishing Limited, 2003).
3. The information for Edward Stott's date of birth is that given on the Birth Certificate. For some reason, the date of 1859 is often cited in various sources.
4. *Rochdale Observer* (13th December 1856), p.1. (SA)
5. A5/Box B. (SA)
6. A number of overlapping factors caused the crisis. In the first instance, there had been an overproduction of woven cotton at a time of shrinking world markets, which had led to the stockpiling of raw cotton. This resulted in the market being flooded with finished goods, which resulted in a dramatic fall in price, and which coincided with a fall in the demand for raw cotton. However, due to the American Civil War, cotton imports were restricted resulting in the price for raw cotton disproportionately increasing. All of these factors changed the social circumstances of the workforce, with the mill workers becoming unemployed and, in many cases, impoverished.
7. *New Annals of Rochdale*, pp.243-244. (SA)
8. Elizabeth Stazicker, Archivist, The King's School, Ely.
9. *The Sussex Daily News* (21st March 1918).
10. 'Preface', *Memorial Exhibition of Paintings and Drawings by the late Edward Stott, ARA.*, catalogue published to accompany the Rochdale Art Gallery exhibition (March to April 1920) (SA); 'Obituary', *Manchester The Guardian* (22nd March 1918). (SA)
11. J. Stanley Little, 'On the Work of Edward Stott', *The Studio*, Vol. VI, No. 32 (November 1895), p.72.
12. William Knight Keeling was a founder member of the Academy which was established in 1859 for the purpose of organising annual exhibitions to be held in Manchester City Art Gallery. Keeling's third Presidency took place from 1865 to 1877. He was also an artist and illustrator.
13. A number of sources confirm this. For example, A.C.R. Carter, 'Edward Stott and his work', *The Art Journal* (October 1899), p.295; Laurence Housman, 'Mr Edward Stott, Painter of the Field and of the Twilight', *Magazine of Art* (January 1900), p.530; J. Stanley Little, op. cit., p.72. Stanley Little states that Stott attended evening classes at Manchester so as 'to educate himself in the rudiments of art-knowledge.'
14. Housman, ibid., p.530.
15. A.C.R. Carter, op. cit., p.295. Thomas Agnew first established his business in Manchester in 1817, with the London gallery opening in 1860.
16. Jeanne Sheehy, 'The flight from South Kensington: British Artists at the Antwerp Academy. 1877-1883', *Art History*, Vol. 20, No. 1 (March 1997), pp.125-126.
17. Ibid., p.126. Artists such as Frank Bramley, William Logsdale, William Wainwright and Edwin Harris were mentioned.
18. McConkey, *Impressionism in Britain*, op.cit., pp.198-199 and p.140.
19. Sheehy, 'The flight from South Kensington', op. cit., pp.124-125.
20. For a good insight into the training art students would have received in London, see H. Cliff Morgan, 'The Schools of the Royal Academy', *British Journal of Educational Studies*, 21:1 (1973); Alice Strickland, 'Opening Doors: The Entry of Women Artists into British Art Schools, 1871-1930', in *The Concept of the 'Master' in Art Education in Britain and Ireland, 1770 to the Present*, edited by Matthew C. Potter (Farnham and Burlington: Ashgate Publishing Limited, 2013); Irish Wien, 'Naturalising Tradition: Why Learn from the Masters?', in *The Concept of the 'Master' in Art Education in Britain and Ireland, 1770 to the Present.*
21. Sheehy, 'The flight from South Kensington: British Artists at the Antwerp Academy. 1877-1883', op. cit., p.125. Alexander Stanhope Forbes and Henry Herbert La Thangue studied at Lambeth College of Art and the Royal Academy Schools of Art before going to Paris. Forbes went to the atelier of Bonnat, whilst La Thangue went to Gérôme's atelier. See, also, McConkey, *Impressionism in Britain*, op. cit., p.126 and p.146.
22. George Halkett, 'Edward Stott, A.R.A., An Appreciation and Some Recollections', *Nash's Pall Mall Magazine*, Vol. 37, Issue 155 (March 1906); Shirley Fox, *An Art Student's Reminiscences of Paris in the Eighties* (London: Mills and Boon, 1909); D.S. MacColl, *Life, Work and Setting of Philip Wilson Steer* (London: Faber and Faber Ltd., 1945); Ysane Holt, *Philip Wilson Steer* (Mid Glamorgan: Seren Books, 1992); Philip Wilson Steer Archive, Courtauld Institute of Art. (CI/PWS)
23. Albert Ludovici, *An Artist's Life in London and Paris* (London: T. Fisher Unwin, 1926); Barclay Day, *Magazine of Art* (1882). I have been unable to find out who Barclay Day is and the name may well be a pseudonym.
24. Arthur Kennedy, 'In the Studio of Carolus-Duran', *The Contemporary Review*, 53 (May 1888); Albert Boime, *The Academy and French Painting in the Nineteenth Century* (London: Phaidon, 1971).
25. Kennedy, ibid., p.704.

26. Day, 'Studio-life in Paris', *Magazine of Art* (1882), p.510.
27. Ibid., pp.510-511.
28. Boime, op. cit., p.49.
29. Shirley Fox, op. cit., p.101.
30. At Bonnat's atelier, the entrance fee was 25 Francs, and the yearly subscription fee was 360 Francs payable monthly. At the Académie Julian, where students were taught by Bouguereau, the fees payable were 50 Francs a month for the whole day, or 200 Francs for six months, or half a day for half the cost. See Barclay Day, 'L'Atelier-Bonnat', *Magazine of Art* (1882), p.138; Letter from Philip Wilson Steer to his mother dated Monday, October 1882. No further date supplied. (CI/PWS/6/10 (1)).
31. Halkett, op. cit., p.283; Letter from PWS to his brother Harry dated 21st November 1882, and his mother dated 29th November 1882. (CI/PWS/6/10 (3&4))
32. Day, 'L'Atelier-Bonnat', op. cit., p.138; Ludovici, op. cit., p.22. Ludovici recalled that in the atelier he attended, there was a half-circle of about 50 or 60 students sat on low stools, with the painters standing behind them three or four deep.
33. Fox, op. cit., p.101.
34. Letter from PWS to his mother dated 6th November 1882. (CI/PWS/6/10 (2))
35. Fox, op. cit., p.102.
36. Ludovici, op. cit., p.23. Ludovici gives an account of what could happen. The new student would be stripped of his clothes which were subsequently hidden. His body would then be painted Prussian blue and striped Indian red.
37. Letter from PWS to his mother or brother dated 18th January 1883. (CI/PWS/6/10 (8))
38. Fox, op. cit., p.103.
39. Kennedy, op. cit., p.704 and p.708.
40. Ibid., pp.705-706.
41. Ibid., p.706.
42. Stippling involved the application of densely packed minute dots of a single colour to give the appearance of a smooth finish. This method was in keeping with the academic atmosphere of the Royal Academy Schools in which the aim was to produce work with a 'high' finish. See Ysanne Holt, *Philip Wilson Steer*, op. cit., p.161.
43. Letter from PWS to his mother dated 7th December 1882. (CI/PWS/6/10 (5))
44. Halkett, op. cit., p.283. The reference to M. Collin must be Raphaël Collin. As to the reference to M. Courtois, this is probably Gustave Claude Étienne Courtois. See *Benezit Dictionary of Artists* (Paris: Editions Gründ, 2006).
45. Halkett, ibid., p.284.
46. Ibid., p.284.
47. Pierre-Henri de Valenciennes (1750-1819) was considered to be a pivotal figure in the practice of plein-air painting. He advocated working directly from the motif in order to gain a truthful understanding of the transient effects of nature. Among his students were Achille-Etna Michallon and Jean-Victor Bertin who continued the tradition and encouraged their students likewise.
48. Ludovici, op. cit., p.2. M. Charles had been a pupil of the portrait painter, Cogniet, who came to look at the students' work and advised that they should leave the studio and go to the quarries and quays to study the human form in motion.
49. Kimberley Jones, *In the Forest of Fontainbleau. Painters and Photographers from Corot to Monet* (New Haven and London: Yale University Press, 2008), p.9.
50. Ibid., p.712.
51. Halkett, op. cit., p.285.
52. Carter, op. cit., p.295.
53. Boime, op. cit., p.104.
54. Fox, op. cit., pp.73-74.
55. Stanley Little, op. cit., p.72.
56. Ysanne Holt, *Philip Wilson Steer*, op. cit., p.20.
57. Boime, op. cit., p.23.
58. Ibid., p.23.
59. Halkett, op. cit., p.285.
60. Fox, op. cit., p.114.
61. Stanley Little, op. cit., p.72. Interestingly, many years later Stott would have a painting selected to contribute to the British Fine Art section of the St. Louis exhibition of 1904. The painting in question was *Sunday Morning* (1901).
62. Carter, op. cit., p.295.
63. Box K (SA).
64. For a good insight into the history of the Salon, See Boime, op. cit.
65. Ibid., p.16. Translated, *juste milieu* means 'middle ground' or 'happy medium'.
66. Ibid., p.17.
67. Other artists included Alfred Philippe Roll, Albert Besnard and Eugène Carrière.
68. John Forbes-Robertson, 'The Salon of 1881 – 1', *Magazine of Art* (1881), p.379.
69. Ibid., p.379.
70. Fox, op. cit., pp.157-158.
71. Ibid., p.159.
72. The former painting has also been given the title of *In the Fields, Auvers-sur-Oise* in auction catalogues.
73. See exhibition catalogues of the Paris Salon, published under the direction of F.G. Dumas (Paris, Boulevard Saint-German: Libraire d'Art L. Baschet). The paintings were exhibited with their French titles. See Footnote 1.
74. Henri van Laun, 'The Paris Salon', *TIME* (June 1883), p.713.
75. Halkett, op. cit., p.285.
76. Kennedy, op. cit., p.709.
77. Richard Shiff, *Cézanne and the End of Impressionism. A Study of the Theory, Technique, and Critical Evaluation of Modern Art* (Chicago and London: The University of Chicago Press, 1984), p.101.
78. Ibid., p.101, quoting Eugène Fromentin, *Les Maîtres*

d'autrefois (Paris: 1876), pp.238-39. Fromentin was known for his paintings of North African life, in particular scenes of Algiers.

79. An alternative viewpoint regarding Stott's spatial handling in this painting is put forward by Kenneth McConkey, who states that Bastien-Lepage was the influence. See *Impressionism in Britain*, op. cit., p.198.
80. Shiff, op. cit., p.102.
81. Ibid., quoting Étienne-Joseph-Théophile Thoré, 'Salon de 1844', *Les Salons*, 3 Volumes (Brussels: 1893).
82. Kennedy, op. cit., p.712.
83. Ibid., p.712.
84. Ibid., p.712.
85. Historically, the term 'cottar' was used to denote a person of lowly status who was either landless or had insufficient land to be able to provide for his family, and so had to find part-time work. As regards the 'kail' or cabbage, this was the staple diet of the Scots cottar from the eighteenth century. See Laura Newton, 'Cottars and Cabbages: Issues of National Identity in Scottish 'Kailyard' Paintings of the Late Nineteenth Century', *Visual Culture in Britain*, Vol. 6, No. 2 (Manchester University Press, 2005), p.51 and p.54.
86. Ibid., p.56.
87. For example, James Guthrie painted *The Cottar's Garden* (1881) and *A Hind's Daughter* (1883), George Henry produced *In a Cottar's Garden* (1885) and William Macgregor, who was an associate of the group, painted *A Cottage Garden, Crail* (1883). The Scottish artist J.R. Reid also produced an early version of the theme in 1877, with the title of *In the Cabbage Patch*. For a good account of the Glasgow Boys, see Roger Billcliffe, *The Glasgow Boys* (London: Frances Lincoln Ltd., 2008), published to accompany the Royal Academy exhibition of 2008.
88. Ibid., p.36.
89. See, for example, Roger Brown, *William Stott of Oldham, 1857-1900: 'a comet rushing to the sun'* (London: Paul Holberton, 2003); Adrian Jenkins, 'William Stott of Oldham', *The Burlington Magazine*, Issue 1213 (2004), pp.273-274.
90. Kenneth McConkey, 'From Grez to Glasgow: French Naturalist Influence in Scottish Painting', *Scottish Art Review*, Vol. 15, No. 4 (1982). McConkey also cites George Clausen's painting, *Winter Work*, as another possible influence.
91. Anne Dinnage, 'Reminiscences', p.28. (SA)
92. Ibid., p.28.
93. For a good account of the history of the Forest of Fontainebleau, see Kimberley Jones, *In the Forest of Fontainebleau. Painters and Photographers from Corot to Monet*, op. cit.
94. Kenneth McConkey, '"The Pallid Gleam of the Imagination." Coastal Art Colonies in Britain at the turn of the Twentieth Century', *Painting at the Edge. British Coastal Art Colonies 1880-1930*, edited by Laura Newton (Bristol: Sansom & Company Ltd., 2005), p.12.
95. McConkey, *Impressionism in Britain*, op. cit., pp.23-25.
96. McConkey, "The Pallid Gleam of the Imagination.' Coastal Art Colonies in Britain at the turn of the Twentieth Century', op. cit., pp.13-14.
97. McConkey writes that Stanhope Forbes lived out his Breton colony experience in Newlyn which was, for him, an 'English Concarneau', ibid., p.16.
98. Bastien-Lepage had urged every young painter to find their vocation in his or her own 'corner of the world' which, for him, was his home village of Damvillers. McConkey, ibid., p.15.
99. Gabriel P. Weisberg, *Beyond Impressionism. The Natural Impulse in European Art 1860-1905* (London: Thames and Hudson, 1992).
100. See Richard Scott, 'Walberswick "An Eye for the Quiet Beauties of Nature"', *Painting at the Edge. British Coastal Art Colonies 1880-1930*, op. cit, pp.81-2; D.S. MacColl, *Life Work and Setting of Philip Wilson Steer*, op cit., p.24.
101. Stott produced a chalk drawing of Steer in the 1890s, and Steer reciprocated with a chalk drawing of Stott in 1894. The sketch by Steer is in the National Portrait Gallery, whilst the sketch by Stott was left to Anne Dinnage under the terms of Stott's Will. It was purchased by Mr and Mrs Arthur Grogan, whose collection has subsequently been dispersed. I assume that Stott's sketch of Steer is now in a private collection.
102. Scott, op. cit., p.85.
103. Ibid., p.81. The areas of Walberswick and Southwold began to attract artists in the 1880s, and access was made easier by the opening of the Southwold Railway in 1879, which linked Halesworth to the coast. By 1881, a station was then added at Walberswick which facilitated travel from London to Walberswick, with one change at Halesworth.
104. Edward Stott struggled financially in the early years, and he borrowed money from Osborne. As Osborne wrote in a letter to his niece, Violet Stockley, 'I have lent Stott £3 until his people send him some so I am short until he pays me. It is all right, I know, as he is a sterling good fellow and would do nothing dishonourable.' See Jeanne Sheehy, *Walter Osborne* (Ballycotton, Co. Cork: Gifford & Craven, 1974), pp.21-22.
105. This was an aspect of Osborne's work also identified by Richard Scott when he described the children in Osborne's painting of 1885, *An October Morning*, as being 'slightly posed.', op. cit., p.85.
106. The location of Stott's scene is likely to be the Vale of Evesham near to where Stott was living in North Littleton. See the exhibition catalogue, *An American in Brittany* (Dublin: Milmo-Penny Fine Art Limited, 2008), pp.14-15. The painting does not appear to have been exhibited at any time, nor are there any details as to provenance. It must be assumed that it is now privately owned.

107. See AAD/2000/5/33, Articles of Agreement between The Piccadilly Art Galleries Company Limited and the Institute of Painters in Oil Colours. Archive of the Royal Institute of Painters in Oil Colours, V&A, Blythe House. (IOP/BH/V&A).
108. Osborne sent in *The Cloisters, Lincoln Cathedral* and *An Old Waterway, Lincoln* to the 1884-5 exhibition. *The Return of the Flock* was shown at the 1885-6 exhibition, where it was sold for £25 to W.A. Duncan. For the 1886-7 exhibition, he exhibited *An Old Byeway, Wells-next-the-sea*, which sold to George Allen for £25. See Institute of Painters in Oil Colours. Exhibition Catalogues, Published by the Galleries, Piccadilly (IOP/BH/V&A).
109. This work came up for sale at Sotheby's on the 22nd May 2014, where it sold for £674,500.
110. *Magazine of Art* (1884), p.135.
111. *The British Architect* (26th November 1886), p.481. The painting was originally purchased by E. Thornly of Portman Square, London, directly from the exhibition for £50. Its current whereabouts is unknown and must be assumed to be in a private collection.
112. See, for example, 'Pictures of the Year IV', *Magazine of Art* (1880), p.500; *Illustrated London News* (8th May 1880), p.45.
113. *The Spectator* (12th June 1880), p.751, quoted by Kenneth McConkey, 'Rustic Naturalism at the Grosvenor Gallery', in *The Grosvenor Gallery. A Palace of Art in Victorian England*, edited by Susan P. Casteras and Colleen Denny (New Haven and London: Yale Center for British Art, 1996), p.134.
114. For a discussion of Clausen's Childwick Green series of paintings, see Anna Gruetzner Robins, 'Living the Simple Life: George Clausen at Childwick Green, St. Albans', in David Peters Corbett, Ysanne Holt and Fiona Russell (Editors), *The Geographies of Englishness. Landscape and the National Past 1880-1940*, The Paul Mellon Centre for Studies in British Art. The Yale Center for British Art (New Haven and London: Yale University Press, 2002).
115. *The Standard* (17th December 1883), p.2. The critic also viewed Bastien-Lepage's country figures as 'uncompromising to the verge of brutality,' with Clausen considered to be 'just as veracious.', p.2.
116. *Pall Mall Gazette* (19th December 1883); *Magazine of Art* (January 1885), p.134. The critic disliked the painting, stating that 'If it exists at all, it exists not as a picture, but as material for a picture…it is excessively ugly, and seems to have been painted for its ugliness sake and nothing else.'
117. *The Graphic* (5th December 1885).
118. Julie F. Codell, 'Constructing the Victorian Artist: National Identity, the Political Economy of Art and Biographical Mania in the Periodical Press', *Victorian Periodicals Review*, Vol. 33, No. 3 (Fall 2000), p.285.
119. Laurel Brake, *Subjugated Knowledges: Journalism, Gender and Literature in the Nineteenth Century* (London: MacMillan, 1994), pp.10-11.
120. Gruetzner Robins, 'Living the Simple Life: George Clausen at Childwick Green, St. Albans', op. cit., p.3
121. Edward Stott letters, ca. 1893-1916. Series II. Letters to Herbert Gilchrist (Folder 2), Special Collection (870011). Getty Research Institute Library (GRIL). It is not known which painting Stott destroyed. Stott underlined the word in his letter.
122. Edward Stott Letters, ca. 1893-1916. Series I. Letters to James Little (Folder 1) (GRIL).
123. Stott to Little (9th December 1893).
124. Stott to Little (9th December 1893); Stott to Little (undated).
125. Stott to Gilchrist (28th October 1909).
126. Stott to Gilchrist (16th November 1911). I have been unable to discover who Cognan is. The reference to 'Girten', however, is to the landscape artist Thomas Girtin (1775-1802) who was a friend and rival of Turner.
127. McConkey, *Impressionism in Britain*, op. cit., p.64.
128. The painting was purchased by Mr P. Emerson of Southwold for £30, although it was listed in the exhibition catalogue with a sale price of £40. It is now in a private collection, with ownership details held by the Fine Art Society.
129. La Thangue complained about the rejection of his bronze picture frame and asked to have the painting removed from the exhibition. He received a letter from the Secretary informing him that he must adhere to the rules. A.M. Rossi complained about the poor hanging position of his painting, despite its being chosen for illustration in the exhibition catalogue. See AAD/2005/5/8, Council Meetings Minute Book No. 1, 19th November 1884. (IOP/BH/V&A).
130. Other members who resigned were Walter Crane, J. Absolom, L.P. Smythe, L. Wood and W. Simpson. Mark Fisher resigned in January 1887.
131. See Lot Note for *The Orchard, Quimperlé* by Stanhope Forbes, in *Victorian and Edwardian Art*, Sotheby's Auction Catalogue (London, 27th June 2006), p.92. The contributor to the Lot Note is unknown.
132. In the spring of 1882, Arthur Tooth's gallery had included Bastien-Lepage's painting in their exhibition and Forbes may well have seen the painting there. Clausen certainly had, and the two may have discussed it when Clausen went out to see Stanhope Forbes in Brittany in 1884, after La Thangue had left. Ibid., p.94.
133. The date of the pastel is unknown. However, the initials 'EAF' in the lower right-hand corner stand for Elizabeth Adela Forbes, which dates this work after her marriage to Stanhope Forbes in 1889. The pastel came up for sale at Sotheby's London on 25th November 2004, and was illustrated in the auction catalogue with accompanying Lot Note, pp.130-31. The work had previously been exhibited at Penlee House Gallery and Museum, Penzance,

and Djanogly Art Gallery, Nottingham, as part of the touring exhibition *Singing From the Walls* which took place from July to December 2000. See exhibition catalogue by Judith Cook, Melissa Hardie and Christiana Payne, *Singing from the walls: the life and art of Elizabeth Forbes* (Bristol: Sansom and Company, 2000).

134. This painting came up for sale at Sotheby's, New York, on 4th May 2016, and was illustrated in the auction catalogue *19th Century European Paintings*.
135. Extract from Martin Heidegger, *The Origin of the Work of Art*, reprinted in 'Philosophers Rumble Over Van Gogh's Shoes', by Scott Horton, *Harper's Magazine* (5th October 2009), npn., harper.org.
136. *Glasgow Herald* (3rd May 1880).
137. McConkey, 'Rustic Naturalism at the Grosvenor Gallery', *The Grosvenor Gallery. A Palace of Art in Victorian England*, op. cit., p.131.
138. Ibid., p.130.
139. Ruskin's comments were published in his pamphlet of July 1877, *Fors Clavigera*. Whistler responded to these insults by issuing a libel action against Ruskin, with the matter coming to court the following year in November 1878, having been postponed on several occasions due to Ruskin's ill health. See *Whistler. A Retrospective*, edited by Robin Spencer (New York: Wings Books, 1991), p.124 and p.14.
140. Much of the Gallery had been financed by Blanche Lindsay who was wealthy in her own right. When they separated at some point in 1880, Coutts Lindsay lost his moral and financial support. See Colleen Denney, 'Introduction', *The Grosvenor Gallery. A Palace of Art in Victorian England*, op. cit., p.4.
141. Ibid., p.4.
142. McConkey, *Impressionism in Britain*, op. cit., p.138.
143. Roger Billcliffe, *The Glasgow Boys*, op. cit., pp.206-8.
144. Along with George Henry, the other Glasgow Boys who joined in 1887 were Thomas Millie Dow, James Paterson and Edward Walton. James Guthrie joined in 1889, and Edward Hornel briefly exhibited in 1891 and showed one work which was co-painted with George Henry. The title of the painting was *The Angel and the Shepherds*. See Charles Baile de Laperrier, *A Dictionary of Artists and their works in the Annual Exhibitions of the New English Art Club Exhibitions 1886-2001* (Calne: Hilmarton Manor Press, 2002).
145. By the end of the 1880s, the Gallery was in decline. George Clausen advised Coutts Lindsay to bring in the Glasgow Boys, and in 1890 they exhibited for the first and last time as the Gallery subsequently closed down. See Denney and McConkey, *The Grosvenor Gallery. A Palace of Art in Victorian England*, op. cit., pp.6-7 and p.142.
146. The painting in question was *A Galloway Landscape*. McConkey, *Impressionism in Britain*, op. cit., p.138.
147. *The Art Journal* (August 1884), p.242. No surviving image exists of this work, and neither is its current whereabouts known or its provenance.
148. Sir Duncan Oppenheim was Chairman of British American Tobacco from 1953 to 1966. He was also an artist in his own right who mainly worked in watercolour and acrylic. He was best known for his paintings of air raid incidents in Westminster, and exhibited with the London Group and the Royal Academy. See 'Obituaries', *The Telegraph* (11th January 2003).
149. Kenneth McConkey, *The New English. A History of the New English Art Club* (London: The Royal Academy of Arts, 2006); Anna Gruetzner Robins, 'Defining Impressionism at the New English Art Club', *A Fragile Modernism. Whistler and his Impressionist Followers*, Paul Mellon Centre for Studies in British Art (New Haven and London: Yale University Press, 2007).
150. McConkey, ibid., p.29.
151. Catalogue. Exhibition of Pictures at the New English Art Club, at the Marlborough Gallery, 53 Pall Mall (1886).
152. *Liverpool Mercury* (13th July 1886).
153. *Pall Mall Gazette* (13th April 1886).
154. *Liverpool Mercury* (13th July 1886).
155. McConkey, *The New English. A History of the New English Art Club*, op. cit., p.32.
156. Ibid., p.37.
157. Ibid., pp.36-7. La Thangue wanted to make the New English Art Club more inclusive and wide-ranging, and aspired to organising an exhibition in which every artist in Britain could vote for the selecting and hanging juries. This was called the 'Bigger' or 'National Movement', and aimed to outdo the Royal Academy. La Thangue's grand scheme was rejected and he subsequently resigned.
158. *Daily News* (5th April 1887).
159. This painting was probably a companion piece to *Winter's Night, Sussex Village*, which was exhibited at the Grosvenor Gallery in 1887. I make this assumption based on the fact that there are a number of similarities between the two images in terms of brushwork, colour, and the fact that both paintings were of similar dimension and executed in oil on panel.
160. J. Stanley Little, 'On the work of Edward Stott', op. cit., p.74.
161. *Liverpool Mercury* (10th October 1887).
162. McConkey, *The New English. A History of the New English Art Club*, op. cit., p.163.
163. Sickert considered Bastien-Lepage to be a painter of 'Paris *machins*', which were large-scale paintings suitable for the Salon. He went on to describe Bastien-Lepage as an 'inveterate *salonnier*, with the ideals and the limitations of the typical uncultured Paris art student. Sickert also disliked the 'mechanically obtrusive square-brush-work of the Parisian schools of art', preferring the work of Millet whom he considered to be a truthful artist and not out for financial gain. Sickert expressed these views

in 1891, but had clearly held them for a while and they appeared to extend to any artist who showed the influence of Bastien-Lepage. See 'Modern Realism in Painting' (1891), reproduced in *Jules Bastien-Lepage and his art: A Memoir*, edited by André Theuriet (1892), reproduced in *Walter Sickert. The Complete Writings on Art*, edited by Anna Gruetzner Robins (Oxford: Oxford University Press, 2000), pp.86-88.

164. Sickert wrote of Tuke's painting, *All Hands to the Pump* (1888-9), that it showed 'carefully copied models'. Of Tuke he wrote that 'Mr Tuke is, of all the groups in England,... who are following what I believe to be fallacious French methods, far and away the ablest and most artistic.' These comments were expressed in an article with the title 'The Royal Academy', published in the *New York Herald* (16th May 1889), in Gruetzner Robins, ibid., pp.48-50.
165. Sickert, 'The Royal Academy Exhibition', *Art Weekly* (10th May 1890), in Gruetzner Robins, ibid., p.62.
166. Anna Gruetzner Robins, *A Fragile Modernism. Whistler and his Impressionist Followers*, op. cit., pp.111-112.
167. The missing paintings comprise *Amberley, Nr. Arundel* (c.1888), *Breakfast Time* (c.1888), *Winter Food* (c.1888), *A Village Street* (c.1889), *Returning to the Fold* (c.1889) which was originally owned by James Gresham, C.E., J.P., *Spring Blossoms* (also known as *A Spring Idyll*) (c.1890) originally owned by J. Dowmunt, *A Souvenir of Amberley Fair* (c.1891), *A Peaceful Evening* (1891), *November Twilight* (1893), *Blue, Gold and Scarlet* (1893), *Storks: Harmony in Blue and Silver* (1893), *The Little Gleaners* (1894), *In the Moonlight* (1894), and a pastel study of a naked child (1895).
168. As stated in Footnote 167, *Returning to the Fold* and *November Twilight* are both missing. However, a black and white reproduction of these two works can be found in the Stott folder in the Witt Library, Courtauld Institute of Art.
169. J. Stanley Little, 'On the work of Edward Stott', op. cit., p.75.
170. *Morning Post* (13th April 1892).
171. George Moore, 'The New English Art Club', *The Speaker* (16th April 1892), p.46.
172. Ibid.
173. *Liverpool Mercury* (19th September 1892).
174. J. Stanley Little, 'On the work of Edward Stott', op. cit., p.80
175. Edward Stott, 'Some Remarks on Impressionism', *The Art Journal* (1893), pp.103-4. The word 'charter' appears in the original transcript, but it may be a misprint and possibly should be 'character'. Other artists who responded by letter were Francis Bate, Walter Sickert, George Clausen, H.B. Brabazon, Fred Brown and Sydney Adamson.
176. Sickert. 'The Royal Academy Exhibition', *Art Weekly* (10th May 1890), in Gruetzner Robins, *Walter Sickert. The Complete Writings on Art*, op. cit., p.63.
177. *Glasgow Herald* (7th April 1893).
178. *Daily News* (11th April 1893).
179. *Glasgow Herald* (7th April 1893).
180. *Daily News* (11th April 1893)
181. The title of this painting, and *Storks: Harmony in Blue and Silver*, must surely be an acknowledgement of Whistler.
182. *The Graphic* (14th April 1894). There are no surviving images of these paintings, nor details pertaining to provenance or current whereabouts.
183. *Glasgow Herald* (8th April 1895).
184. *The Saturday Review* (20th April 1895).
185. Ibid.
186. John Maddocks purchased five paintings: *Bathers* (c.1890), *The Horse Pond* (1891), *The Ferry Boat* (1887), *Changing Pastures* (1893), and *The Labourer's Cottage* (1893). C.T. Harris purchased four paintings: *Peaceful Evening* (1891), *Trees Old and Young* (1899) (version 2), *A Moonlight Idyll* (1902), and *Folding Time* (1904). Only one painting was purchased by Harris privately and that was *The Gleaners* (1903). For background on John Maddocks, see Kristi Holden, 'George Clausen and Henry Herbert La Thangue. Rural Painting, Urban Patronage', *Apollo*, Vol. 149, No. 444 (February 1999), p.17. Maddocks' collection was sold on Saturday, 30th April 1910, by Christie, Manson and Woods. See *Catalogue of choice Modern Pictures of the British and Continental Schools, the Property of John Maddocks, Esq., of Heath Royal, Putney Heath (sold owing to his having disposed of his residence.* As regards C.T. Harris, very little is known about this collector of Stott's work. Harris' collection was sold on the 28th November 1913, also by Christie, Manson and Woods, following his death, and sold for the benefit of the Memorial Fund of King's College Hospital. A number of Harris' paintings were purchased by the fine art dealer, W.W. Sampson, who also purchased some of Maddocks' collection. A brief reference to Sampson was found on the University of Glasgow website: exhibitionculture.arts.gla.ac.uk, accessed 1st September 2015.
187. 'New Gallery Notes. No.1, 1888', *The New Gallery 1888. An Illustrated Catalogue of the Summer Exhibition at the New Gallery, 121 Regent Street*, edited by Henry Blackburn (London: Chatto and Windus, May 1888).
188. Ibid.
189. Other artists on the Committee were W.B. Richmond, H. Herkomer, A. Gilbert, E. Onslow Ford, J.W. North, Alfred Parsons and the architect, E.R. Robson.
190. *Pall Mall Gazette* (8th May 1888).
191. Bridgeman Images have given the painting the title of *Springtime*. However, as a result of searching through the original New Gallery exhibition catalogues, the illustration of the work in the catalogue and the accompanying title identifies it as *Trees Old and Young, Sprouting a Shady Boon for Simple Sheep*.
192. The poem was originally published in 1818, but a collection of Keats' poems were published in *The Poetical Works of John Keats*, with notes by Francis T. Palgrave (London: Macmillan, 1884).

193. The lines in the poem read 'Soon as the morning trembles o'er the sky/And unperceived, unfolds the spreading day/ Before the ripen'd field the reapers stand/In fair array.'
194. Rosamund Marriott Watson wrote under the male pseudonym of Graham R. Tomson. The lines come from her published work of 1889 entitled *The Bird-Bride. A Volume of Ballads and Sonnets* (London and New York: Longmans, Green and Co., 1889). See www.1890s.ca., accessed 17th February 2015.
195. New Gallery exhibition catalogue (1888).
196. For purposes of accuracy, the title should be *As twilight melts beneath the moon away.*
197. See a series of undated paintings such as *Old Mill, Pulborough*; *Road near Arundel*; *Plumpton Church, Sussex*; *Eve on the Arun*; *Morning on the Sussex Downs*, and *Arundel, West Sussex.* Waterlow had studied in London, Germany and Switzerland. He exhibited at the Royal Academy in 1871, and was President of the Society of Painters in Water-Colours. He became an Associate of the Academy in 1890, achieving full Academician status in 1903. In *Benezit Dictionary of Artists*, Vol. 14 (Paris: Éditions Gründ, 2006).
198. New Gallery Exhibition Catalogue (1888).
199. George Faulkner Wetherbee was an American artist who spent much of his life in England, but also travelled throughout Europe. He studied in Antwerp and London. His early work was influenced by Bastien-Lepage, and also shows a visual alliance with certain examples by Clausen and Hall. His Sylvan scenes of boys bathing, as well as his paintings of rural subject matter, suggest an artistic connection or affinity with artists such as Tuke and Stott.
200. I have over-simplified matters here for the sake of clarity, but an excellent introduction and explanation of modernism in its various forms can be found in Charles Harrison, *Modernism* (London: Tate Gallery Publishing Limited, 1997).
201. Anne Dinnage wrote in her diary that she would sometimes travel up to London to see her cousins and then meet up with Stott where they would then have lunch, visit the galleries and sometimes see a show. Dinnage Diary, p.15 (SA).
202. Ysanne Holt, *British Artists and the Modernist Landscape*, op. cit., pp.14-15.
203. In the letter, Stott refers to the artist W.J. Laidlay's publication 'Lena Laird' which was published in 1901, hence my suggested dating.
204. Letter from Stott to Osborne, 2nd December 1917. MS 2597, Special Collections, The Sir Duncan Rice Library, University of Aberdeen.
205. *National Observer* (4th May 1895); *Daily News* (7th May 1895).
206. The title could be a loose reference to the myth of Narcissus, as it is known that Stott was interested in mythological subject matter. See Dinnage Diary, page 7 (SA).
207. Dinnage Diary, p.1; Census Return (1881).
208. A.C.R. Carter 'Edward Stott and his work', op. cit., p.294.
209. Census Return (1891).
210. For a list of the various employments, trades and services, see The Reverend Noel E. Staines, *Dear Amberley. A Guide to Amberley and History of the Parish* (Amberley: 1968), p.19; Census Returns; Kelly's Directories of Sussex.
211. There were three schools. A National School in Amberley for mixed and infant pupils, a mixed Catholic School in Houghton Bridge, and a Catholic Infants' School in Houghton. On the social side, there were two recreation rooms. One in Amberley used for reading, games and other purposes, and the St. Edmund's Recreation Club at Houghton Bridge which was for working men and boys, also used for reading and games. St. Edmund's also had a lending library with 150 books. See Kelly's Directories of Sussex (1899 and 1905). The two public houses were The Cricketers and the Houghton Bridge Inn.
212. P.H. Ditchfield, *Our English Villages. Their Story and their Antiquities* (London: Methuen & Co. Ltd., 1889), p.4.
213. Raymond Williams, *The Country and the City* (Nottingham: Spokesman, 2011), p.46. First published by Chatto and Windus, London, 1973.
214. Geoffrey Best, *Mid-Victorian Britain 1851-75* (London: Fontana Press, 1987 [1979]), p.84.
215. Alun Howkins, *Reshaping Rural England: A Social History 1850-1925* (London: HarperCollins Academic, 1991), p.61.
216. Maple sought to turn Childwickbury into a place of leisure and pleasure. See Anna Gruetzner Robins, 'Living the Simple Life: George Clausen at Childwick Green, St. Albans', in *The Geographies of Englishness. Landscape and the National Past 1880-1940*, op. cit., pp.6-7 and p.23.
217. Further changes also occurred in 1891 when Maple bought the common at Childwick Green and thus denied the villagers their age-old rites of access, and replaced feudal privileges with philanthropic acts instead. As Gruetzner Robins noted, out of the 39 families listed as living there in 1881, only four remained in 1891. Ibid., p.23.
218. The railway line was initially laid from Pulborough to Ford in 1863. It was considered to be a great feat of engineering because the rail crossed the river four times, and tunnels were cut through the chalk hills at North Stoke. There were talks of running the line on the west side of the river, with a tunnel under Arundel Park which would provide Bury with a station. However, the Duke of Norfolk would not allow this and so a railway line was built on the east side which gave Amberley a station. The residents of Houghton Bridge and Bury were unhappy at this because it meant they had to pass through a Toll Gate at Houghton Bridge to get to the station See Staines, op. cit., p.1.
219. On the 3rd October 1891, the *West Sussex Times* reported that on the previous Sunday 300 anglers came

from London to fish for roach, bream and dace, with a competition set by the two Amberley public houses, The Cricketers and the Houghton Bridge Inn. A week later, the fishing competition took place with 900 members of the London angling clubs arriving at 8.30 a.m., by special train. This was reported by the newspaper on the 10th October 1891. On the 9th June 1894, the *West Sussex Times* reported that an 'anglers' train runs every Sunday morning to Pulborough and Amberley, leaving London Bridge at 7 a.m. On 7th July 1894, it was reported that 1000 anglers and friends had journeyed to Pulborough and Amberley on the Sunday. Both notices were also mentioned in the *Angling News*.

220. P.H. Ditchfield, *The Cottages and the Village Life of Rural England* (London: J.M. Dent & Sons Ltd., 1912), p.67. Ditchfield also wrote that the County of Sussex was noted for its fish: Chichester lobster, Shelsey cockle, Arundel mullet and Amberley trout. Isaak Walton (c.1594-1683) was an English writer who wrote *The Compleat Angler*, which was first published in 1653 and added to over a 25 year period. The book celebrated the art and spirit of fishing in prose and verse.

221. Weiss and three colleagues made initial short flights on a man-lifting glider that had been built in the Houghton Bridge village hall. See Staines, op. cit., p.54.

222. Even as late as 1916, two years before Stott died, he was still enquiring about property that was coming up for sale. In a letter to Anne Dinnage dated 7th May 1916, sent from the Arts Club, 40 Dover Street, London, Stott wrote 'From your letter I could not understand if the Shorter property is to be sold on the 13th or 18th. Neither do you mention where the sale is to take place.' See Box K (SA).

223. Dinnage Diary, p.20 (SA).

224. Ibid., pp.21-22.

225. Both occasions were the cause of much merrymaking which resulted in drunken behavior. At the Gala Day, Alfred and Richard Ruff were charged with being drunk and disorderly. At 8.30 p.m., they were turned out from the field where the amusements were taking place, whereupon a general riot started with 12 or more couples fighting. On the day of the Queen's Jubilee, an Amberley resident refused to leave the Cricketer's Arms whereupon he was arrested. In Court, he pleaded guilty to drunken behaviour. The Defendant apologised, particularly as it was the Queen's Jubilee. He was let off, but with costs to pay amounting to 8 shillings. This was reported in the *West Sussex Times* on 3rd July 1897.

226. The painting was exhibited at the New English Art Club in 1891. No further information exists.

227. J. Stanley Little, 'Amberley. The Pearl of Sussex', *Khaki* (Christmas, 1916), p.570. *Khaki* was a naval and military magazine.

228. Amberley Castle was erected as an Episcopal palace in 1368 by William Rede, the Bishop of Chichester. However, he rarely used it as London was preferred. The castle passed into the hands of Lord Zouche in 1872 and was then acquired by the Duke of Norfolk in 1893. It was tenanted by a farmer to protect it from further decay, and used to shelter his cattle. See Kelly's Directory (1899), pp.18-19; Ditchfield, *The Cottages and the Village Life of Rural England*, op. cit., p.68.

229. The Williamson Art Gallery in Birkenhead recently came into possession of a substantial portfolio of sketches by Stott, which had previously been owned by Arthur Grogan.

230. Both paintings are assumed to be in private collections.

231. Richard Roe, *The Solicitors' Journal*, Vol. 122 (5th May 1978), p.292. 'Withies' were pliable twigs or branches usually from the Willow tree.

232. Carter, op. cit., p.295. His reference to 'grad-grind' is likely to have come from Charles Dickens' novel *Hard Times*, where Thomas Gradgrind viewed industrialisation and mechanisation as a positive and progressive thing, even though it dehumanised people. Conversely, creativity, imagination and emotions, were dismissed as unimportant.

233. Dinnage Diary, p.22 and p.25 (SA).

234. Stott was a fine skater. When the flood water froze over the meadow below Houghton village, he would skate there. Also, in his first years of living at Hope Cottage, he hired a horse and went riding every evening in the summer. He then took up cycling, but gave it up after he suffered an accident. Stott also thought a great deal about his weight and health and was influenced by anything he heard on the subject. Dinnage diary, p.25 and pp.8-10 (SA).

235. Sketch Book 1, Box A5, ST/1 (SA).

236. Carter, op. cit., p.296.

237. Sketch Book 1, Box A5, ST/1 (SA).

238. Sketch Book 1, Box A5, ST/1 (SA).

239. Nina Lübbren, *Rural artists' colonies in Europe, 1870-1910* (Manchester: Manchester University Press, 2001), p.50.

240. *Ploughing, Early Spring* was exhibited at the New English Art Club in 1891, and is now in the Rochdale collection. Its companion piece, *Ploughing in Early Spring* (1892), was exhibited at the New Gallery in 1892, and is now in a private collection following its sale at Sotheby's in October 1997.

241. *Harvesting* was never exhibited, and is currently privately owned. As regards Stott's paintings of gleaners, he produced two works: *Gleaners* (c.1894) and *The Gleaners* (1903). The former work was exhibited at the New English Art Club in 1894, and then at the New Gallery in 1898. The New Gallery exhibition catalogue described the scene as one of 'children returning from harvest fields, with level rays of sun showing light touches on the figures.' No further information exists as to the painting's current whereabouts. The latter work was also not exhibited and had previously been owned by Charles T. Harris. Its current whereabouts is also unknown. However, a black

and white image exists which shows the subject matter to be of a young woman and a girl stood in a harvested field, with gleaning being carried out in the background.

242. Lübbren cites two examples – a work by the Dutch artist, Anton Mauve, with the title of *Changing Pastures* (date unknown), and a painting by an American artist called John Leslie Breck, with the title of *Autumn Giverny* (1889), op. cit., p.50 and p.52.
243. *West Sussex Times* (22nd August 1891 and 31st October 1891).
244. This painting is in the University of Hull art collection and is presently undated. It was also not exhibited in its time. However, in terms of subject matter, it closely resembles a painting exhibited at the New Gallery in 1888 with the title of *Homewards* (now lost), of which an illustration by Stott appeared in the exhibition catalogue. This painting depicts a young boy leading a cow down a country lane. Based on this information, I suggest that a date of circa 1888 could also be applied to *The Young Cowherd*. Furthermore, the painterly and impressionistic handling of this work is also evident in an undated and unexhibited work which has the title of *A Boy Riding a Pony on a Forest Track*, given the alternative title of *Farm Boy* when it came up for auction in 2009 by Burstow and Hewett auction house, and I suggest that a date of circa 1888 can also be applied to this painting.
245. For an early overview of key modern Dutch landscape painters, see E.G. Halton, 'The Collection of Mr Alexander Young – IV. The Modern Dutch Pictures', *The Studio*, Vol. 39, No. 166 (January 1907), pp.287-300.
246. Anonymous, *The Art Journal* (June 1901).
247. I explore this aspect of Stott's work in Chapter Six, 'Edward Stott and Modernism', *Edward Stott (1855-1918): The Forgotten Artist*, unpublished PhD Thesis, University of Northumbria at Newcastle (May 2015).
248. *The Times* (19th May 1898), p.8.
249. Ibid., p.8.
250. I am drawing on my own evidence here.
251. W.H. Hudson, *Nature in Downland* (Macdonald Futura Publishers, 1981), p.36. First published by J.M. Dent & Sons Ltd., 1923. Hudson was an author, naturalist and ornithologist.
252. Frank Rinder, 'The Royal Academy Exhibition of 1902', *The Art Journal* (July 1902), p.216.
253. Bawcombe had begun shepherding for his father at the young age of 6 and, having caught a chill early in life through long exposure to wet and cold weather, had contracted rheumatic fever which left him lame. W.H. Hudson, *A Shepherd's Life. Impressions of the South Wiltshire Downs* (California: Linden Publishing Inc., 2004), p.39. First published by Methuen & Co. Limited (London, 1910).
254. Ibid., p.42.
255. Dinnage Diary, p.22 (SA).
256. Ysanne Holt, *British Artists and the Modernist Landscape*, op. cit., p.17.
257. *The Observer* (17th April 1904).
258. I use the word 'paternalistic' in the sense of being protective rather than as being patriarchal or authoritarian.
259. W.H. Hudson, *A Shepherd's Life. Impressions of the South Wiltshire Downs*, op. cit., p.95.
260. P.H. Ditchfield, *Country Folk. A Pleasant Company* (London: Methuen & Co. Ltd., 1923), p.191.
261. Both of these paintings, and *Snow on the Hills*, are now lost.
262. *The Saturday Review* (25th May 1889), p.639.
263. Ibid. The exhibition catalogue gave a brief description of the colours used.
264. *The Saturday Review* (25th May 1889), p.639.
265. *The Guardian* (22nd April 1899), p.10.
266. *Daily News* (22nd April 1899).
267. *The Times* (25th May 1899).
268. *The Art Journal* (June 1899), p.185. The critic aligned Stott with the artist G.F. Watts, writing that 'If Mr Watts painted landscapes he would share Mr Stott's vision.' As Watts was a highly regarded artist at the time, this was indeed high praise.
269. Alun Howkins, *Reshaping Rural England. A Social History. 1850-1925*, p.102. The italic emphases are by Howkins.
270. Parliamentary Papers: Second Report by the Honorable E.B. Portman, Royal Commission on the Employment of Children, Young Persons and Women in Agriculture, 1867-68, Vol. XVII, p.95 (1867) (BL).
271. See Anna Gruetzner Robins 'Living the Simple Life: George Clausen at Childwick Green, St. Albans', op. cit., p.20, drawing on Jefferies' essays on country life which were serialised in the 1870's.
272. Ibid., p.15. Chapman can be identified in at least three of Clausen's Childwick Green paintings: *Daydreaming*, *Winter Work* and *A Woman of the Fields*.
273. Kenneth McConkey, Lot Note for *The Mushroom Gatherers*, in 'Victorian and Edwardian Art', *Sotheby's Sale Catalogue* (London, 11th December 2007), p.122. McConkey's comment was to do with the young female mushroom gatherer. However, his description is fitting for Clausen's and La Thangue's country children generally.
274. The painting was part of a series that La Thangue produced of this theme, of which the most significant work was *A Sussex Cider Press* (1898). See Kenneth McConkey, Lot Note for *In the Orchard, 'Haylands', Graffham*, in 'Victorian and British Impressionist Pictures Including Drawings & Water-Colours', *Christie's Sale Catalogue* (London, 16th December 2009).
275. Stott made three studies for the *Cider Press*: *Study for the 'Cider Press'*, which was exhibited at the Fine Art Society in 1910 and is now owned by the Cecil French Gallery, *Study of Horse for 'Cider Press'*, and *Interior of Barn for 'Cider Press'*, both exhibited at the Fine Art Society in 1919, but current whereabouts unknown. With regards to the completed painting, *The Cider Harvest*, a photocopy of

this little-known work can be found in the Stott box file of images at the Witt Library, Courtauld Institute, with a reference made to the Baroda collection as its last known location.

276. A black and white image of *The Gleaners* can be found in the Stott folder, Witt Library, Courtauld Institute.
277. Other examples would include *The Team* and *Youth and Age.*
278. The date and whereabouts of this work is unknown, but a photocopy of the painting can be found in the Stott Archive.
279. *Daily News* (7th May 1895).
280. Ibid.
281. New Gallery exhibition catalogue (1895).
282. This later work was bequeathed by the Felton Bequest to the National Gallery of Victoria in 1914.
283. James Stanley Little wrote that the River Arun was fast flowing and very deep in parts. It often burst its banks and overflowed into the Brooklands, which resulted in the villagers having to get about in punts, using hawthorn bushes and dwarf oaks which remained above the water level as landmarks. See Little, *Khaki*, op. cit., p.572.
284. In July, Edward Gosden was fishing on the bank of the Arun, near Houghton Bridge, when he fell in and drowned. The *West Sussex Times* reported on the 5th July 1890, that the sad event 'created quite a sensation in the village.' That same month, a group of pupils from Littlehampton Congregational Sunday School went to Amberley for their annual treat. Leonard Helyer, along with some of his companions, left the group to go swimming. Helyer plunged in and almost immediately called for help and then sank. His body was found an hour later. This was reported in the *West Sussex Times* on the 26th July 1890. In April 1896, William Lee went out in his boat. He was last seen near Bury on late Sunday afternoon, and the boat was found at Bury on Monday morning. A drag of the river found his body on Tuesday between Bury and Amberley. Foul play was ruled out, and cause of death was listed as 'accidental death by drowning', as reported by the *West Sussex Times* on 25th April 1896.
285. Christiana Payne, *Toil and Plenty. Images of the Agricultural Landscape in England 1780-1890* (New Haven and London: Yale University Press, 1993), p.7.
286. Tim Barringer, *Men at Work. Art and Labour in Victorian Britain*, The Paul Mellon Centre for Studies in British Art (New Haven and London: Yale University Press, 2005), p.111. Co-incidentally, the landscape in the background of *Harvest Moon* is the Weald which unites the North and South Sussex Downs.
287. Ibid., p.111.
288. It is outside the scope of this publication to explore the possible connection between Stott and an English tradition, as my aim has been to purposefully argue for a continuing French influence. However, certain of Stott's paintings can feasibly be viewed as a continuum of similar subject matter painted by Samuel Palmer, of whom Linnell was a close friend, and also the work of George Heming Mason.
289. *Daily News* (7th April 1900).
290. Ibid.
291. Ibid.
292. Frank Rinder 'The Royal Academy of 1900', *The Art Journal* (June 1900), p.161.
293. *The Guardian* (14th May 1900), p.10.
294. Ibid., p.10.
295. Ibid., p.10.
296. Ibid., p.10.
297. David Croal Thomson Papers, 1879-1931. Series 1. Letters from artists, dealers and friends (boxes 1-5). Special Collection (910126) (GRIL). David Croal Thomson (1855-1930) was a Scottish-born art expert, writer and editor. He ran the Goupil Gallery in London from 1885, and then in 1897 left the Goupil to join Thomas Agnew's & Sons. In 1908, he became a partner in the French Gallery until 1918, whereupon he opened his own firm Barbizon House. He worked as sub-editor of the *Year's Art*, which was a subsidiary of the *Art Journal* which he became editor of. He also contributed to the *Magazine of Art*, *Scotsman* and *The Studio*. See *Dictionary of Nineteenth-Century Journalism*, General Editors: Laurel Brake and Marysa Demoor (Gent: Academia Press, 2009; London: The British Library, 2009), p.624.
298. David Croal Thomson Papers (GRIL).
299. Stott to Thomson (7th June 1913).
300. Stott to Thomson (20th June 1913).
301. Stott to Thomson (7th November 1913).
302. Stott to Thomson (26th December 1913). The painting came up for sale on 8th December 2012 at Mainichi Auction house in Tokyo, where it sold for 400,000 JPY ($4,849). The price achieved was under the estimate figure.
303. *Birmingham Daily Post* (8th May 1894).
304. Ibid.
305. For further reading on foreign exhibitors to German exhibitions, see Shearer West, *The Visual Arts in Germany 1890-1937. Utopia and Despair* (Manchester and New York: Manchester University Press, 2000); Robin Lenman, *Artists and Society in Germany 1850-1914* (Manchester and New York: Manchester University Press, 1997); Maria Makela, *The Munich Secession. Art and Artists in Turn-of-the Century Munich* (Princeton, New Jersey: Princeton University Press, 1900); Matthew Potter, *The Inspirational Genius of Germany. British Art and Germanism 1850-1939*, op. cit.
306. West, ibid., pp.16-19; Potter, ibid., p.176.
307. There were two exhibiting groups in Munich. The traditionally inclined exhibited at the Genossenschaft exhibitions, whilst the progressives exhibited at the Secessionist shows. I have been unable to ascertain which exhibition the painting appeared in, but due to the subject

matter it is likely to have been the Genossenschaft show.

308. *The Guardian* (25th April 1896).
309. The medal can be found in the Stott Archive.
310. Letter from Stott to Poynter (23rd September 1899), MSL/1917/229/251 NAL
311. Letter from Stott to Spielmann, MSL/1999/2/2286.
312. *The Guardian* (1st May 1894), p.9.
313. M.H. Spielmann, 'At the Royal Academy Exhibition, 1901. III – The Figure Subjects', *Magazine of Art*, July 1901, p.442.
314. Ibid.
315. I am grateful to Dr. Matthew Potter for bringing this to my attention.
316. For my discussion of Stott's contribution to Internationalism, see Chapter Six, 'Edward Stott and Internationalism', *Edward Stott (1855-1918): The Forgotten Artist*, op. cit.
317. See A.E. Lütticke, 'The Work of Max Liebermann, *The Studio*, Vol. 32, No. 137 (15th August 1904).
318. Dinnage Diary, p.4 (SA)
319. See Martin Pugh, *State and Society. British Political & Social History 1870-1992* (London, New York, Sydney, and Auckland: Arnold, 1997 (1994)).
320. Susan Kingsley Kent, *Gender and Power in Britain*, 1640-1990 (London: Routledge, 1999), pp.147-8.
321. Ibid.
322. The following texts unpack the complexities of the 'separate spheres' debate in some detail: Mary Poovey, *Uneven Developments. The Ideological Work of Gender in Mid-Victorian Britain* (London: Virago Press, 1989, first published by the University of Chicago Press, 1988); Martha Vicinus, *Independent Women. Work and Community for Single Women. 1850-1920* (London: Virago Press, 1985, first published by the University of Chicago Press, 1985); Peter N. Stearns, "Working-Class Women in Britain, 1890-1914", in *Suffer and Be Still. Women in the Victorian Age*, Martha Vicinus (Editor), (Bloomington and London: Indiana University Press, 1973).
323. On these points, see Susan Kingsley Kent, op. cit., p.229; A. James Hammerton, *Cruelty and Companionship. Conflict in Nineteenth-Century Married Life* (London and New York: Routledge, 1992).
324. Susan Kingsley Kent, ibid., p.233.
325. Ibid., p.233.
326. Major Maurice cited Germany as a role model whose ideology was that a mother's role should be devoted to 'kinder, küche, kirche' (children, kitchen, church). See Anna Davin, "Imperialism and Motherhood", in *Tensions of Empire: Colonial Cultures in a Bourgeois World*, Frederick Cooper and Anna Laura Stoler (eds.) (Berkeley: 1997), p.94. The concern over the declining health of the male population, and the onus placed on mothers to restore it, resulted in a number of child welfare measures being introduced in the early part of the twentieth century which were augmented by a number of voluntary organisations promoting public health and domestic hygiene. See Davin, ibid, p.89.
327. Ibid., p.90.
328. The precedent, however, can be traced back to earlier European examples found in the work of, say, the eighteenth-century French artist Jean-Baptiste Greuze, and the seventeenth-century Dutch artist Pieter de Hooch. See Christiana Payne, *Rustic Simplicity. Scenes of Cottage Life in Nineteenth-Century British Art* (London: Lund Humphries Publishers in association with The University of Nottingham Arts Centre, 1998), published to accompany the exhibition held at the Djanogly Art Gallery 1998.
329. Ibid., p.18.
330. Ibid., p.18.
331. Ibid., p.5.
332. In January 1906, Stott finally became an Associate of the Royal Academy. Three years previously in 1903, his name had been put forward for an Associateship. There were three vacancies at that time and the leading candidates were J.H.F. Bacon, Arnesby Brown, W.L. Coton, Frank Brangwyn and Edward Stott. Stott passed through all the rounds of voting, but was beaten in the final round by Arnesby Brown's 28 votes to Stott's 23. The reviewer for *The Academy and Literature* wrote that 'The election was therefore somewhat disappointing. We had hoped to see Mr Stott elected.' *The Academy and Literature*, No. 1603 (24th January 1903). The *Magazine of Art* also expressed disappointment, writing that 'we cannot but regret that the merits of Mr Stott have not yet received full recognition, for the Academy would be the stronger for the inclusion of the peculiarly reticent and genuine poetry of Mr Stott's individual and personal art.' *Magazine of Art* (January 1903), p.57.
333. Census Records (1901).
334. Dinnage Diary, p.4 (SA).
335. Dinnage, 'Reminiscences', p.13 (SA).
336. During the first year of Stott's residence with the Dinnage family, he lunched every day with a fellow artist called Gascoigne who would also join them for the occasional evening meal. The friendship ended when Gascoigne married. Dinnage Diary, p.20 and p.6. Although I found no mention of a Gascoigne or Gascoyne listed on any of the Census Returns for the Amberley area, it could be George Gascoyne who lived and worked in London, and painted rural images and farming scenes such as *Plough Horses in a Wheat Field*, *Autumn Labour* and *Return from Work*. In Benezit, Vol. 5, op. cit., pp.1364-5; BBC My Paintings; Mutual Art.
337. Dinnage Diary, p.20. The underlining is by Anne Dinnage.
338. The letter was sent from 1 Pembroke Cottages, Edwards Square, Kensington. Housman also thanked Dinnage for a blackcurrant pudding she had sent him, which he remarked was a kind thought 'after all these years.' This suggests

that they had not kept in touch after his falling out with Stott and one questions why she felt the need to get back in touch with Housman now, bearing in mind Stott's temperamental and over sensitive nature.

339. Anne Dinnage liked to draw and paint, and was encouraged by Stott who would give her materials. However, she decided not to pursue it as it took up too much of her time and, as she stated, 'might prevent my looking after him and his affairs properly', further adding that he was not a good teacher because he lacked patience. Dinnage Diary, p.4 (SA).
340. Stott to Little (10th October 1893) (GRIL).
341. Stott to Little (9th December 1893).
342. Stott to Little (undated)
343. J. Stanley Little, 'The Wealden Painters at the Summer Exhibitions', *West Sussex Gazette* (9th June 1892).
344. Stott to Little (undated) (GRIL).
345. Stott to Little (9th December 1893).
346. Stott to Little, 20th June 1900.
347. Dinnage Diary, p.15 (SA).
348. Stott also produced a work with the title of *God's Acre.* No other information exists pertaining to this painting.
349. Stott to Little (20th June 1900). The other painting was to be an 'apple blossom picture'.
350. M.H. Spielmann, 'At the Royal Academy Exhibition, 1901', *Magazine of Art*, July 1901, p.442.
351. See exhibition publication, St. Louis International Exhibition. 1904. Issued by The Royal Commission. Entered at Stationers' Hall (1906), p.123.
352. In the Stott folder held by Manchester City Art Gallery, I came across a letter from a Mrs Eileen Davies who said that the young girl in the painting was her mother, Alice Kennard. Born in Amberley in 1888, Alice Kennard's father was a master thatcher and, according to her daughter, it was Alice's father who made her model for Stott. She did not enjoy modelling as it meant standing around for hours. Her daughter recounts that on one occasion her mother told her that Stott came to the house asking for her to sit for him. She was out playing, but had to come back.
353. Letter to Spielmann, MSL/1999/2/2289 NAL.
354. Dinnage Diary, p.14. She also said that Stott kept his little models quiet with biscuits and sweets.
355. *The Times* (4th May 1908), p.13.
356. P.G. Konody, 'The Triumph of Mr Stott', *Observer* (3rd May 1908).
357. Marion Hepworth Dixon, 'Edward Stott: An Appreciation', *The Studio*, Vol. 55, No. 227 (February 1912), p.4.
358. Ysanne Holt, *British Artists and the Modernist Landscape*, op. cit., p.17.
359. P.G. Konody, 'A Critical Survey', *Observer* (2nd May 1909), p.23. It is interesting that Konody has used the term 'modernist'. In the context of the time, I suggest it is used to mean up-to-date and not how it is now understood.
360. Ibid., p.23.
361. He writes further that whilst Spanish Old Masters, such as Murillo, hold little interest for him, he admired the Venetians and Rembrandt.
362. *Observer* (30th April 1911).
363. Ibid. Translated, the Italian word 'morbidezza' means softness.
364. *Observer* (3rd May 1914).
365. *The Times* (5th May 1917), p.9.
366. Dinnage Diary, p.9 and p.29. Stott was in the habit of going for daily walks in all weathers. He was also trying out new diets and 'cures'. One of the cures he tried was the Kneipp Water cure which was introduced to him by his German friend, the artist Robert Meyerheim. The idea was to 'tread water' and Stott would run about in the paddock in the morning dew in his bare feet. Anne Dinnage recalls that he eventually abandoned this habit but until the end of his life he continued to put on his socks and vest whilst his body was still wet.
367. This tells of when Joseph fled to Egypt with Mary and Jesus after a visit by the Magi to warn the Holy Family that Herod intended to kill all the children of that area, and was the final episode in the Nativity of Jesus.
368. Dinnage Diary, p.14 (SA).
369. *The Times* (25th May 1899).
370. *The Art Journal* (June 1899).
371. Laurence Housman, *The Guardian* (11th May 1906). The painting was purchased by Captain Audley Harvey, who was a prodigious collector of British art, and hung in the dining room of his house in Primrose Hill, London. Reviewing Harvey's collection, A.J. Finberg wrote that 'The two most important English works in this room are Stott's 'Washing Day' and Oliver Hall's 'Le Pont Rouge: Albi', and further added of Stott's work that 'The figures are beautifully arranged and there is a charm and completeness about the whole which make it most delightful to contemplate.' See A.J. Finberg, 'Captain Audley Harvey's Collection', *The Art Journal* (April 1911), pp.97-103; peerage.com, accessed 6th September 2015. Harvey also purchased other paintings by Stott from the Royal Academy exhibitions. These included *Flamingos* (1908), *Where the Dark Earth Sleeping Lies* (1908), and *Hagar and Ishmael* (1911).
372. P.G. Konody 'Leading Pictures of the Year', *Observer* (2nd May 1909), p.8.
373. Clement Greenberg, 'Modernist Painting', reproduced in *Modern Art and Modernism. A Critical Anthology*, edited by Francis Frascina and Charles Harrison (London: Paul Chapman Publishing Limited in association with The Open University, 1982), p.6. Original source: *Art and Literature*, no.4, spring 1965.
374. Ysanne Holt, *British Artists and the Modernist Landscape*, op. cit., p.18.
375. Ibid., p.18.

376. *The Times* (30th April 1910), p.10.
377. *Observer* (1st May 1910), p.16.
378. A.C.R. Carter, 'The Royal Academy. A General Survey', *The Art Journal* (June 1910), p.164.
379. See oxforddnb.com, accessed 6th September 2015; en.m.wikipedia.org, accessed 6th September 2015; Getty Provenance Index for Duveen archive.
380. A.C.R. Carter, 'The Royal Academy. A General Survey', *The Art Journal* (June 1910), p.164.
381. Ibid., p.164.
382. Sarai (Sarah), Abraham's wife, was unable to give him children and so she gave her Egyptian slave, Hagar, to him to have his child. Sarai subsequently mistreated Hagar who turned against her mistress and was dismissed. On the road, she was visited by an angel who told Hagar to return and, when her child was born, she should call him Ishmael. At the age of 14, Ishmael was freed from Abraham's house along with his mother. Abraham gave them bread and water for their journey into the wildnerness, and the subject matter for Stott's painting is based on this aspect of the story.
383. Hepworth Dixon described the painting as 'perhaps one of the most tender and translucent of all his canvasses.', 'Edward Stott: An Appreciation', op. cit., p.9.
384. *The Carpenter's Shop* was originally owned by A.G. Anderson and is now owned by the Royal Academy having been purchased from the owner using the Stott fund. The *Adoration of the Shepherds* is now lost.
385. P.G. Konody, 'The Academy', *Observer* (4th May 1913), p.6.
386. Ibid., p.7. Both paintings were hung in the Academy's 'Gem Room' which was reserved for smaller paintings and often crowded together on the walls.
387. Tim Barringer, "'Not a "modern" as the word is now understood'? Byam Shaw, imperialism and the poetics of professional society", in *English Art 1860-1914. Modern artists and identity*, edited by David Peters Corbett and Lara Perry (Manchester: Manchester University Press, 2000), p.66.
388. Stott to Little (December 1910) (GRIL)
389. For a good overview of the events leading up to the war, and of the general political situation abroad and nearer to home, see Martin Pugh, "Crisis and Controversy in Edwardian Britain", *State and Society. British Political & Social History 1870-1990*, op. cit.
390. I am grateful to Dr. Lesley Twoomey for pointing this out.
391. Stott produced a few paintings featuring the Amberley landscape in this formally specific way, and in their 'other worldly' aspect they border on fantasy.
392. Roger Fry, 'An Essay in Aesthetics' (1909), reproduced in Roger Fry, *Vision and Design*, edited by J.B. Bullen (Mineola, New York: Dover Publications, Inc., 1981), p.22.
393. Ibid., pp.23-4. The other elements comprise mass, space, light and shade, which Stott's paintings also attend to.
394. Stott completed a handful of paintings which showed him experimenting with colour and atmosphere, particularly scenes bathed in mist, or moonshine breaking through clouds. See, for example, *Starlight* and *Where the Dark Earth Sleeping Lies.*
395. *The Guardian* (30th April 1916), p.5.
396. Ibid., p.5.
397. Abraham was the chief Patriarch, along with his son Isaac and Isaac's son, Jacob.
398. I am grateful to Dr. Matthew Potter for pointing out the similarities. Watts' self-portrait is held in the National Portrait Gallery. Also, Stott had been linked more than once to Watts by the critics.
399. Its inclusion in the chapter is acceptable because, in catacomb paintings during the Roman Empire, Orpheus was symbolic of Christ. See James Hall, *Illustrated Dictionary of Symbols of Eastern and Western Art* (London: John Murray (Publishers) Ltd., 1994), p.175.
400. Dinnage Diary, p.7 (SA).
401. Ibid., p.29.
402. Ibid., p.32.
403. Ibid., p.33. Anne Dinnage also wrote that towards the very end, Stott reverted to his Lancashire dialect and began to speak of his parents. Friends came to visit, but he did not recognise them. Evidently, at one point, his sisters wrote to say they were coming to see him, but this made him very agitated.
404. P.G. Konody, *Observer* (5th May 1918), p.3.
405. Dinnage Diary, p.21 (SA).
406. Probate of Will (18th June 1918).
407. Reviewing Shackleton's pictures at the Goupil Gallery, the critic wrote that Shackleton's 'work was modelled probably in the first instance by association, with Mr Edward Stott.' *The Athenaeum*, No. 4295 (19th February 1910), p.223.
408. As reported in *The Rochdale* (31st March 1920).

BIBLIOGRAPHY

Primary Sources

ARCHIVES

Kelly's Directories of Sussex, Horsham Library
King's School Archive, Ely
Parliamentary Papers, British Library
Philip Wilson Steer Archive, Courtauld Institute of Art (CI/PWS)
Royal Institute of Painters in Oil Colours, Blythe House, V&A (IOP/BH/V&A)
Stott Archive, Rochdale Arts and Heritage Resource centre (SA)
Stott image file, Witt Library, Courtauld Institute of Art
Stott letters to Sir Edward Poynter and Isidore Spielmann, National Art Library, V&A
Stott letters to J. Stanley Little, Herbert Gilchrist and David Croal Thomson, Getty Research Institute Library, Los Angeles (GRIL)

NEWSPAPERS

Birmingham Daily Post
Daily News
Glasgow Herald
Illustrated London News
Liverpool Mercury
Manchester Guardian
Morning Post
National Observer
Pall Mall Gazette
Rochdale Observer
The Academy and Literature
The Graphic
The Guardian
The Observer
The Rochdale
The Saturday Review
The Standard
The Sussex Daily News
The Times
West Sussex Times
West Sussex Gazette

JOURNALS

Magazine of Art
Nash's Pall Mall Magazine
New Annals of Rochdale
The Art Journal
The Athenaeum
The British Architect
The Contemporary Review
The Studio
Time Magazine

AUCTION HOUSE AND EXHIBITION CATALOGUES

Christie, Manson and Woods, *Catalogue of choice Modern Pictures of the British and Continental Schools, the Property of John Maddocks, Esq., of Heath Royal, Putney Heath (sold owing to his having disposed of his residence* (London: Saturday, 30th April 1910).
~ *Catalogue of Paintings owned by C.T. Harris, sold by the Executors of C.T. Harris' Estate for the benefit of the Memorial Fund of King's College Hospital* (London: 28th November 1913).
Grosvenor Gallery
New Gallery (1888-1902) including 'New Gallery Notes. No. 1, 1888', *The New Gallery 1888. An Illustrated Catalogue of the Summer Exhibition at the New Gallery, 121 Regent Street,* edited by Henry Blackburn (London: Chatto and Windus, May 1888).
Paris Salon (1882-1886), F.G. Dumas (Paris, Boulevard Saint-German: Libraire d'Art L. Baschet).
Rochdale Art Gallery, *Memorial Exhibition of Paintings and Drawings by the late Edward Stott, ARA* (March to April 1920)
Royal Institute of Painters in Oil Colours (1884-5/1885-6/1886-7)
St. Louis International Exhibition. 1904. Issued by The Royal Commission. Entered at Stationers' Hall (1906).

AUTHORED TEXTS

Anon., 'Obituary', *Manchester Guardian* (22nd March 1918).
Anon., 'Preface', *Memorial Exhibition of Paintings and Drawings by the late Edward Stott, ARA.*, Exhibition Catalogue, Rochdale Art Gallery (March to April 1920).
Carter, A.C.R., 'Edward Stott and his work', *The Art Journal* (October 1899).
~ 'The Royal Academy. A General Survey', *The Art Journal* (June 1910).
Day, Barclay, 'Studio-life in Paris', *Magazine of Art* (1882).
~ 'L'Atelier-Bonnat', *Magazine of Art* (1882).
Dinnage, Anne, 'Reminiscences' (undated)
~ Diary (undated)
Ditchfield, P.H., *Our English Villages. Their Story and their Antiquities* (London: Methuen & Co. Ltd., 1889).
~ *The Cottages and the Village Life of Rural England* (London: J.M. Dent & Sons Ltd., 1912).
~ *Country Folk. A Pleasant Company* (London: Methuen & Co. Ltd., 1923).
Finberg, A.J., 'Captain Audley Harvey's Collection', *The Art Journal* (April 1911).
Forbes-Robertson, John, 'The Salon of 1881–1', *Magazine of Art* (1881).
Fox, Shirley, *An Art Student's Reminiscences of Paris in the Eighties* (London: Mills and Boon, 1909).
Halkett, George, 'Edward Stott, A.R.A., An Appreciation and Some Recollections', *Nash's Pall Mall Magazine,* Vol. 37, Issue 155 (March 1906).
Halton, E.G. 'The Collection of Mr. Alexander Young – IV. The Modern Dutch Pictures', *The Studio,* Vol. 39, No. 166 (January 1907).
Hepworth Dixon, Marion, 'Edward Stott: An Appreciation', *The Studio,* Vol. 55, No. 227 (February 1912).

Housman, Laurence, 'Mr. Edward Stott, Painter of the Field and of the Twilight', *Magazine of Art* (January 1900)
Kennedy, Arthur, 'In the Studio of Carolus-Duran', *The Contemporary Review*, 53 (May 1888).
Konody, P.G., 'The Triumph of Mr. Stott', *Observer* (3rd May 1908).
~ 'A Critical Survey', *Observer* (2nd May 1909).
~ 'Leading Picture of the Year', *Observer* (2nd May 1909).
~ 'The Academy', *Observer* (4th May 1913).
~ *Observer* (5th May 1918).
Laun, Henri van, 'The Paris Salon', *Time* (June 1883).
Little, J. Stanley, 'The Wealden Painters at the Summer Exhibitions', *West Sussex Gazette* (9th June 1892)
~ 'On the Work of Edward Stott', *The Studio*, Vol. VI, No. 32 (November 1895).
~ 'Amberley. The Pearl of Sussex', *Khaki* (Christmas, 1916).
Ludovici, Albert, *An Artist's Life in London and Paris* (London: T. Fisher Unwin, 1926).
Lütticke, A.E., 'The Work of Max Liebermann', *The Studio*, Vol. 32, No. 137 (15th August 1904).
MacColl, D.S., *Life, Work and Setting of Philip Wilson Steer* (London: Faber and Faber Ltd., 1945).
Moore, George, 'The New English Art Club', *The Speaker* (16th April 1892).
Parliamentary Paper: Second Report, Portman, Honourable E.B., Royal Commission on the Employment of Children, Young Persons and Women in Agriculture, 1867-68, Vol. XVII, p.95 (1867).
Rinder, Frank, 'The Royal Academy of 1900', *The Art Journal* (June 1900).
~ 'The Royal Academy Exhibition of 1902', *The Art Journal* (July 1902).
Spielmann, M.H., 'The New Gallery', *The Graphic* (29th April 1899).
~ 'At the Royal Academy Exhibition, 1901', *Magazine of Art*, July 1901.
Stott, Edward, 'Some Remarks on Impressionism', *The Art Journal* (1893).

Secondary Sources

BOOKS, JOURNALS, AND CATALOGUES

An American in Brittany, Exhibition Catalogue (Dublin: Milmo-Penny Fine Art Limited, 2008).
Anon., Lot Note for 'The Orchard, Quimperlé', in *Victorian and Edwardian Art*, Sotheby's Auction Catalogue (London, 27th June 2006).
Barringer, Tim, '"Not a 'modern' as the word is now understood'? Byam Shaw, imperialism and the poetics of professional society', in *English Art 1860-1914. Modern artists and identity*, David Peters Corbett and Lara Perry (Editors) (Manchester: Manchester University Press, 2000).
~ *Men at Work. Art and Labour in Victorian Britain*, The Paul Mellon Centre for Studies in British Art (New Haven and London: Yale University Press, 2005).
Benezit Dictionary of Artists (Paris: Editions Gründ, 2006).
Best, Geoffrey, *Mid-Victorian Britain 1851-75* (London: Fontana Press, 1987 [1979]).
Billcliffe, Roger, *The Glasgow Boys* (London: Frances Lincoln Ltd., 2008).
Boime, Albert, *The Academy and French Painting in the Nineteenth Century* (London: Phaidon, 1971).
Brake, Laurel, *Subjugated Knowledges: Journalism, Gender and Literature in the Nineteenth Century* (London: MacMillan, 1994).
Brown, Roger, *William Stott of Oldham, 1857-1900: 'a comet rushing to the sun'* (London: Paul Holberton, 2003).
Casteras, Susan P. and Denney, Colleen (Editors), *The Grosvenor Gallery. A Palace of Art inVictorian England* (New Haven and London: Yale Center for British Art, 1996).
Codell, Julie F., 'Constructing the Victorian Artist: National Identity, the Political Economy of Art and Biographical Mania in the Periodical Press', *Victorian Periodicals Review*, Vol. 33, No. 3 (Fall 2000).
Cook, Judith, Hardie, Melissa and Payne, Christiana, *Singing from the walls: the life and art of Elizabeth Forbes*, Exhibition Catalogue (Bristol: Sansom and Company, 2000).
Corbett, David Peters, Holt, Ysanne and Russell, Fiona (Editors), *The Geographies of Englishness. Landscape and the National Past 1880-1940*, The Paul Mellon Centre of Studies in British Art. The Yale Center for British Art (New Haven and London: Yale University Press, 2002).
Davin, Anna, 'Imperialism and Motherhood', in *Tensions of Empire: Colonia Cultures in a Bourgeois World*, Frederick Cooper and Anna Laura Stoler (Editors) (Berkeley: 1997).
Denney, Colleen, 'Introduction', *The Grosvenor Gallery. A Palace of Art in Victorian England* (New Haven and London: Yale Center for British Art, 1996).
Falkenheim, Jacqueline V., *Roger Fry and the Beginnings of Formalist Art Criticism* (Ann Arbor, Michegan: UMI Research Press, 1980 (1973)).
Fry, Roger, 'An Essay in Aesthetics', *Vision and Design*, edited by J.B. Bullen (New York: Dover Publications Inc., 1998).
Greenberg, Clement, 'Modernist Painting', reproduced in *Modern art and Modernism. A Critical Anthology*, edited by Francis Frascina and Charles Harrison (London: Paul Chapman Publishing Limited in association with The Open University, 1982). Original source: *Art and Literature*, no. 4, spring 1965.
Gruetzner Robins, Anna, 'Living the Simple Life: George Clausen at Childwick Green, St. Albans', in David Peters Corbett, Ysanne Holt and Fiona Russell (Editors), *The Geographies of Englishness. Landscape and the National Past 1880-1940*, The Paul Mellon Centre for Studies in British Art. The Yale Center for British Art (New Haven and London: Yale University Press, 2002).
~ (Editor), *Walter Sickert. The Complete Writings on Art* (Oxford: Oxford University Press, 2000).

~ *A Fragile Modernism. Whistler and his Impressionist Followers*, Paul Mellon Centre for Studies in British Art (New Haven and London: Yale University Press, 2007).
Hall, James, *Illustrated Dictionary of Symbols of Eastern and Western Art* (London: John Murray (Publishers) Ltd., 1994).
Harrison, Charles, *Modernism* (London: Tate Gallery Publishing Limited, 1997).
Holden, Kristi, 'George Clausen and Henry Herbert La Thangue. Rural Painting. Urban Patronage', *Apollo*, Vol. 149, No. 444 (February 1999).
Holt, Ysanne, *Philip Wilson Steer* (Mid Glamorgan: Seren Books, 1992).
~ *British Artists and the Modernist Landscape* (Aldershot: Ashgate Publishing Limited, 2003).
Howkins, Alun, *Reshaping Rural England: A Social History 1850-1925* (London: HarperCollins Academic, 1991).
Hudson, W.H., *Nature in Downland* (Macdonald Futura Publishers, 1981). First published by J.M. Dent & Sons Ltd., 1923.
~ *A Shepherd's Life. Impressions of the South Wiltshire Downs* (California: Linden Publishing Inc., 2004). First published by Methuen & Co. Limited (London, 1910).
Jenkins, Adrian, 'William Stott of Oldham', *The Burlington Magazine*, Issue 1213 (2004).
Jones, Kimberley, *In the Forest of Fontainbleau. Painters and Photographers from Corot to Monet* (New Haven and London: Yale University Press, 2008).
Kent, Susan Kingsley, *Gender and Power in Britain, 1640-1990* (London: Routledge, 1999).
Laperrier, Charles Baile de, *A Dictionary of Artists and their works in the Annual Exhibitions of the New English Art Club Exhibitions 1886-2001* (Calne: Hilmarton Manor Press, 2002).
Lenman, Robin, *Artists and Society in Germany 1850-1914* (Manchester and New York: Manchester University Press, 1997).
Lübbren, Nina, *Rural artists' colonies in Europe, 1870-1910* (Manchester: Manchester University Press, 2001).
Makela, Maria, *The Munich Secession. Art and Artists in Turn-of-the Century Munich* (Princeton, New Jersey: Princeton University Press, 1900).
McConkey, Kenneth, 'From Grez to Glasgow: French Naturalist Influence in Scottish Painting', *Scottish Art Review*, Vol. 15, No. 4 (1982).
~ *British Impressionism* (Oxford: Phaidon, 1989).
~ 'Rustic Naturalism at the Grosvenor Gallery', in *The Grosvenor Gallery. A Palace of Art in Victorian England*, edited by Susan P. Casteras and Colleen Denney (New Haven and London: Yale Center for British Art, 1996).
~ *Impressionism in Britain* (London and New Haven: Yale University Press in association with the Barbican Art Gallery, 1999).
~ '"The Pallid Gleam of the Imagination"'. Coastal Art Colonies in Britain at the turn of the Twentieth Century', *Painting at the Edge. British Coastal Art Colonies 1880-1930*, edited by Laura Newton (Bristol: Sansom & Company Ltd., 2005).
~ *The New English. A History of the New English Art Club* (London: The Royal Academy of Arts, 2006).
~ Lot Note for *The Mushroom Gatherers*, in 'Victorian and Edwardian Art', *Sotheby's Sale Catalogue* (London, 11th December 2007).
~ Lot Note for *In the Orchard, 'Haylands', Graffham'*, in 'Victorian and British Impressionist Pictures Including Drawings & Water-Colours', *Christie's Sale Catalogue* (London, 16th December 2009).
Morgan, H. Cliff, 'The Schools of the Royal Academy', *British Journal of Educational Studies*, 21:1 (1973).
Newton, Laura, 'Cottars and Cabbages: Issues of National Identity in Scottish 'Kailyard' Paintings of the Late Nineteenth Century', *Visual Culture in Britain*, Vol. 6, No. 2 (Manchester University Press, 2005).
~ Editor, *Painting at the Edge. British Coastal Art Colonies 1880-1930* (Bristol: Sansom & Company Ltd., 2005).
Payne, Christiana, *Toil and Plenty. Images of the Agricultural Landscape in England 1780-1890* (New Haven and London: Yale University Press, 1993).
~ *Rustic Simplicity. Scenes of Cottage Life in Nineteenth-Century British Art* (London: Lund Humphries Publishers in association with The University of Nottingham Arts Centre, 1998).
Pugh, Martin, *State and Society. British Political & Social History 1870-1992* (London, New York, Sydney and Auckland: Arnold, 1997 (1994).
Roe, Richard, *The Solicitor's Journal*, Vol. 122 (5th May 1978).
Scott, Richard, 'Walberswick "An Eye for the Quiet Beauties of Nature"', *Painting at the Edge. British Coastal Art Colonies 1880-1930*, edited by Laura Newton (Bristol: Sansom & Company Ltd., 2005).
Sheehy, Jeanne, *Walter Osborne* (Ballycotton, Co. Cork: Gifford & Craven, 1974).
~ 'The Flight from South Kensington: British Artists at the Antwerp Academy. 1877–1883', *Art History*, Vol. 20, No. 1 (March 1997).
Shiff, Richard, *Cézanne and the End of Impressionism. A Study of the Theory, Technique and Critical Evaluation of Modern Art* (Chicago and London: The University of Chicago Press, 1984).
Spencer, Robin (Editor), *Whistler. A Retrospective* (New York: Wings Books, 1991).
Staines, The Reverend Noel E., *Dear Amberley. A Guide to Amberley and History of the Parish* (Amberley: 1968).
Strickland, Alice, 'Opening Doors: The Entry of Women Artists into British Art Schools, 1871–1930', in *The Concept of the 'Master', in Art Education in Britain and Ireland, 1770 to the Present*, edited by Matthew C. Potter (Farnham and Burlington: Ashgate Publishing Limited, 2013).
Webb, Valerie, *Edward Stott (1855-1918): The Forgotten Artist,*

unpublished PhD Thesis, University of Northumbria at Newcastle (May 2015).
Weisberg, Gabriel P., *Beyond Impressionism. The Natural Impulse in European Art 1860-1905* (London: Thames and Hudson, 1992).
West, Shearer, *The Visual Arts in Germany 1890-1937. Utopia and Despair* (Manchester and New York: Manchester University Press, 2000).
Wien, Iris, 'Naturalising Tradition: Why Learn from the Masters?' in *The Concept of the 'Master' in Art Education in Britain and Ireland, 1770 to the Present*, edited by Matthew C. Potter (Farnham and Burlington: Ashgate Publishing Limited, 2013).
Williams, Raymond, *The Country and the City* (Nottingham: Spokesman, 2011). First published Chatto and Windus, London, 1973).

ONLINE REFERENCES

Art UK (formerly BBC Paintings)
Blouin Sales Index
Census Returns
Duveen family – en.m.wikipedia.org; oxforddnb.com
Duveen archive – Getty Provenance Index
harper.org – article by Scott Horton, 'Philosophers Rumble Over Van Gogh's Shoes', *Harpers Magazine* (5th October 2009), npn.
Captain Audley Harvey – peerage.com
Mutual Art
W.W. Sampson – exhibitionculture.arts.gla.ac.uk
Rosamund Marriott Watson – www.1890s.ca

INDEX OF WORKS BY EDWARD STOTT

Numbers in **bold** relate to illustrations

INDEX